THE WIZARD FROM VIENNA

Franz Anton Mesmer

THE
WIZARD
FROM
VIENNA

BY

VINCENT BURANELLI

 Coward, McCann & Geoghegan, Inc.   New York

SBN: 698–10697–0

Library of Congress Cataloging in Publication Data

Buranelli, Vincent.
    The wizard from Vienna.

    1. Mesmer, Franz Anton, 1734–1815. 2. Mesmerism.
I. Title.
BF1127.M4B87   1975   615'.8512'0924[B]   75–24072

PRINTED IN THE UNITED STATES OF AMERICA

To my friends
John and Elisabeth Davidson

Contents

Illustrations may be found following page 160

PREFACE

The reputation of Franz Anton Mesmer has had its ups and downs during the two centuries since he came forward as a new kind of specialist in psychotherapy and abnormal psychology. Today that reputation is on the upgrade. Hypnotism, the offspring of Mesmerism, is flourishing once again after a long eclipse by psychoanalysis, and Mesmer's place as an earlier Freud is increasingly accepted by members of the psychiatric profession that he did more than anyone else to found.

But Mesmerism has had a much wider influence than that, ramifying from dynamic psychology into revolutionary politics, the occult sciences, and Gothic literature. All these elements must be covered in any systematic account of the man and his thought, and such is the purpose of this book.

I would like to thank John Leypoldt of the Photographic Services, Princeton University Library, for his assistance with the illustrations, and I am especially indebted to my wife, Nan Gillespie, for research in the German sources.

CHAPTER 1

The Academy and the Master

In 1811, when Napoleon controlled most of Europe and all of Germany and dragooned Prussian soldiers into the Grand Army of France for his coming invasion of Russia, the savants at the Academy of Science in Berlin occupied themselves with a special problem of their own—the doctrine of Franz Anton Mesmer.

The point at issue was the hypnotic trance, which Mesmer had discovered forty years earlier. A mass of data collected since then raised questions and suggested paradoxes about thought, memory, sense perception, and personality. Scientists and physicians who investigated the phenomenon found it endlessly perplexing.

The fully hypnotized subject appeared to be sound asleep, yet his thought processes might be, with regard to certain ideas, more acute than ever. He conversed rationally and performed complex acts without remembering anything when he woke. His senses hallucinated at the command of the hypnotist, when he "saw" objects that were not there and failed to see things right before his eyes.

Deep layers of his personality revealed themselves during the trance. He could recall long-forgotten events, often far back in his childhood, by somehow switching from his conscious mind to his subconscious. Most astonishing of all, he became susceptible to posthypnotic suggestion, carrying out when awake orders given to him during hypnosis and doing so in total ignorance of the cause or the meaning of his behavior.

The Berlin academicians, mulling over these claims, agreed that it would be useful at the start if they could reach some kind of consensus on the theory used by the master, Mesmer himself, to account for the trance. And so they poured over his writings, chopped texts, debated earnestly, and divided into various camps defending various readings.

13

Some agreed with Johann Kaspar Lavater, the Swiss founder of physiognomy, or the pseudoscience of reading character in the lines of the face and the structure of the features. Lavater described Mesmer as one for whom the trance implied a spiritual basis of mental events such that the mind of the hypnotist exercised a direct influence on the mind of the subject. Others agreed with Augustin Wilhelm Hufeland, who thought that Mesmer tended toward a materialistic theory of abnormal psychology and that his doctrine was about not mental persuasion or force of will, but the physical effect of one human being on another. Around the Lavater and Hufeland groups circled the academicians who refused to view the problem in such stark terms, who argued that Mesmer must have found a place for both mentalist and materialist factors. The debate grew warm.

And then somebody suggested asking Mesmer.

The suggestion, apparently so obvious, caused a ripple of surprise at the academy. Most of the academicians found it hard to believe that Mesmer was still alive. The discussion of his doctrine had proceeded on the tacit assumption, gradually and insensibly introduced among them during twelve years of silence on his part, that he must have died obscurely during his wandering in the backwater provinces of Switzerland and the Holy Roman Empire.

Actually, Mesmer had four more years to live, all of which he spent in the vicinity of Lake Constance. Now an old man, he never strayed far from his modest home, where his housekeeper presided, took care of his needs, and protected him from inconvenient intrusions on his privacy. He welcomed his close friends and kept in touch with his relatives along the shore of the lake. At home by himself, he played tunes on the glass harmonica or worked at a book that occupied him off and on for many years. As regularly as possible he drove out in his horse and carriage to attend private musicales and public concerts.

Visitors told engaging anecdotes about his pet canary, which lived in an open cage and woke him every morning by flying across his bedroom and landing on his head. During breakfast the bird perched on the sugar bowl and accepted lumps from his hand. When he got up, it would fly back to the cage and go to sleep when he stroked it.

The canary submitted to his hypnotic powers, as did the patients he took in his capacity of a physician specializing in nervous illnesses and neuroses. Local medical men were prominent among his acquaintances.

Mesmer lived in Meersburg in 1811, as ignorant of what the Berlin academicians were doing as they were of what he was doing. Although appreciating their attention, when he learned of it, and pleased by correspondence and visits from them, he felt disinclined to enter the debate about his doctrine. They could read his ideas in his book when it came out. As for a trip to the Prussian capital at their invitation, he begged off, saying that his seventy-eight years precluded so long a journey over bad roads. He did not want to interrupt the placid existence to which he had become accustomed for so long.

Now in his declining time of life, he lived contentedly far from the great world represented by the academicians. No one ignorant of his past could ever have guessed that he once had cut a larger figure in that world than any of them.

He had followed a rough, twisting, murky path to reach the quietude of Meersburg. Along the way he had become the focal point of a noisy international controversy. By the time the French Revolution broke out he was the most celebrated, notorious, adulated, vilified physician in Europe, termed a savior and a charlatan, a genius and a quack, a Hippocrates and a Cagliostro. He had founded a school, attracted fervent partisans, created virulent enemies, indulged in furious polemics, and added a new word to the dictionary—the word "mesmerism."

CHAPTER 2

Background

The basic ideas of Mesmerism—hypnotic trance, suggestion and autosuggestion, healing rays, stroking medicine—were in no sense original with the man who gave his name to the system. Mesmer contributed the controlled use of these ideas in a scientific, systematic manner capable of developing into something new, modern psychotherapy. Their naïve, unsystematic use dated from the dawn of history and never vanished from human experience down the ages. The facts have always been available, in the trivialities of everyday life no less than in medical psychology.

On the most ordinary level, the "hypnotic stare" of a powerful personality coercing someone psychologically is an example of Mesmerism. World leaders have often had this dominating quality to a consummate degree. It was remarked of Caesar, William the Conqueror, Napoleon, and Churchill, not to mention Adolf Hitler. (We could go behind humanity to an example from worldwide folklore, that of the bird immobilized by the stare of the approaching serpent; whether this is a scientific fact or not, animal hypnotism is certainly a fact.)

Group psychology presents quasi-hypnotic suggestion on another level, control of the individual's will by the mass emotion around him, which happens in aggregations from armies to political conventions. Often enough the individual who has gone along with mob fury will, in the cold light of dawn, wonder what on earth could have made him do so. On April 4, 1789, when the members of the Éstates-General at Versailles began a stampede to divest themselves of their age-old privileges in an orgy of class guilt and atonement, one aristocrat begged the presiding officer to suspend the session because these ordinarily sensible men had clearly gone off their heads. The session was not suspended, the privileges were

17

voted out in a grand display of mass psychology, and some of those who were carried along on the tide of emotion lived to regret it.

Euripides dealt with the true hypnotic trance more powerfully than any other writer. In his play *The Bacchae*, during the orgiastic rites in honor of the god Bacchus, the queen mother Agave leads her raving bacchantes to the slaying of her son, whom they all, in their inspired mania, believe to be a lion. Then Agave carries his head around in her arms until the ultimate horror of recognition when she comes out of her trance. The playwright's moral is broader than a warning against barbarous religion. It is a warning against a human frailty, the temptation to abdicate reason in favor of hypnotic hallucinations.

The Greek oracles submitted to the trance with less lethal consequences, although their psychology was the same as that of the bacchantes—namely, to close the normal faculties of perception and judgment and let them be replaced by the inspiration of the deity.

The most celebrated, the Oracle of Delphi, was located on the slopes of Mount Parnassus where cold vapors billowed up through clefts in the rocks. To begin a "consultation," the prophetess, in flowing robes and gold ornaments, entered the sanctum sanctorum and sat in a chair poised on a tripod standing over the heaviest outpouring of vapor. She took deep breaths until the trance supervened. Her face became contorted, her voice shrill, her gestures spasmodic. She intoned words that made no sense to the uninitiated—the kind of gibberish that has been so marked a feature in the annals of hypnotism and abnormal psychology. A priest of Delphi stood beside her during the trance. Recording her gibberish, he made an interpretation for the client, waiting nervously to hear what the god had to tell him through the prophetess, who, like many a subsequent practitioner of the occult arts, could not divine the significance of her revelation.

The Cumaean Sibyl, who lived in a cave in the volcanic rock overlooking the Bay of Naples, is important for an understanding of the oracular trance because Virgil gives a description of her in the throes of divination. He says in the *Aeneid* that she shook from "a spasm" in which her features assumed a wild expression, her breast heaved tumultuously under possession by "the mighty godhead," and the sounds that came from her throat were "more than human." In her trance the Cumaean Sibyl, unlike her sister at Delphi, spoke intelligibly, although her voice bore no resemblance to her normal speech—an example of dual personality without lapse into irrationality.

The cold vapor of Delphi, the volcanic fumes of Cumae, were fundamental in bringing on the hallucinatory state, comparable to LSD in our time and opium at all times. The seer at the Oracle of Ammon at Siwa deep in the Sahara Desert seems to have relied on self-hypnosis alone. His secret conference with Alexander the Great apparently took place without external aids to inspiration, judging from the little ancient historians tell us about this famous interview.

While the trance was appearing in a striking form in religion, Greek medicine made its own discoveries. Hippocrates talks much of the relationship between doctor and patient and of the vital necessity of making that relationship one of mutual respect. The patient's mental and moral attitudes can be decisive in certain cures. The doctor, therefore, should concern himself with them as much as with setting broken bones or prescribing remedies. Suggest to the patient that he will get well, convince him of the fact, and you entice him into becoming a partner in the healing process. A soothing touch may alleviate his pain. He may fall asleep at a command.

All this is in the realm of psychological medicine, which Hippocrates formulated in terms that are not outmoded today.

The power of parapsychology was displayed in antiquity's greatest hospital at Epidaurus. The shrine being dedicated to Asclepius, the god of healing, the sick congregated here to invoke his aid against their afflictions. The number of startling cures was past counting. The lucky ones went home grateful to Asclepius when they should have been self-congratulatory since the cures came from within themselves, from their capacity for autosuggestion and self-hypnosis.

Medicine and religion came together most astoundingly in the ministry of Christ, whom the Gospels explicitly call a healer, as well as a worker of miracles. No one has ever had similar authority over the ill, and therefore, no one has had such success in healing. The examples of his curing by a touch or a gesture are too well known to need recounting here. He Himself spoke of faith as part of the healing process, thereby recognizing the place of the subjective factor.

The significance of Christ in medicine is that He set a precedent for the Middle Ages. The Catholic Church maintained hospitals. Faith healers handled difficult cases. Saints performed miracles, and priests performed exorcisms in behalf of suffering humanity, but whatever the explanation of such acts in the aggregate, no one can miss the fact that some medieval miracles were instances of suggestion at work, that some exorcisms were successful through hypnotism, not the casting out of demons.

The data from numerous sources over some 2,000 years began to fall into a modern pattern during the Renaissance. By the sixteenth century medical psychology was growing into an autonomous subject.

One man stands at the origin of the trend—Philippus Theophrastus Bombastus von Hohenheim, who simplified matters for us by calling himself Paracelsus. He was a true man of the Renaissance in the sense that he stood between two worlds, the medieval and the modern, and bore the impress of both. Fantastic and scientific notions jumbled together in his mind.

He was an alchemist who believed lead could be turned into gold by the Philosopher's Stone. He was also an iatrochemist—that is, a pioneer in applying chemistry to medicine. Convinced of the reality of sorcery, he ruled it out of his medical practice on the ground that most illnesses have a natural origin, therefore require natural remedies.

Paracelsus furthered scientific medicine by calling for experiments rather than reliance on the written word. He furthered medical psychology by expounding a functional, dynamic theory of mind, will, emotions, and perception. His statements on the subjective factor in medicine have a modern ring:

> The spirit is the master, the imagination is the instrument, the body is the plastic material.
> The moral atmosphere surrounding the patient can have a strong influence on the course of his disease.
> It is not the curse or the blessing that works, but the idea. The imagination produces the effect.

Paracelsus used magnets to concentrate in his patients what he believed to be a cosmic fluid with healing properties. He must have been something of a naïve hypnotist, the only explanation of his boast that he could cause specific dreams. This makes him seem like a Mesmer beforetime, and Mesmer was called another Paracelsus by his enemies. The allegation was false, as we shall see. The element of truth is that Paracelsus did play a critical role in the medical psychology Mesmer inherited.

Paracelsian medicine attracted physicians for the next century. Jan Baptista van Helmont of Brussels, the foremost name in the tradition, practiced as both alchemist experimenting with transmutation and iatrochemist for whom the principal problem was to isolate in the laboratory the remedies—drugs, ointments, chemical elements—already existing in nature in a confused or corrupt condition.

In England, William Maxwell elaborated the theory of a healing cosmic fluid (Mesmer would be accused of plagiarizing from him, too). In Ireland, Valentine Greatraks became known as the Stroking Doctor for his success in healing by touch.

Europe was prepared for a phenomenon like Greatraks because the Royal Touch for the King's Evil (scrofula, or tuberculosis of the lymphatic system) was still an annual ceremony of the British and French monarchies, a holdover from the Middle Ages. William of Orange "touched" for scrofula at the end of the seventeenth century. He was an unbeliever in the power attributed to him, who is said to have muttered under his breath after going through one performance: "May God give you better health and more sense!" Yet his successors continued the rite. Young Samuel Johnson, the future Dr. Johnson of English letters and Boswell, was taken to be "touched" by Queen Anne, a pilgrimage to court that did him no good, for, as his mature portraits reveal, the swelling of the glands in his neck remained.

The Royal Touch died out because of loss of faith in the healing power of monarchs. That certain of their subjects possessed the power was proved in every generation. Remarkable cures crowded the medical record. Valentine Greatraks provided the best example of healing by touch.

Greatraks was a prodigy if only because he was neither a physician by training nor a religious mystic by inspiration, but simply an Irish country gentleman who lived under the Stuarts and until his mid-thirties during the reign of Charles II had no thought of doing more than cultivating his acres, seeing to the welfare of his tenants, and preaching Protestantism to Catholics. He felt repelled by unsightly illnesses, scrofula in particular. The descent of his medical vocation upon him left him baffled:

> About four years since, I had an impulse or a strange persuasion in my own mind (of which I am not able to give a rational account to another) which did frequently suggest to me that there was bestowed on me the gift of curing the King's Evil; which for the extraordinariness of it I thought fit to conceal for some time, but at length I communicated this to my wife, and told her that I did verily believe that God had given me the blessing of curing the King's Evil, for whether I were in private or publick, sleeping or waking, still I had the same impulse. But her reply was to me, that she conceived this was a strange imagination.

There the matter might have rested for the Irish squire and his dubious wife:

> But to prove the contrary, a few days after, there was one William Maher of Salterbridge in the parish of Lissmore that brought his son William to my house, desiring my wife to cure him, who was a person ready to afford her charity to her neighbours according to her small skill in surgery. On which my wife told me that there was one that had the King's Evil very grievously in the eyes, cheek and throat; whereupon I told her that she should now see whether this were a bare fancy or imagination as she thought or the Dictates of God's Spirit on my heart. And thereupon I laid my hands on the places affected, and prayed to God for Jesus' sake to heal him, and then I bid the parent two or three days afterwards to bring the child to me again, which accordingly he did, and then I saw the eye was almost whole, and the node, which was almost as big as a pullet's egg, was suppurated, and the throat strangely amended; and to be brief (to God's glory I speak), within a month discharged itself and was perfectly healed, and so continues, God be praised.

Moved by his success, Greatraks tried "touching" more of the ill. He cured scrofula, fever, palsy, hysteria, convulsions, St. Vitus' dance. Patients sought him out, among them John Flamsteed, later the Astronomer Royal, who admitted that "not finding any amends, I determined to depart." This was one of Greatraks' failures. Nonetheless, Flamsteed saw the Stroking Doctor work cures, and "for my part, I think his gift was of God."

Greatraks also failed when he came to England to "touch" Lady Conway for chronic headache. However disappointed the Conways were, Lord Conway was so satisfied with the healing art of the Irishman as exemplified by his success in Gloucestershire that he persuaded Henry Stubbe to publish the facts. Stubbe gave a natural explanation of the effect when Greatraks stroked a painful or diseased area of a patient's anatomy:

> God had bestowed upon Mr. Greatraks a peculiar temperament, or composed his body of some particular ferments, the effluvia whereof being introduced sometimes by a light, sometimes by a violent friction, should restore the temperament of the debilitated parts, reinvigorate the blood, and dissipate all the heterogeneous ferments out of the bodies of the diseased, by the eyes, nose, mouth, hands, and feet.

Stubbe thus believed that something physical passed from the Stroking Doctor to the patient. His analysis appealed to Robert Boyle. The Father of Chemistry commented:

> What you say of the subtlety of the effluvia, and of the great efficacy they are capable of, will not be much struck at by a Corpuscularian. And if I could think it proper here to add some of the instances of that kind, which I have lying by me in my notes about Occult Qualities (as they are commonly called), perhaps they would afford no despicable confirmation both to what you here say and to what I have elsewhere written about the power of invisible corpuscles.

Writing today, Boyle would replace "corpuscles" with "subatomic particles." The meaning would be the same in either case. The theory was that Greatraks healed because invisible but real entities streamed from him to the person he massaged. Paris remembered the Stroking Doctor a century later when Mesmer made a similar claim for himself.

Another stroking healer brings us right into the Mesmer era—Father Johann Gassner, the Austrian exorcist, older than Mesmer by seven years. Gassner as a young man suffered from nervous complaints—headaches, cramps, fits of trembling, dizzy spells, difficulty in breathing—that bothered him when he was performing his religious duties. He overcame them by prayer, fasting, and self-exorcism, which proved to his satisfaction that they were of diabolical origin and that he could control the demons responsible.

He extended his treatment to his parishioners, exorcizing those who failed to respond to ordinary medical treatment. The Church had always used exorcisms, but Gassner dispensed with the bell, book, and candle ceremony, influenced his patients through his powerful personality and priestly vocation, stroked their stricken areas with holy water, and relieved them of their infirmities without the ugliness, horror, or depravity so frequently seen in cases of diabolical possession.

Gassner had an extraordinary ability to control the autonomic nervous systems of those he healed. Before witnesses, some of them skeptical when he started, he ordered one woman to increase her heartbeat to 120 per minute and then to slow it down until no pulse could be detected. She obeyed both times, and the second time a physician pronounced her dead because her heart had stopped. Gassner commanded the demon to leave, whereupon the woman came to her senses and rose to her feet. She was alive and well and permanently cured.

A nun who had been compelled to leave her convent because she suffered from convulsions came to Gassner desperate for relief. He went through his solemn ritual with her and intoned in Latin; "If there is anything preternatural about this illness, I command in the name of Jesus that it manifest itself at once." The nun went into convulsions, which Gassner took to be the writhing of the demon possessing her. Again the exorcist commanded the demon to leave. Again he was obeyed. Again the cure was complete.

The healing process in the worst cases came to a chilling climax with the expulsion of the preternatural being preying on the victim. A multitude of the less ill profited from Gassner's ministrations in less harrowing exhibitions, but anyone severely afflicted had to be severely shaken by the cure because, in his view, the malignant demon would not depart without a struggle. There had to be a violent crisis—another superficial resemblance to Mesmerism, where the explanation was scientific, not religious.

Gassner settled in Bavaria, enjoying the patronage of the Bishop of Ratisbon, and cured many difficult cases in the privacy of the confessional and at public demonstrations. He soon became an embarrassment, the storm center of a furious quarrel.

The quarrel turned ᴑn the question of what occurred when he "stroked" the sick. One commission of theologians endorsed his "laying on of hands" in his own terms—he was casting out devils. A second commission expressed doubt about possession being so common. The medical profession took a stand against him. A few physicians believed he might be right, but most denied the reality of possession and accused him of fostering dangerous illusions in unbalanced minds. Caught in the middle of the dispute, solicitous about the sick souls as well as sick bodies in his diocese, concerned that the truth should prevail, the bishop finally decided to allow Gassner to continue practicing, merely ordering him to confine himself to patients referred to him by their local clergy.

The debate raged in 1775 when the Elector of Bavaria put the problem to a Viennese doctor just arrived in Munich. The new arrival was Franz Anton Mesmer, who had an explanation (negative) for Gassner and all those who professed to cure nervous, mental, and psychosexual ailments except by animal magnetism.

CHAPTER 3

The Gamekeeper's Son

Mesmer belonged to the frontier region where Lake Constance divides Switzerland from the German lands to the north.

He was born at Iznang, a Swabian town on the westernmost arm of the lake, on May 23, 1734. His ancestors had lived in Swabia for generations, his father, Anton Mesmer, being related to the Mesmers of the Black Forest, while his mother, Maria Ursula Michel, came from the Michels of Meersburg on the northern shore of the lake. The parents' names indicate a strongly Catholic family tradition, and since Anton Mesmer served as gamekeeper to the Bishop of Constance, a pious home atmosphere might be taken for granted even if we did not know that Maria Mesmer encouraged at least some of her nine children to enter the Church. One son, Johann, fulfilled her fondest hopes by becoming a priest. Franz Anton, the third of the nine, started out along the route of his mother's preference only to get sidetracked into a worldly vocation.

Little is known about Mesmer's home life. He himself never discussed it as far as we know, a silence prompting speculation that he had some reason for disliking and resenting his childhood experience. Psychological interpretation of the great psychologist cannot, when applied to his formative years, go beyond that without becoming guesswork. Poverty was not the problem. His father's job carried responsibility and raised the family above the peasant class, giving it respectability, status, and a degree of comfort.

Tradition and probability converge on one point, that Mesmer never shook off the effects of the physical surroundings in which he grew up. The wide expanse of Lake Constance is the dominating feature of the Iznang landscape, and in the distance to the south rises the majestic backdrop of the Swiss Alps, always holding the eye and the imagination whether they tower in sharp outline under bright sunshine or loom through the mist in snow or rain. The Rhine River, rising in the Alps, flowing through Swiss glaciers into the lake, emerges at the western end not far from Iznang en route to the spectacular Schaffhausen Falls. This is Rhine wine country, rich with ripening grapes at harvesttime. No biographer has questioned the impact of such a setting on the senses and emotions of an impressionable child.

In later life Mesmer added autobiographical details, picturing himself as precociously susceptible to every impulse from a vernal wood. He was, if we can believe him, beguiled by nature from infancy, as if destiny were giving him a presentiment that his interest in the woodland and its denizens would bear fruit in the discoveries of his maturity. Perhaps he seemed a little more remarkable to himself in retrospect than he had been at the time. Still, his father, the gamekeeper, no doubt talked to him about the cunning and the oddities of nature as the pair made the rounds of the bishop's wooded domain, and the idea is not incredible that, before leaving Iznang, Mesmer had in the back of his mind serious questions about natural law and scientific explanation.

The works of man influenced him scarcely less than the works of nature, for the Lake Constance area had historical roots going back to Roman times. Relics of the distant past were everywhere in the lakeside towns—reminders of the time of Charlemagne, of the establishment of the Holy Roman Empire, of the Crusades, the Teutonic Knights, the Reformation, the periods of Gothic and Baroque architecture. The island of Reichenau out in the lake held the tomb of Charles the Fat, Charlemagne's grandson, who died there in 888 after his deposition for failing to halt the Viking incursions. Radolfzell cherished the relics of the somewhat legendary saint from whom it took its name.

The city of Constance had been an episcopal see since the early Middle Ages, rising to prominence under a line of bishops who accumulated ecclesiastical and secular authority until they ranked as both powerful churchmen and princes of the Holy Roman Empire. The medieval cathedral and the Renaissance town hall were the city's most prominent buildings, along with the Kaufhaus where the fifteenth-century Council of Constance held the sessions that put an end to the Great Schism in the Catholic Church. Constance later belonged to the Swabian League promoting reforms in the

Empire, and joined the Protestant Schmalkaldic League during the Reformation. After the tumult and violence of the Reformation died down, Constance returned to its Catholic and imperial allegiance, and so it remained into the eighteenth century, no longer a center of European events but still a valued outpost of Maria Theresa's Empire.

Mesmer retained an abiding affection for this German-Swiss region with its age-old towns, crooked buildings, narrow winding streets, and villagers whose lives had scarcely changed in centuries. He returned to it periodically as to a sanctuary where he could relax, collect his thoughts, mull over his problems, and plan his strategy for a return to the larger, stormier world of Vienna and Europe.

Since his father had the ear of the Bishop of Constance, Mesmer grew up with distinct advantages. The two prelates who held the see during his childhood were highborn aristocrats as their names imply—Johannes Franziskus Schwenk von Stauffenberg and Damian Hugo von Schönborn. Visiting them at the episcopal residence, the gamekeeper's son learned to conduct himself among the lordly and the venerable without self-consciousness, the origin of the ease and assurance so notable when he dealt with the nobles and crowned heads of Europe. He benefited from the direct patronage of Bishop von Schönborn, who agreed with his mother that so intelligent a child should be educated for the Church.

In 1743 nine-year-old Franz Anton Mesmer entered a school run by monks to begin the studies that would prepare him for the university and ultimately the priesthood. These teachers gave him his primary education, six years of languages, classical literature, the Catholic catechism, and music. The latter subject became his passion at the monastic school when he began to read scores and play an instrument.

The pupils at this institution received no formal training in modern history, although they were expected to know something about Austria's majestic House of Hapsburg that had given their Empire rulers since the thirteenth century. They could not go unaware of the War of the Austrian Succession, the din of which echoed in their classrooms as their own Hapsburg ruler, Maria Theresa, lost the province of Silesia to Frederick the Great of Prussia. This welter of campaigning and fighting, and the evils consequent thereon, filled the years during which Mesmer passed from childhood into adolescence (1740–48). The talk of masters and boys at school was of their august empress and her gallant struggle to maintain the territorial integrity of the Holy Roman Empire. The boys, if not the monks, learned to hate the Prussian ogre who had despoiled her, and the Empire, of Silesia.

In 1750 Mesmer went up from his monastic school to the University of Dillingen in Bavaria, where he studied philosophy for four years before proceeding on to theology at the University of Ingolstadt, also in Bavaria. Both Dillengen and Ingolstadt were Jesuit institutions, the latter one of the most celebrated of those run by the sons of St. Ignatius, the master educators of Europe for the past two centuries. At the end he had received from his Jesuit professors an introduction to modern thought, especially scientific thought, as well as a solid grounding in the traditional systems of the Church.

The Jesuits taught Aristotelian logic and Thomistic metaphysics, to which they added the philosophy of their illustrious pupil of the past century Descartes. They even touched upon such non-Catholic writers as Christian Wolff, systematizer and expounder of the philosophy of Leibniz. In short, the Catholic Church had not yet fixed upon St. Thomas Aquinas as its official philosopher or declared Thomism mandatory in its schools, so that Mesmer entered an intellectual milieu alive with different possibilities. The Aristotle-Aquinas tradition left no important deposit in his thinking, which took rather to the comprehensive cosmological speculations of those modern philosophers, Descartes principally, who tried to interpret all physical reality in the same terms, dropping the Aristotelian notion that earthly and heavenly bodies are essentially different.

This intellectual bias made him receptive to the new scientific ideas. At Ingolstadt he learned Copernican astronomy and Cartesian mathematics. His professors repeated Galileo's experiments with moving objects, expounded Kepler's laws of planetary motion, debated Newton's physics, and noted the refinements added by lesser men to the pioneering work of the masters.

Mesmer, judging from his mature thought, always preferred general ideas to more precise and limited concepts. He preferred Galileo's astronomy to his work on the pendulum; Descartes' theo-

ry of gigantic vortices swirling through the universe to his analyti-
cal geometry; Newton's theory of universal gravitation to his optics.
In reading Descartes, Mesmer came across a point of immense importance to his later thinking: the conviction that medicine could
be turned into an exact science by extending cosmological laws to
the physiology of the human body.

Mesmer's penchant for grandiose speculation has led to the inference that he went beyond his formal courses at Dillingen and Ingolstadt and studied the occult sciences associated particularly with
the name of Paracelsus, the reputed magician and medical innova-
tor of the sixteenth century. It has been assumed that he had some
acquaintance with existing societies preaching hermetic doctrines
and the "wisdom of the East" such as the Rosicrucians and the
Freemasons. His familiarity with the Faust legend can be confidently assumed since every German university student knew about the
man who sold his soul to the devil.

Even if all this be granted, the conclusion does not follow that the
occult sciences dictated the development of Mesmerism later on.
Mesmer began as a scientist in the ordinary sense, his guides being,
not Paracelsus and Faust, but Descartes and Newton. His early interest in extrasensory perception came from an attitude understandable in our time—namely, that good evidence existed for its
reality. Only in his later years, long after his formulation of Mesmerism, did he give way to fantastic speculations about the occult
sciences.

One thing he certainly failed to carry away from the university
was his religious vocation. Realizing he had no aptitude or desire
for the priesthood, he refused to accept holy orders or a place in
the Church.

He turned first to the law. Having entered the University of
Vienna in 1759, he pursued a course of legal studies for about one
year, just long enough to learn that service in the courts held no
more attractions for him than service to the Church. He lacked the
type of mind that can find a home amid paperwork, in the study of
formulas, precedents, and conflicting opinions. His interest and
ability lay in science, so that, shifting once more, he at last found
the vocation for which he had been searching. He would be a physician.

In 1760 he began six years of medical studies in Vienna. This was an exciting time historically, for the Seven Years' War was raging and Frederick the Great defeated the Austrians at the Battle of Liegnitz almost as Mesmer started working toward the degree of Doctor of Medicine. The conflict continued until 1763, by which time he was halfway to his goal.

It was an exciting time to be a medical student in Vienna. Maria Theresa had started a complete renovation in the teaching of medicine at the university during the 1740s, and the changes were firmly established by the 1760s. Some of the best minds in Europe were on the faculty.

The man behind this achievement, Gerhard van Swieten, was a Dutchman who had taken his degree at Leiden in his homeland, where he had been a pupil of the century's foremost physician, Hermann Boerhaave, a central figure in breaking the hold of ancient texts on modern medicine. Boerhaave disproved the doctrine of the four humors expounded by the Roman physician Galen and used by Ben Jonson in his famous play—*Every Man in His Humour*—the doctrine that the sanguine, choleric, phlegmatic, and melancholic temperaments are connected with the predominance in individuals of blood, yellow bile, phlegm, or black bile. Boerhaave described the body as composed of solids and fluids, disease being a matter of changes in the tissues or imbalance in the fluidic mixtures. He wrote on the circulatory system, the nervous system, functions of the brain, and the possibility that electrical impulses or magnetic attractions caused glandular secretions. He founded a clinic and perfected the technique of deciding cures through meticulous case histories of his patients.

Boerhaave's monumental achievement brought pupils from all over Europe to sit at his feet, including his compatriot Gerhard van Swieten, who became his assistant and probably would have been his successor in the Leiden chair except for religion. Van Swieten was a Catholic, a fact that ruled him out even in comparatively tolerant but staunchly Protestant Holland. He therefore accepted a call to Vienna in 1745 to become personal physician and librarian to Maria Theresa. His extraordinary ability caused her to appoint him president of the Medical Faculty in 1748 with a commission to reorganize the whole medical system, by now encrusted with outmoded ideas and usages.

Van Swieten was a perfect official of the imperial government.

He even resembled the empress, each being a portly figure with a broad face, double chin, heavy eyelids, and matter-of-fact expression—as solid and sober as the Empire they represented. Van Swieten added that specifically masculine affliction, a progressively receding hairline.

He brought the Vienna Medical School under imperial control, so that the empress appointed professors following his advice. Licenses and salaries were now decided by the state, not by the Medical Faculty, to the annoyance of its members. Van Swieten let them *be* annoyed and went his way—erecting new buildings, opening new laboratories, establishing new chairs, founding a clinic like the one in Leiden. Between administrative duties, he lectured to students and wrote his magisterial *Commentaries* on Boerhaave's *Aphorisms on Diagnosing and Curing Illnesses*. In 1758 Maria Theresa rewarded her medical counselor by naming him a baron of the Holy Roman Empire. He remains in medical history the founder of the Old Vienna School.

In 1756, having accumulated too many duties to perform them all properly, Van Swieten turned his chair in medicine over to another Dutchman, Anton de Haen, a man similar to him in nothing but a genius for medicine. De Haen was a thin, pale, intense individual with a prominent nose and chin, a prissy mouth, and a waspish disposition—Galen's and Ben Jonson's "choleric man." He managed to hold science and superstition side by side in his mind. A pupil of Boerhaave, he became Europe's best teacher of clinical medicine, making his students keep exhaustive case histories of patients in the wards. He performed autopsies, used the thermometer, resorted to electrotherapy to cure nervous ailments, and published an annual report on his clinic. But De Haen at the same time believed in the preternatural causes of disease and held that some of his patients suffered from diabolical possession.

The chair in pharmacology established by Van Swieten went to Anton von Stoerck, the bright young man of the faculty who had taken his medical degree as recently as 1757. Stoerck was Mesmer's friend, as well as his teacher. They were of an age, the professor being only three years older than the pupil, and both came from the Swabian hinterland of the Holy Roman Empire. Their common interests gave rise to a mutual regard that endured for some fifteen years. Stoerck served as a witness at Mesmer's wedding. Mesmer celebrated with Stoerck the latter's appointment by the empress to the presidency of the faculty after Van Swieten's death in 1772.

This amity finally soured in the heat of Mesmer's notoriety, something no one could have predicted, least of all the two principals, when Stoerck was showing Mesmer how to use drugs and how to distill curative potions from poisons.

The triumvirate of Van Swieten, De Haen, and Stoerck dominated the science of medicine in Vienna during Mesmer's student years. Enlightened and advanced for the most part in their diagnosis and treatment of illnesses and injuries, they were not revolutionaries, but rather cautious practitioners who taught strict adherence to the rules and no nonsense. They were the leaders of the Old Vienna School.

Mesmer followed their lectures and demonstrations for six years in the four-square stone building with its drafty corridors, high-ceilinged rooms, and large surgical amphitheater where they held forth. He learned from them about Boerhaave, Sydenham, and other doctors who had recently revised their science. He followed their own contributions by hearing Van Swieten on corrosive sublimate as a cure for syphilis, De Haen on the use of electric shocks to alleviate the convulsions of St. Vitus' dance, and Stoerck on the chemical reasons why hemlock can be medicinal rather than lethal. Then there were the ordinary professors who took him through the basics of anatomy, physiology, infectious diseases, obstetrics, and medical ethics.

Mesmer received as good an education as that available to medical students anywhere in Europe. He completed his courses to the satisfaction of his teachers, passed his examinations, and wrote a dissertation that brought him, later on, under the suspicion of purveying occult mysticism.

Writing in Latin, the language of the learned, he gave this earliest product of his pen the title *Dissertatio Physico-medica de Planetarum Influxu,* which may be translated *A Physico-medical Inquiry Concerning the Influence of the Planets.* In later years he referred to his dissertation as *The Influence of the Planets on the Human Body,* a title that has the virtues of brevity and precision and that, since the author himself sanctioned it, may properly be used.

His choice of a subject seems surprising for a candidate for the degree of Doctor of Medicine. He proposes to show how the heavenly bodies affect human beings, an enterprise under a dark shadow in the Age of Reason, increasingly left to astrologers, occultists, and charlatans while rational men got on with science. The temptation to become mystical remained strong in Germany. The homeland of Faust and Paracelsus was also the place where the secret society of the Rosicrucians began, and its members, late in the eighteenth century, were still planning the perfection of humanity through the "wisdom of the pyramids" handed down from the seers of ancient Egypt and presumably preserved since then by an apostolic succession of secret devotees. Many a German student still dabbled in occult mysticism.

This cannot have been true of Mesmer. He was no mystic. Everything else aside, he would never have been tolerated as such by the medical faculty of the University of Vienna, not even by De Haen, whose diabolism was in the Catholic, not the occult, tradition. Mesmer's degree would never have been approved by Van Swieten, who as head of the medical faculty was promoting scientific medicine and as an adviser to the empress was bent on suppressing all practitioners of the occult arts, the Rosicrucians in particular. The university men were the more suspicious of the occultism precisely because of the contemporary interest in it. They were on their guard. Since Mesmer passed his doctoral examination with the assent and compliments of his examiners, he clearly had a different ambition than to defend antique lore or the quasi-scientific doctrines of Paracelsian medicine.

His purpose was to explain in a strictly scientific manner the influence of the heavens on the earth, more specifically, the effect of gravitation on human physiology. The project was so far from being mystical, so unexceptional in the eighteenth century, that Mesmer was able to borrow whole sections of his theory from the respected English physician Richard Mead.

Gravitation was a puzzle for scientists. Unanimous agreement existed that all bodies attract one another according to the theory of Sir Isaac Newton. But what is the cause of gravitation? Newton left that question open, refusing to commit himself to a material or an immaterial cause.

Mesmer opts for a material cause, but one rarefied to the point of intangibility, undetectable by our senses. He uses the phrase "universal fluid" for this cause and claims that as a hypothesis it explains not only gravitation, but also magnetism, electricity, light, heat, and whatever else the universe may hold of a related nature. All things are immersed in this fluid as in a cosmic sea.

Now, just as the seas of the earth have tides, so does the universal fluid, which is subject to great surges across interstellar space and through the heavenly bodies in a never-ending ebb and flow. It passes through the earth and everything on the earth. It sets up "tides" in the bloodstream and the nerves of human beings.

This is where astronomy joins medicine. The direct influence of the universal fluid and its indirect influence by way of the heavenly bodies make us healthy or ill. Mesmer comments on "this force, which is the cause of universal gravitation and, no doubt, the basis of all bodily properties; which, in effect, in the smallest particles of fluids and solids of our bodies, contracts, distends and causes cohesion, elasticity, irritability, magnetism, and electricity; a force which can, in this context, be called *animal gravitation*."

That last phrase sounds a permanent note in Mesmer's thinking. He infers the existence of the universal fluid, here termed "animal gravitation," but he has not yet related its immense import to his medical science. The idea lay dormant in his mind, ready to give him, when defined, systematized, and put to practical use, the basis for a new science of abnormal psychology. He never went back on what he said in *The Influence of the Planets on the Human Body*. Each of his major works extends the theory, finding more meanings and implications in it. When he went from "animal gravitation" to "animal magnetism," he founded Mesmerism.

This development was not something Mesmer excogitated from his inner consciousness. It sprang from his medical practice when he was drawn by certain difficult cases to begin experimenting with novel methods of treatment. Six years elapsed before this trend began. Meanwhile, he kept his theory of a universal fluid in the back of his mind as an intellectual toy to play with at odd moments, never guessing how it would suddenly revolutionize his medical concepts.

When he published his doctoral dissertation, he imagined that a unique, all-pervasive force reaches out across astronomical distances, joins physical bodies to one another, keeps the cosmos in a dynamic tension, gives rise to secondary causes like gravitation, and finally affects human beings by penetrating their bodies.

Could the universal fluid be "channeled" in such a way as to make it available to the physician? Mesmer saw no answer to that question as he opened his medical practice in Vienna.

He had a good sendoff. His diploma, signed by Van Swieten and Stoerck, referred to him as "the very learned Master Anton Mesmer" and mentioned his achievements in fulsome terms. No charges of occultism sullied his reputation. He was ready to join the medical fraternity.

The founder of Mesmerism, like the founder of psychoanalysis at a later date, emerged from the Vienna School of Medicine (for Freud it was, of course, the New Vienna School) without any thought except of setting up in the conventional type of medical practice.

Mesmer was a mature man of thirty-two, broad and deep in his culture, holder of the PhD and the MD, professionally equipped in philosophy, theology and medicine, knowledgeable in the sciences, experimental and speculative. Well advanced in music, his passionate avocation all these years at the university, he now played the cello and the clavichord with flair and personalized technique.

CHAPTER 4

Dr. Mesmer's Vienna

Mesmer the physician and psychologist was in his maturity a man of one idea, which might not unfairly be termed an *idée fixe*—the cure of psychosomatic illnesses by animal magnetism. He devoted the best part of his life to an earnest, passionate, often belligerent, and sometimes petulant campaign for the recognition and acceptance of his discovery by the medical profession. What he tells us of himself is almost entirely associated with his grand design. Our knowledge of his private life comes from other sources—the testimony of friends and enemies, public records, journalistic accounts, and, of course, inference based on human nature and its probabilities.

The hiatus in Mesmer's life falls between his reception into the medical profession (1767) and his undertaking to treat the patient whose malady led him to the theory of animal magnetism as a practical medical cure (1773). This is the period when he appears most human, when he is very much a Viennese enjoying the pleasures of the city.

His doctoral dissertation appeared in print during the probationary year he had to put in before becoming a fully qualified member of his profession with a place in the corporation of physicians, the Vienna Faculty of Medicine. During this year and immediately afterward he pursued his studies; attended lectures and conferences; watched diagnoses, operations, and deaths at the hospitals; followed case histories at the clinic; treated his own patients; and consulted his colleagues about difficult cases.

Van Swieten was too occupied with administrative duties to spare him much time, but he remained a close associate of his old professors De Haen and Stoerck. De Haen was the most important from the standpoint of Mesmer's medical practice. The master clinician

39

made him an expert in the case history method, and Mesmer spent long hours at bedsides in the clinic observing patients who suffered from all the ailments native to the human organism. He took notice in particular of those afflicted with mental or nervous derangement. Lunacy, epilepsy, paralysis, hysterical blindness, chronic nightmares, pathological coughing and trembling, fits of depression and panic—he saw how frequently conventional medicine failed to cure them.

Even the latest thing, De Haen's electrotherapy, succeeded in only a minority of cases. Patients were peculiarly difficult to treat when the apparatus of batteries, wires, and electrodes disturbed them, when they feared the shocks they were about to receive. Emotions, attitudes, and trust in, or suspicion of, the doctor determined the fate of the cure in many cases. Yet psychology was irrelevant to the treatment of strictly physical ailments like broken bones and damaged organs. Mesmer had read of this distinction, but experience brought the point home to him more forcefully than ever before. He ruminated about it.

Meanwhile, his private life underwent a transformation. On January 10, 1768, he married Maria Anna von Bosch, a member of the Austrian aristocracy with connections in the imperial army. Being a daughter of Georg Friedrich von Eulenschenk (an officer in the army medical corps), Maria Anna possessed wealth inherited from her father and her late husband to go with the high social status they bequeathed her.

Since she was ten years older than Mesmer, some of his acquaintances raised their eyebrows at his choice of a wife. However, at thirty-four he had reached the age of discretion in affairs of the heart, and he looked for a settled life with a compatible partner, not for youthful romance. Maria Anna charmed him. He felt comfortable with her. There were definite gains for him in their union. He liked to entertain, and she, reared in a big house in Vienna, knew how to play the hostess. His profession was medicine, and she, the daughter of a physician, could be understanding and helpful in his vocation.

Even the fact that she had a teenage son was no drawback in Mesmer's eyes. He treated Franz von Bosch as if he were his own son, giving him personal affection, advice, and guidance. Mesmer was a good family man who would have made an affectionate father. His stepson was the surrogate for the children he never had.

Finally, in judging Mesmer's marriage there is the question of Maria Anna's wealth and status. Money tempted Mesmer throughout his life, and his wife brought it to him in abundance, releasing him from his worries about making a living, permitting him to set up a medical practice to suit his own taste. He wanted to move in fashionable Viennese society, and through her he did so without waiting, toadying, or social climbing.

Mesmer went into marriage wholeheartedly, conscientiously, and confident that he had made the right decision.

The wedding of Dr. Franz Anton Mesmer and Maria Anna von Bosch was Vienna's most splendid for the year 1768, not a difficult achievement given the somber atmosphere left by the recent visitation of the plague. Empress Maria Theresa was still in mourning. The Viennese, nevertheless, were eager for a splash of color in their lives after the drabness and danger of the past months. They turned out in crowds to see the ceremony in historic St. Stephen's Cathedral when the Archbishop of Vienna presided in the full ecclesiastical magnificence of the Catholic Church. Army officers were there, brilliant in their uniforms, drawn by the Eulenschenk and Bosch connections. Members of the Faculty of Medicine and other departments of the university came to see their colleague become a married man. A concourse of onlookers outside the massive doors of the cathedral cheered the couple as they emerged and drove off.

Returning from their honeymoon, the Mesmers moved to the Landstrasse near the Danube, where they lived in an elegant mansion belonging to Frau Mesmer's family, overlooking the Prater, Vienna's Hyde Park or Bois de Boulogne. They began their participation in the social and musical life of Vienna. They entertained at home; they circulated through the city's high society of princes, ambassadors, landed magnates, and prosperous merchants.

Mesmer was a social animal who enjoyed intimate sessions with his friends when they talked at length about a myriad of subjects—political, scientific, philosophical—and he could prove by his vast knowledge that he kept his large library for use, not ostentation. A good conversationalist, he enjoyed dialectical give-and-take in a good-natured way.

Still, he could turn stubborn all of a sudden. He had a habit of introducing abstruse problems such as the cause of gravitation, and from there he would go into the theories of his doctoral dissertation that "engaged" him in the existentialist sense. Then he would become argumentative, dogmatic, warmly determined to extort agreement from an opponent or at least to have the last word. His friends accepted this combativeness as an engaging eccentricity in which they might as well indulge him. He seems to have kept his friendships intact until the scandal surrounding animal magnetism.

The Mesmers had numerous relatives in the city among the Eulenschenks, the Bosches, and the Mesmers. The doctor's stepson lived with them for a few years, as did his mother-in-law, evidently without any serious friction. Various members of the Mesmer family, who, like the doctor, had come from Swabia to Vienna in search of a career, lived nearby. Joseph Mesmer, a cousin, obtained a prominent place in the Austrian education system when Van Swieten was overhauling the schools and bringing them up to date. Another cousin entered the service of the Archbishop of Salzburg. The Eulenschenks, Bosches, and Mesmers were, therefore, an interlocked clan radiating a degree of influence through the capital of the Holy Roman Empire, and their headquarters were in the mansion on the Landstrasse where Dr. Mesmer held forth.

That influence extended into court circles even though the Mesmers were not on a personal footing with Maria Theresa or Joseph II. They were close to those close to the empress. Through Van Swieten they were in touch with his colleagues in the imperial service. Chancellor Wenzel Anton von Kaunitz, the most powerful figure in the Holy Roman Empire outside the royal family, was an acquaintance on whom they could call for minor favors. The narrow circle of those at the top in Vienna made it possible for the Mesmers to know most of them to a greater or lesser degree.

Unfortunately, Mesmer never knew that royal object lesson in abnormal psychology, Grand Duchess Isabella of Parma. Isabella, arriving in Vienna in 1760 to marry Joseph, proved to be the strangest individual in the strange family history of the Hapsburgs. She was a prey to morbid depression, subject to shattering nervous crises, and hounded by a chronic death wish. Her only relief came from the passionate emotion she bestowed, not on her husband, but on one of his sisters. After the birth of a daughter in 1762, she went into a depression that left her unable to cope with herself any longer. Van Swieten lavished his enormous fund of medical knowledge and his advanced therapeutic techniques on Isabella without achieving more than a temporary alleviation of her condition. Obviously willing the event, she died in 1763. Isabella's problem never became common knowledge outside the royal family, and a mere medical student, as Mesmer then was, could not have heard more than dim echoes of the tragedy.

Kaunitz was another, lesser, indeed comical study in neurosis. The chancellor suffered from severe hypochondria. A cough or a sneeze, his own or somebody else's, upset him, and he took to his bed when he heard of illness among his associates. A patron of the Mozarts, he refused to let them come anywhere near him when Wolfgang was recovering from a mild and no longer contagious case of smallpox—the small red spots on his face frightened the chancellor. Kaunitz's worry over his own health was so extreme that he, a gentleman of culture and refinement, lost all sense of the proprieties when taking care of himself. Playing the host at stately banquets at his residence, he had the engaging habit of summoning a bowl of water, brushes, and other dental implements and carefully, thoroughly, and meticulously cleaning his teeth at the table in front of his guests. Mesmer's thoughts on the chancellor's antics, which he may have seen at first hand and certainly knew about, can only be guessed at.

Maria Theresa, Joseph II, Kaunitz—these were the three major figures during Mesmer's Viennese decade (1768–78). They presided over a city rising into an era of splendor and opulence, over a people regaining their equilibrium after suffering from war and pestilence. The Seven Years' War had ended in 1763, and there would be no major conflict for Austria until the outbreak of the French Revolution. The one big international imbroglio resolved itself in 1772, when Austria took part, with Prussia and Russia, in the dismemberment of their common neighbor and victim. This was only the First Partition of Poland, with two more to come before the eighteenth century ended.

Life was good in Vienna, and growing better. The city was becoming the Vienna so familiar to the Western world, the sparkling, light-hearted, carefree metropolis on the slopes between the Vienna Woods and the Danube.

Within the old walls, the line where the Ringstrasse now runs, lay the heart of the old city, a complex of buildings, medieval and modern, dominated by the towering spire of St. Stephen's. The cathedral dated mainly from the fourteenth century. Since then, the Renaissance had come and gone, leaving an architectural heritage of its own, and then the eighteenth-century master Fisher von Erlach added the next great phase. Working in the Baroque style, he built two gems—the Karlskirche, a church with a dome and Roman pillars, and the exquisite royal library—but his masterpiece stood on the outskirts of Vienna, ornate Schönbrunn Palace, the residence of the Hapsburgs. His successor, Lukas von Hildebrandt, added churches, monasteries, mansions, gardens, and the beautiful Belvedere Palace done for Austria's foremost soldier, Prince Eugene of Savoy. When Mesmer lived in Vienna, the delicate Rococo style prevailed in the elegant town houses of the titled and wealthy.

The people were pleasure-mad according to many visitors. Mesmer, with a view overlooking the Prater, could witness scenes such as those reported by Michael O'Kelly, the Irish tenor who created secondary roles in Mozart operas (and spelled his name "Ochelli" while singing in Italy). O'Kelly wrote after his visit to Vienna in 1783:

> The Prater I consider the finest promenade in Europe, far surpassing in variety our own beautiful Hyde Park. It is about four miles in length; on each side of the road are fine chestnut trees, and a number of avenues and retired drives. These roads, on spring and summer evenings, are thronged with carriages. On all sides, as in our Hyde Park and Bushy Park, deer are seen grazing, and gazing at the passing crowds. At the end of the principal avenue is an excellent tavern, besides which, in many parts of this enchanting spot, there are innumerable cabarets, frequented by people of all ranks in the evening, who immediately after dinner proceed thither to regale themselves with their favorite dish, fried chickens, cold ham, and sausages; white beer, and Hofner wines, by way of dessert; and stay there until a late hour: dancing, music, and every description of merriment prevail; and every evening, when not professionally engaged, I was sure to be in the midst of it.

O'Kelly sang in the Viennese opera, attended the theater, and watched the "procession of sledges" through the city over the snow in the depths of winter. He was among the first to mention a heady new dance, the waltz.

The city saw its population pass the 150,000 level during the 1770s. The residents were multinational and polyglot, for this was the capital of the Holy Roman Empire, which spilled across boundaries, provinces, nations, nationalities, peoples, and races. To Vienna came representatives from half of Europe—cultured Germans, musical Italians, melancholy Slavs, romantic Bohemians, booted and befurred Magyars from the plains of Hungary. They mingled in a bewildering welter under the dominating forces of Austrian might and Viennese culture.

If Mesmer had been looking for an example of his "harmony" principle in politics, he could have found it in the Hapsburg government of the Holy Roman Empire. Maria Theresa ranks among the greatest members of her house if only because of her success in holding the allegiance of non-Austrians. At her moment of peril at the beginning of the War of the Austrian Succession, she had gone to the Diet at Pressburg and thrown herself on the mercy of the Hungarian nobles, who responded with all the impetuous gallantry of the Magyar people. After that, the empress always found men willing and eager to defend her and her cause to the bitter end.

But she had trouble with her co-ruler. Joseph II did not see eye to eye with his mother because they adopted different approaches to religion. Maria Theresa was a fervent Catholic of the old school, committed wholeheartedly to the system that had come down from the Counterreformation—the system of Papal authority, Jesuit guidance, and the Index of Prohibited Books. Joseph, on the contrary, was touched by the skeptical mentality of the Age of Reason.

The difference between empress and emperor should not be exaggerated. They parted company, not at the center of religion where faith was concerned, but on the fringes where politics was concerned. The emperor had his way. Joseph wanted to curtail historic rights of the Catholic Church in Austria, and Maria Theresa, an old woman and a still-grieving widow, would not oppose her son no matter how much she disliked what he was doing.

He closed monasteries she patronized. When the empress found the lodges of the Freemasons proliferating in Vienna and elsewhere in the Empire, mindful that the Popes had condemned Freemasonry, she started a campaign to have them eradicated. The emperor countermanded the order because he supported the Masons as a counterweight to Papal political power. Joseph admired the

Masonic principle of scientific government, although it is unnecessary to believe that he borrowed the principle from the Masons, for
it was a cliché of the Age of Reason.

Many Catholics felt as Joseph did. Kaunitz, no Mason, was a leading proponent of scientific government, of regularizing the administration of the Holy Roman Empire along more rational lines.
Kaunitz also backed Van Swieten, another good Catholic, in the latter's campaign to wrest control of Austrian education from the Jesuits. Here again there was no question of faith. Austrian Catholics
were not the only segment of the Church opposing the order. A
broad attack across Europe led to its suppression by the Pope in
1773, the year after Van Swieten's death. Meanwhile, Van Swieten
had, to Joseph's satisfaction and Maria Theresa's dismay, diminished the Index of Prohibited Books to a quarter of its former size.

It is impossible to say precisely how Mesmer felt about Catholic
faith at this time. It is certain that he sided with Joseph II, Van
Swieten, and Kaunitz and held that the Catholic Church should be
renovated in the light of modern, rational, scientific ideas. His own
thought had moved, independently, into the Age of Reason.

Rationalism is not always rational. Joseph II, advocating a single
language for the Holy Roman Empire as a rational move, could not
understand why Slavs, Bohemians, and Magyars did not share his
belief that German should be the language. Spokesmen for science
are not always scientific, as the inoculation controversy showed.

Back in 1717, Lady Mary Wortley Montagu had seen the Turks
inoculating healthy people to keep them from catching smallpox
and had promoted the method on her return to England. Wide-
spread opposition developed within the medical profession, the
leaders of which claimed that inoculation would only spread the
disease. But the doctors who did use it succeeded so well that eventually the idea caught on that giving an individual a mild case of
smallpox would prevent him from suffering an acute attack. England became the leading nation of the West in immunology.

Continental physicians resisted longer. Boerhaave refused to endorse inoculation, as did his pupils Van Swieten and De Haen.
Then, in 1768, following the death of her daughter and daughter-
in-law and apprehensive of more fatalities in the royal family,
Maria Theresa clutched at one straw within reach and summoned

Jan Ingenhousz to inoculate her children and grandchildren. Ingenhousz was a Dutchman who had learned the treatment in England. His success and his scientific explanation convinced Van Swieten, who bowed to the royal will and the medical evidence, putting his immense prestige behind inoculation for smallpox. The Faculty of Medicine remained divided. Stoerck agreed with Van Swieten. De Haen disagreed—he could prescribe exorcisms, but it seemed to him a gross superstition to introduce small doses of a disease into the bloodstream of a healthy human being. It is one of the oddities of the history of ideas that De Haen was publishing annual reports of his clinical studies that set a model for medical literature, teaching physicians everywhere how to draw up and employ exhaustive case histories.

Mesmer heard the medical debates of 1767–68. If he took part in them, he followed Van Swieten and Stoerck, for he had an open mind about new theories, and the soundness of inoculation was conclusive to anyone willing to examine the evidence.

Mesmer remained abreast of the new techniques of his profession. He pursued his private practice from his home, where besides an office and dispensary he maintained a research laboratory. Here he examined his patients, diagnosed their ailments, and prescribed remedies. Here, too, he carried out experiments in medicine and chemistry. Most of his prescriptions, treatments, and cures were ordinary enough, nothing to alarm his patients or his colleagues. He diagnosed his cases according to the knowledge of the time and took remedies, as any doctor would, from the books by the best authorities. He resorted to bleeding and blistering for a host of ailments, used opium as a general anodyne, and measured out such specifics as antimony for scrofula, sassafras for diabetes. Even his advanced experimental medicine was in the current mode. Other physicans besides De Haen tried electrotherapy, a branch of the science growing so rapidly that it now provided the contents for a biennial report published in Paris. Mesmer's work at the hospitals caused no comment.

It must have seemed to his associates that he had outgrown the intellectual wild oats sown in his doctoral dissertation on the planetary influences and that he had justified those who thought he would buckle down to the realities once he had a medical practice of his own. Van Swieten, dying in 1772, never heard of him as a radical or maverick in their profession. Stoerck, replacing Van Swieten at the head of the Faculty of Medicine, considered his former pupil, now his colleague and his friend, an eminently sound practitioner. Mesmer's reputation was that of a fashionable Viennese physician with a taste for science and music.

CHAPTER 5

Mesmer and Mozart

Eighteenth-century Vienna was a city where musical circles crossed those at court, where members of the professions performed in public, and where composers turned out masterpieces for the delectation of wildly applauding audiences.

Both Emperor Joseph II and his brother, who would succeed him as Leopold II, played instruments at intimate musicales in Schönbrunn Palace. Van Swieten played the bass viol at private gatherings, often in ensembles that included professors from the university. Dr. Leopold Auenbrugger, the inventor of medical percussion, the method of striking the chest cavity to determine the condition of the internal organs from the sound, wrote the libretto for an opera by Antonio Salieri, one of the most popular composers of the time. Wealthy citizens deemed it an honor to patronize the masters. The powerful Esterházy family maintained Haydn. Dr. Mesmer came to the aid of Mozart.

When Mesmer moved to the Landstrasse, he intended to cultivate music in a lordly way. He landscaped the grounds of his estate in the approved French manner with gardens, groves, walks, fountains, and posturing statury, to which he added a small outdoor theater for musical performances. Much of his time away from his medical practice he devoted to playing the cello, the clavichord, and the glass harmonica, an old instrument recently improved by Benjamin Franklin. His position enabled him to hold open house once every week and to attract an opulent assembly of music lovers.

Mesmer presided over these festivities, a tall, portly figure in his thirties with, as his portraits reveal, brown hair and eyes, broad cheekbones, high forehead, straight nose, double chin, and a mouth turned up at the corners even in repose, giving him an expression at once quizzical, sardonic, and obstinate. Gregarious,

49

amiable enough to have a wide circle of friends, he knew how to entertain his guests with style and aplomb, aided and abetted by his wife, who had grown up amid the whirl of social Vienna.

Mesmer's musicales took place in the drawing room of the mansion or, if the weather was pleasant, in his open-air theater. He often took an instrumental part in an ensemble with the professionals, accompanying them through established classics like Purcell and Palestrina, introducing works by Gluck, Haydn, or lesser composers then exciting the Viennese ear. The audience usually included acquaintances knowledgeable enough about their host's vanity to ask him for a solo on the glass harmonica, his own choice for a display of his virtuosity.

Dr. Mesmer and Frau Mesmer on other occasions attended private musical sessions in the homes of their friends, there being a constant coming and going of this kind among the Viennese upper classes. They frequently saw performers and composers debut at these sessions and heard reports about the best, the worst, and the most notorious. They picked up gossip about who would be arriving in the city or leaving, who had made a hit or suffered a fiasco in Paris or Rome, London, or The Hague.

 Some time during the 1768 season the Mesmers became aware of the *Wunderkind* of European music, Wolfgang Amadeus Mozart.

Leopold Mozart of Salzburg came to Vienna that year, bringing with him his two children, Maria, age sixteen, and Wolfgang, just twelve, the latter being in the eyes of the proud father "the greatest wonder of which Europe or the world can boast." The judgment was no hyperbole, but rather a simple statement of fact. This most astounding of child prodigies performed on the keyboard at the age of four, invented little tunes at the age of five, became a professional instrumentalist at six, and composed music of real distinction at twelve.

Some rare genetic combination must have fallen into place in the Mozart children. Maria herself was a prodigy of whom more notice would have been taken had it not been for the dazzling genius of her younger brother. Although lacking his creative gift, she too had begun to play when just out of infancy, and now, in 1768, she ranked, as he did, among the instrumental virtuosi of the period.

The young Mozarts had been making European concert tours under parental guidance since 1762, when during their first visit to

the Austrian capital they performed at the imperial court and delighted Empress Maria Theresa. Six-year-old Wolfgang, slipping
on the polished floor of Schönbrunn Palace, was assisted to his feet
by Archduchess Maria Antonia, soon to Gallicize her name to Marie Antoinette and marry the heir to the throne of France. The
youngsters were petted and caressed by the empress, the members
of the royal family, and the throng of courtiers who surrounded
the throne. It was a triumphal visit, one that made Leopold Mozart
feel his children were on their way to fame and fortune. After that,
Wolfgang and Maria had been heard and applauded in the Versailles of Louis XV, the London of George III, and the courts of
Holland and Germany.

Leopold Mozart planned another Viennese tour for 1767, but
the outbreak of the plague forced him to retreat with his family to
Olmütz until the following year, when the capital seemed safe
again. He then returned in high expectation of an even better reception than before. He knew from experience that Vienna was the
place, beyond any other in Europe, to make a success in music. He
had mingled with composers, performers, and connoisseurs who
abounded in the lordly metropolis of the Holy Roman Empire. He
confidently believed his children could satisfy a Viennese taste that
ran largely to the German symphony and Italian opera, of which
the two contemporary masters were, respectively, Haydn and
Gluck.

This was, then, the moment to exploit what Vienna had to offer,
beginning at the top with the empress, who had been so gracious to
him and his miraculous little prodigies on their first visit.

His timing proved unfortunate. The plague had visited Schönbrunn Palace, leaving a pall over it, and concerts would not be
given there during the period of mourning decreed by Maria
Theresa. She and Joseph II did in fact receive the Mozarts in private audience, but nothing resulted except some complimentary
words and a medal—no commission, no pension, no appointment.

Disappointed, Leopold turned to Vienna itself, the city of musicians, patrons of musicians, and audiences intoxicated with music.
Surely, he thought, the Viennese would accord a fitting welcome to
his twelve-year-old genius? Here again he miscalculated.

Wolfgang's age no longer commanded the interest of earlier
days. At six he was an amusing little creature, sumptuously dressed

in court costume complete with velvet waistcoat and powdered wig, sitting sedately at the clavier and fingering out his own compositions. At twelve he had been in the public eye for so long that the novelty had worn off. Patrons no longer considered him a staggering phenomenon to be captured for their musicales.

Nor were professional musicians willing to accord Wolfgang the type of reception his father would have considered fitting. Composers, having come to Vienna to make a success for themselves, bidding against one another for patronage and commissions, lacked any incentive to promote the career of a competitor. Performers wondered aloud whether they would compromise their reputations by doing the works of one who, after all, lacked the sophisticated skills of mature musicians and could not begin to rival the creative ability of Gluck and Haydn. Impresarios doubted the box-office success of a twelve-year-old, who might charm an intimate circle at a private party but could scarcely cause a rush to buy tickets when audiences had so many other entertainments to spend their thalers on.

Although an undercurrent of sincerity ran through all this, Leopold Mozart naturally could see nothing but a dark conspiracy against his son, as he reported to his friend Lorenz Hagenauer back in Salzburg:

> I find that all clavier players and composers in Vienna set themselves against our progress, Wagenseil alone excepted, who, however, being confined to the house by illness, cannot help us or contribute much to our advantage. The chief maxim of these people is to avoid carefully every opportunity to see us and to recognize Wolfgangerl's knowledge. And why? So that whenever they are asked, as they so often are, whether they have heard this boy and what they think of him, they may ever reply that they have not heard him and that there cannot possibly be any truth in it.

Then Joseph II offered modified assistance. Without extending his royal patronage to the Mozarts, he suggested that Wolfgang be commissioned to write an opera for the Vienna opera house. Overwhelmed and delighted by this imperial favor, Leopold Mozart set his son to work on *La finta semplice*, an example of Italian *opera buffa* in the current style. Wolfgang showed that even then he could turn an absurd libretto into an interesting opera by adding to it a grace-

ful score, this one of no great distinction by absolute standards, but
certainly as meritorious as many another musical drama then appearing on the Viennese stage and nothing short of astonishing for
a boy of his age.

His father, confidently expecting *La finta semplice* to go speedily
into production, experienced a series of frustrations that became a
prolonged nightmare. Viennese opera was under the control of impresario Giuseppe Affligio, an Italian adventurer who later, on various counts having to do with money, became of interest to the police of several countries and ended up a convict sweeping the
streets of Pisa. Affligio held his position in Vienna in 1768 because
he knew how to turn a profit at the box office and could produce
plays, concerts, and operas without expecting the court to foot the
bill. Having started rehearsals on *La finta semplice*, he lost faith in it
because, after the fashion of impresarios then, now, and always, he
felt it would not draw the public in sufficient numbers to make it a
profitable venture. Under his inspiration, arguments against stag-
ing the opera began to proliferate in other interested quarters.

Leopold Mozart chronicled the downward spiral of his hopes in
plaintive, suspicious, exasperated letters to Hagenauer. The cast
suddenly decided the arias were not singable. The orchestra objected that a child of twelve could not conduct with professional polish.
The music was called too juvenile to be good, in which case presenting it would be merely a stunt. Alternatively, the music was too
good to be juvenile and therefore evidently composed by somebody else (the doting father, no doubt).

The elder Mozart attributed every criticism to malicious envy.
"As for Wolfgang's opera," he informed Hagenauer, "all I can tell
you is that, to put it shortly, the whole hell of musicians has arisen
to prevent the display of a child's ability."

His suspicions extended to the most illustrious composer then in
Vienna. He named Gluck among those conniving jealously with
Affligio against *La finta semplice*, an absurd accusation since the
creator of the heralded *Orfeo ed Euridice* had no reason to be jealous of anyone, even if that vice had been part of his character,
which it was not. In truth, Leopold Mozart made problems for himself. His constant complaining, however understandable, alienated
those he was trying to cultivate, even the emperor, who refused to
act on an appeal from the aggrieved parent to order the impresario

to stage his son's work. Affligio never did stage it and thereby walked away from a unique niche in the temple of music and Western culture. It would be a great thing to be remembered as the man who produced Mozart's first opera.

Just when the elder Mozart was verging on desperation, relief came from an unexpected source, from neither a member of the royal family nor a professional of the theater, but a doctor.

We cannot tell when the Mesmers met the Mozarts or under what circumstances. Perhaps it was at one of the brilliant musicales held by Prince Golitsyn, the Russian ambassador to Vienna, who more than anyone else gave young Mozart the scope to display his incredible talents before an audience of the great and the powerful, of critics and dilettantes. Perhaps Mesmer's developing interest in psychology, as well as his passion for music, contributed to his decision to patronize this extraordinary boy who could compose delightful melodies for instruments and voices. In any case, when we see Mesmer and the Mozarts together for the first time, they are already friends.

More than that, Mesmer has commissioned a new work by the youthful master, whom he recognized as no freak or nine-day wonder, but an authentic genius destined to grow ever more exalted in composition. Mesmer had the ear and the taste to see what so many in the anti-Mozart cabal could not or would not see: that he was dealing with a composer of the first magnitude in an undeveloped stage.

It seems likely that *La finta semplice* being too big and too intricate for a private performance, Mesmer suggested something more appropriate to the occasion, perhaps even selecting *Bastien und Bastienne* himself, a theme already familiar in the theater, therefore easily followed by any audience. Wolfgang set to work once again and finished the score with his characteristic speed.

This opera is French and German in inspiration rather than Italian—thus far had his international culture and cosmopolitan musical thinking proceeded before he reached his teens. The plot came from Jean Jacques Rousseau's *Le Devin du village*, about a magician who brings a wayward shepherd back to his blushing maiden amid the roundelays of the assembled villagers. A parody of Rousseau appeared on the Paris stage under the title *Les Amours de Bastien et Bastienne*, in which the rude French countryside replaced Arcadia and Rousseau's pastoral scenes were transmogrified into boisterous farce. F. W. Weiskern translated the parody into German, and this became the basis of the libretto for *Bastien und Bastienne*.

In setting the story to music, Wolfgang drew on compositions he had heard in Paris for his approach and style, handled the voice parts in the German *Singspiel* tradition (no florid Italianate passages), and added the inventiveness and grace the world would come to know as quintessentially Mozartean. Some of his finest characterizations begin with this opera. Bastien resembles Masetto in *Don Giovanni*, dim-witted rustics both. Bastienne, witty and a bit sly, is an earlier Susanna of *The Marriage of Figaro*. The third character of *Bastien und Bastienne*, philosophical Colas, will grow into the urbane Don Alfonso of *Così fan tutte*. The scoring for brass and woodwinds to achieve a pastoral simplicity recurs in instrumental and operatic compositions basic to the Mozart canon. Anyone who collects coincidences should listen first to the *Bastien und Bastienne* overture and then to Beethoven's *Eroica*—the same theme opens this slightest of operas and the most titanic of symphonies, where it is called the Prometheus theme.

Such was the work that brought Wolfgang Amadeus Mozart before a fashionable gathering at the Mesmer mansion on an autumn evening (the date remains uncertain) in 1768. While conducting, the composer sat at the clavier, which he played as a member of the orchestra. The musicians took their lead from him, a system rendered easier by the form of the opera, it being made up of spoken dialogue interspersed with songs rather than a continuous musical texture. One can imagine the surprised delight of the first audience to hear this engaging music, the applause following each song, and the ovation at the end. It is unfortunate that no reference to the occasion appears in the surviving letters of Leopold Mozart. For once he would have had nothing to complain about.

The Mozarts returned to Salzburg shortly after this musicale, and the Mesmers did not see them again until 1773, when they paid another visit to Vienna. Five years had turned the child prodigy into a polished young man, as well as a great composer, surprising those who had not seen him since the first performance of *Bastien und Bastienne*. "Nobody recognized Wolfgang," Leopold Mozart wrote to his wife, "for each time I let him go in alone. You can picture to yourself the joy in the Landstrasse at seeing us." The writer (adding an aristocratic "von" that did not belong there) went on to say:

> The Mesmers are all well and in good form as usual. Herr von Mesmer, at whose house we lunched on Monday, played to us on Miss Davie's harmonica or glass instrument and played very well. It cost him about fifty ducats and is very beautifully made. His garden is extremely fine, with views and statues, a theater, an aviary, a pigeon-house and, at the top, a belvedere looking right over the Prater. We dined with them on Saturday and also on Monday.

A month later the elder Mozart reported in another letter to Salzburg about "a big concert in the garden on the Landstrasse," and continued with regard to the Mesmers' home life: "Herr von Mesmer is adding three new rooms on the ground floor in order that he may be able to live downstairs in the winter, since although an enormous amount of wood is burned upstairs, the rooms never get warmed up." There are several references to Rothmule, a country retreat where the Mesmers escaped the heat of the Viennese summer.

Again nothing turned up for the visitors from Salzburg. Again they went back to Salzburg.

Mesmer remained a friend of the Mozarts after that, mentioned in the correspondence of both father and son, and then Wolfgang put a direct reference to the doctor into another opera, *Così fan tutte*, which, appearing in 1790, represents the composer at the summit of his ability.

As Act One of this work moves toward its finale, a distinctive stir begins in the orchestra, down among the woodwinds where oboes, flutes, and bassoons take up a theme that vibrates and flutters. It is one of the happiest moments in the most lighthearted of Mozart's operas. The master scored this passage as an interpretation of events onstage, so that while the music delights the ear for the sound alone, the full meaning needs the assistance of the plot provided by Mozart's libidinous, cynical, greatly gifted librettist, Lorenzo da Ponte.

At this point in the drama, Despina disguised as a doctor draws a huge magnet from under her robe and makes mysterious passes at Ferrando and Guglielmo, who are supposed to have swallowed poison out of unrequited love for Dorabella and Fiordiligi. This scene is the clue to the passage in which the woodwinds sound their vibratory theme, which signifies the flow of animal magnetism from the magnet along the patients' nerves to the stricken areas of their anatomy.

The magnet scene has to be explained today, but it was self-explanatory in 1790. Every audience would comprehend the words Da Ponte has given Despina to go with the stir in the orchestra:

> *Questo e quel pezzo*
> *Di calamità*
> *Pietra Mesmerica,*
> *Ch'ebbe l'origine*
> *Nell' Alemagna,*
> *Che poi si celebre*
> *La in Francia su.*

These words have been translated in different ways to fit the music, but for present purposes the following will do:

> Here and there a touch
> Of the magnet,
> The stone of Mesmer,
> Who was born and bred
> In Germany,
> And became so famous
> In France.

Mozart could always dignify a topical joke with exquisite music, and the magnet scene from *Così fan tutte* is the prime example. It is a mild jest at the expense of his old friend, who, however, might not have appreciated it if he had seen the opera. Mesmer was, in 1790, sensitive to anything that made him look foolish. He was by then an exile from Vienna, forced out by a train of events that began in 1773 and involved him in more than a decade of tumultuous quarrels.

CHAPTER 6

First Steps in Abnormal Psychology

Francisca Oesterlin was a woman in her twenties who lived with the Mesmers during the 1770s. She appears to have been related to Frau Mesmer, perhaps a cousin. The Mozart letters have a number of references to Franzl, the Austrian diminutive for her first name, and the reader can infer from these passages that both Leopold and Wolfgang found her a pleasant, engaging individual. She enjoyed doing little favors for other people, especially with her knitting needles, which she wielded expertly enough to fashion birthday gifts and parting mementos.

She did this, that is, when her nerves permitted. Franzl Oesterlin suffered from a form of psychosomatic illness that today would cause her childhood to be closely investigated. Periodically she felt hysteria welling up within her. Typically, according to Mesmer's clinical description: "Her hysterical fever caused convulsions, spasms of vomiting, inflammation of the intestines, inability to make water, agonizing toothache and earache, despondency, insane hallucinations, cataleptic trance, fainting, temporary blindness, feelings of suffocation, attacks of paralysis lasting for days, and other terrible symptoms."

The illness would reach a convulsive climax, carrying the victim into unconsciousness, and then the break would come. She would begin to breathe regularly again, regain consciousness, and gradually become her normal self, returning to her workaday interests as soon as she felt strong enough.

Since Franzl patently could not take care of herself in her hysterical spasms and since Frau Mesmer would not have her committed to a public institution, she became a permanent houseguest, putting in an appearance when she could, otherwise remaining out of sight until her fit was over. She was lucky in one respect. The

59

head of the house had no wish to be rid of her, quite the contrary. He was a doctor profoundly concerned about her problem.

Mesmer was well schooled in hysteria by now, in its symptoms and stages, and in all the techniques employed to combat it. He could compare a new case to old ones he had seen at the clinic. He could ask De Haen's advice about using electrotherapy, Stoerk's about drugs. And he had the older conventional wisdom that prescribed bleeding, purging, and blistering.

With Franzl, he stayed with the methods to hand until his patient's inability to respond forced him to conclude that orthodox medicine was not enough. She resisted his treatments until she forced him to develop a totally new theory of the neuroses, the theory that gave rise to the first important modern school of abnormal psychology.

Franzl was Mesmer's Anna O.

The Viennese woman known in psychoanalytical literature as Anna O. suffered from a bad case of hysteria involving split personality. She became the patient of Dr. Josef Breuer in 1880, and during sessions lasting over a year he discovered that some of her symptoms vanished when she talked to him at length about them. Applying the technique descending from Mesmer, he hypnotized her, whereupon she recalled many more experiences than emerged frm her conscious memory. Her condition improved remarkably as they proceeded. Breuer consulted Freud, who had but to substitute free association for hypnotism to reach the patient-on-a-couch technique so familiar in psychoanalysis today.

Now, just as Mesmer anticipated Breuer in handling neuroses through hypnotism, so did Franzl become a classical case in abnormal psychology before Anna O.

Mesmer wrote meticulous clinical reports on Franzl, and as they multiplied on his desk, he began to see a regular pattern in her illness. The attacks came and went in an ebb and flow of crisis and alleviation, crisis and alleviation. We do not have his detailed reports, but the cycle in one period can be followed in the letters of Leopold Mozart writing to his wife from Vienna during the summer of 1773:

> *July 21.* We found Fräulein Franzl in bed. She is really very much emaciated and if she has another illness of this kind, she will be done for.

August 2. Fräulein Franzl is now recovered.

August 12. Meanwhile Fräulein Franzl has again been dangerously ill and blisters had to be applied to her arms and feet. She is so much better now that she has knitted in bed a red silk purse for Wolfgang which she has given him as a remembrance.

August 21. Fräulein Franzl has now had a second relapse from which she has again recovered. It is amazing how she can stand so much bleeding and so many medicines, blisters, convulsions, fainting fits and so forth, for she is nothing but skin and bones.

The number of violent attacks within such a short space of time made the elder Mozart feel that Franzl would surely succumb to the next one, but her constitution was stronger than he imagined, and her faith in her doctor kept her from going out of her mind. She clung to life pertinaciously enough to extend her martyrdom for another year, long enough for him to cure her.

As Mesmer observed the ebb and flow of Franzl's attacks, as he learned to diagnose and predict them, the idea he had carried in the back of his mind since his graduate studies began to move into the center of his thoughts again. He saw, ever more strongly, a connection between the hard medical facts of Franzl's case and his grandiose cosmological theory. He judged that he had before him an example of the tidal effect in the nervous system that he had read in Mead and expounded in his dissertation. His patient was being bothered by the effect of the universal fluid, or animal gravitation, ebbing and flowing through her body. His problem now was to find an agent that would enable him to control the ebb and flow, some force acting in a manner analogous to that of the moon controlling the tides of the sea.

His logic led him to magnetism, which he had two good reasons for using on Franzl. Magnets were standard in one broad current of medical science (albeit by no means universally accepted but rather a subject of much dispute in the profession). And secondly, in their polar attraction and repulsion, magnets set up an ebb and flow that could be intepreted as one version of the general tidal effect of which the gravitation of the heavenly bodies was another version. Magnets fell in line with his theory of a universal fluid, for, like gravitation across space, they seemed able to exert action at a distance because they attracted objects they did not touch. As he explained: "The magnetic influence of the heavens affects all parts of the body, and has a direct effect on the nerves. Consequently, an active magnetic force must exist in our bodies."

For his magnets Mesmer went to his friend Maximilian Hell, professor of astronomy at the university, who had the atronomy department manufacture a number in specific shapes, each of which might have a special virtue through its correlation with one part of the body—solid for chest ailments, open-ended for the feet, and so on. We cannot tell how seriously Hell or Mesmer took these hoary analogies at this point. However, Mesmer used the magnets in his treatment of Franzl, with the startling results recorded in his *Memoir*:

> It was on July 28, 1774, that my patient having suffered another of her attacks, I placed three magnets on her, one on the stomach and one on each leg. Almost immediately she began to show severe symptoms. She felt painful volatile currents moving within her body. After a confused effort to find a direction, they flowed downward to her extremities. Alleviation followed and lasted for six hours. A repetition of the attack on the following day caused me to repeat the experiment, with the same success.

Mesmer continued to experiment with magnets on different parts of Franzl's body. He discovered he could turn the "current" in different directions and noted on his anatomical chart which intensified the attacks, which alleviated them. At the end, he could doubt no longer. He felt satisfied that he was generating artificial tides in her nervous system, that he was controlling the ebb and flow of the universal fluid.

This was Mesmer's first insight into the possibility of a cure for hysteria. It was also the reason for the first of the quarrels, controversies, and feuds in which he was to engage for the rest of his life. When he described his success to Professor Hell, the latter attributed the good effects to the magnets and wrote an article in which he claimed the credit for providing Mesmer with the means of helping Franzl Oesterlin. Hell's article destroyed their friendship. Mesmer, never one to let his achievements be stolen from him, issued a heated rejoinder. He may have stressed the fact that magnetism was too widely used for anyone to claim it as his own. His real rebuttal, however, lay elsewhere. He denied that Hell's magnets had the kind of efficacy the professor attributed to them because he denied the efficacy of magnets as such.

Negatively, the magnets could not be the cause of the ebb and flow. Being mineral and therefore unable to act directly on the living nerves, they could be only conductors. Mesmer, in arguing thus, revealed for the first time his ability to miss a non sequitur when his theory was at stake. He knew from his medical practice that minerals do affect physiology—arsenic has quite a marked effect. He slipped past this illogicality because of his determination to find some other agent was at work and using the magnets merely as conductors—to wit, his universal fluid, which, entering the nervous system by way of the magnets, repaired the physiological damage. He was totally convinced that the medical evidence for his cosmological theory had finally emerged from his studies and that he had learned how to "channel" the universal fluid into his patient. In his dissertation he had spoken of "animal gravitation." Now he used the phrase "animal magnetism," the phrase that became permanent in the science and lore of Mesmerism.

It is the proper balance of animal magnetism in the body that makes the difference between health and illness. If there is too much, some should be withdrawn. If there is too little, some should be introduced. When the patient no longer responds to animal magnetism, he may be considered cured because the balance has been restored. It is a matter of, in the metaphor drawn from music, the "harmony" of the body.

If magnets act only as conductors, not agents, the implication is that they can be dispensed with. Mesmer, still experimenting, found that many things could function as conductors of the true agent, the universal fluid. He got much the same reaction from Franzl and other patients suffering from nervous maladies when he used objects made of cloth or wood, things nonmagnetic in the sense of mineral magnetism but, on his interpretation, powerfully magnetic in the sense of animal magnetism. They became so—and this is the substance of the whole thing—because Mesmer himself touched them. He was an *animal* magnet capable of magnetizing things and people with *animal* magnetism in a manner analogous to a *mineral* magnet magnetizing metals with *mineral* magnetism.

Having made what he considered a revolutionary discovery, he decided to make it known to, and accepted by, the medical profession. He appealed to Stoerck, as head of the Faculty of Medicine and personal physician to the empress, to examine the evidence and render a verdict on animal magnetism. Stoerck refused. Mesmer attributed the refusal to an aversion for novelties in medicine and a fear that the faculty would be compromised if one' member became notorious. Stoerck's attitude is understandable. An expert in drugs, he advocated straight physiological medicine. He felt that animal magnetism ran entirely too close to occultism, and he knew that Mesmer was engaged in an acrimonious dispute with another member of the university. Naturally he backed off.

Mesmer rejected Stoerck's appeal to him to stop defending his theory publicly. He carried it to a wider audience when Dr. Johann Cristoph Unzer of Hamburg wrote to him to inquire about his methods. Mesmer's *Letter to a Foreign Physician* (January 5, 1775) recounts the story of Franzl, describes the treatment to which she responded, and argues for the veritable existence of animal magnetism (the phrase occurs here for the first time in his extant writings). Mesmer had enough influence in court circles to have this letter copied and dispatched to scientific institutions in the German states and beyond. It was his bow on the stage of European opinion.

The letter leaves the case history of Franzl short of her complete cure. The *Memoir on the Discovery of Animal Magnetism* (1779) carries her story to the end. Mesmer was out to convince the skeptics. The facts developing from his research were dramatic enough in themselves, and they appealed to the dramatist in Mesmer, who staged with Franzl his first display of his technique.

Ingenhousz was in Vienna. The Anglicized Dutch physician had achieved a European reputation as an expert in medical biology (his place in the history of science is that of the discoverer of photosynthesis, the fact that plants breathe carbon dioxide and return oxygen to the air). He was known to be experimenting with magnetism and consulting with Professor Hell on the subject. He had the virtue for Mesmer of not being tied to the Viennese Faculty of Medicine and its hidebound traditions. Moreover, he expressed to Mesmer his skepticism about animal magnetism, so that if he could be convinced, his about-face might be Mesmer's breakthrough with the medical profession. Therefore, according to the *Memoir*, "I sent Mr. Ingenhousz an invitation to pay me a visit. He accepted and arrived in the company of a young physician. My patient was just then in the midst of a fainting fit. I explained that this was the optimum moment to see for himself that the healing agent I had discovered really did exist."

Mesmer's account of this session is too brief to give us a complete picture of what happened. It would be worth much to have a full clinical report, including whatever questions Ingenhousz may have asked—Mesmer was never very good at remembering hard questions that were put to him about animal magnetism. Short of that, we can readily enough imagine the scene as Mesmer recalled it. The word "scene" is not out of place. Mesmer had the air of a conjurer performing tricks that would amaze his audience.

First, he told Ingenhousz to touch Franzl as she lay on the bed with her eyes closed, apparently unconscious. Nothing happened. Then Mesmer took Ingenhousz by the hands, saying he was communicating animal magnetism to him, and asked him to touch Franzl for a second time. Franzl responded with a convulsive jerk as the visitor's fingertips came in contact with her. When he moved his hand, her bodily tremors followed the direction of the movement. Mesmer accompanied the demonstration with explanations *sotto voce* on the potency of animal magnetism.

In the manner of a conjurer passing from a comparatively simple trick to one more difficult, Mesmer produced six cups. He asked Ingenhousz to select one, which he then proceeded to magnetize with his fingers. When Franzl was touched on the hand with the six cups, she reacted to the magnetized one only, pulling her hand away as if it hurt. Mesmer told Ingenhousz to try the same experiment, and the same result followed. Mesmer held Ingenhousz by one hand and asked him to touch any other cup with his free hand. Of course Franzl reacted to that particular cup at once, and to none of the others, when they were applied to her skin in succession.

To cap it all, there was the action-at-a-distance of animal magnetism. Stepping back from the bed, Mesmer pointed his finger dramatically at his patient lying there. She moved convulsively as if in great pain and arched her body from shoulders to feet into a rigid position until he released her. He placed Ingenhousz between himself and Franzl, gestured at her as before, and caused her to go into the same contortion, proving that the influence flowed through or around Ingenhousz to reach Franzl.

When the demonstrations were over, Mesmer and Ingenhousz had a discussion in which the latter, according to the former, did admit to changing his mind about animal magnetism: "His answer was to the effect that he required nothing more, being now convinced."

That phrase "to the effect" conceals the fact that Mesmer drew an unwarranted conclusion from the demeanor and comments of Ingenhousz, who advised him not to publicize his work for fear of being ridiculed, a piece of advice impossible to understand if he had really been impressed by what he had just seen. This passage in the *Memoir* makes no sense on Mesmer's terms. Anyone reading between the lines can see that he inferred agreement with himself from silence or noncommittal remarks. It was a trait he would reveal again and again in analogous circumstances. Similarly, he was always astounded at skepticism after a display of his art and science of healing.

He reacted with characteristic astonishment when he heard a few days after the Franzl exhibition that Ingenhousz remained a skeptic. It seemed so plain and evident to Mesmer. Surely no one could doubt the facts as they had been presented. And here was Ingenhousz spreading doubt in Vienna, telling one and all that the phenomena of Franzl Oesterlin could have been caused by some magnets he himself had had in his pocket when he saw her. Ingenhousz being a friend of Hell, both being partisans of conventional magnetism in medicine, Mesmer naturally suspected that his two opponents were in collusion to discredit him.

What are we to make of all this? The description of Franzl indicates not, as Mesmer thought, that animal magnetism flowed from him into her, but that she was the first person ever to be mesmerized. It looks as if Mesmer had learned how to use, not the universal fluid of the cosmos, but the power of suggestion. He had discovered unwittingly, how to put a patient into a hypnotic trance.

It may be that some of the oddities in the case escape this explanation. Perhaps Mesmer exaggerated both Franzl's quiescence at the start and her agitation after the treatment began. Perhaps her state was one of semiconsciousness, so that she may have been at least partly aware of what was occurring and reacting as she knew from experience her doctor expected her to. Nonetheless, all the signs point to this as a classical case of hypnosis.

By thus controlling Franzl's symptoms and their cause, Mesmer cured her hysteria, ended her psychosomatic afflictions, and made it possible for her to lead a normal life. She married his stepson.

Mozart, on one of his visits to the Mesmers in 1780, reported in his typical comic vein:

> I write this—where? In Mesmer's garden on Landstrasse 2. The gracious lady is not at home but the former Fräulein Franzl, nowadays Frau von Bosch, is. She has bidden and is actually still bidding me to send you and my sister a thousand respects. Listen, on my honor I hardly recognized her, she is so large and fat. She has three children, two girls and a boy.

Having achieved this astonishing cure, Mesmer decided to make another appeal to the Faculty of Medicine. He met Stoerck and again asked the head of the faculty to come see Franzl Oesterlin for himself. Stoerck demurred and made excuses. He still disliked Mesmer's research as smacking of occultism, and he knew what Ingenhousz was saying after a visit to the infirmary on the Landstrasse. Nor would he form a medical commission to look into the matter as Mesmer requested. He must have felt by now that his old friend was turning into a crank who, if taken seriously, would only keep the faculty in a turmoil because of internal dissension and public notoriety.

All Stoerck would do was to give Mesmer permission to demonstrate his method at the Spanish Hospital in Vienna. Here Mesmer went through his Ingenhousz experience, assuming agreement on the part of the chief physician, who in fact could see nothing in the method and soon stopped paying attention to it. Mesmer attributed the change to the machinations of Ingenhousz, who had the ear of all the physicians in Vienna—except Dr. Mesmer.

Again frustrated by the colleagues who he thought should be the first to support him, Mesmer again appealed over their heads to a wider public. The Franzl cure gave him a reputation as a healer. He took more patients, worked more cures, and became the talk of Vienna. While his fellow physicians became colder to him, those who flocked into his waiting room gave him what he craved—belief in animal magnetism. That belief, since he was actually using the power of suggestion, naturally contributed to his continuing success. Partly it was a matter of faith healing, partly it was his skill as a hypnotist; but he told them it was animal magnetism flowing through their bodies, and they accepted his explanation as absolute truth. He cured mental and nervous afflictions ranging from deep depression to hysterical paralysis.

His fame radiated beyond Vienna, through Austria and the German states, and he was invited to attend notable patients with persistent psychosomatic problems. During 1775 and 1776 he toured his Swabian homeland, Bavaria, Switzerland, and Hungary, savoring the heady experience of being in demand by those whose personal physicians, using orthodox medical methods, had failed to bring them relief.

In Hungary he went to the castle at Rohow to treat the Baron Hareczky de Horka who suffered from spasms of the throat. Horka had been a patient of the best Vienna specialists. Van Swieten had treated him without effecting a cure and then advised him to let time and nature end the spasms. De Haen applied electrotherapy without effecting a cure and then advised Horka to see Mesmer. The advice was not a compliment. De Haen, who denied the reality of animal magnetism, simply felt that Mesmer could not do this particular patient any harm and might by chance do him some good.

So Mesmer was summoned to the Horka castle, to the baron's bedside. We know about the rather astonishing events that took place there because the tutor of the children, Ernst Seyfert, wrote an eyewitness account, the memoir in which Mesmer is called a "wizard" for the first time in print.

Mesmer spent a week with the patient, talking to him, establishing a rapport between them, and laying the groundwork for a full magnetic treatment. When the day came, Seyfert found the baroness distraught, wringing her hands, and, varying the occult terminology, crying that "Mesmer, this witch," was killing her husband. Seyfert hurried into the baron's room:

> Mesmer sat at the right side of the bed on a chair with his left arm turned against the chair. He wore a light gray robe trimmed with gold lace. On one foot he was wearing a white silk stocking. The other foot was bare and plunged into a wooden bucket filled with water. . . . At this bucket sat a violinist in the baron's service named Klowratek with his face turned toward the bed. He held in his left hand the lower end of a metal rod that descended into the water. He rubbed the upper part of the rod along his body in a continuing motion. . . . Both re-

mained silent. Only the baron spoke. He was lying in bed covered only by a wolfskin. He babbled as if he suffered from a raging fever.

Seyfert considered the spectacle slightly ludicrous, and he admits he laughed in spite of Horka's suffering when Mesmer seized the baron by the hand and then by the toe, alternating back and forth in an effort to set up an ebb and flow of animal magnetism through the extremities of the patient.

This scene at the castle in Hungary holds a distinctive place in the Mesmer canon, for its elements will reappear in fully developed Mesmerism. The bucket of water and its metal rod will become the magnetized tub, the baquet, of his perfected technique. The robe of this session will become the robe of the Mesmerian séance. The gravity, the silence, the attempt to create the right atmosphere will remain an essential part of the treatment.

The conclusion of the Horka case also points to the future. Mesmer failed with the baron, who, prodded by his angry wife and urged by his jealous physician, called the Mesmer treatment off. He was the more willing to be persuaded in that he dreaded the fever Mesmer made him feel. He was thus one of the first to short-circuit Mesmer's magnetic technique through fear of the Mesmerian crisis.

Horka, that is, admitted the reality of Mesmer's influence, and so did Seyfert, a confessed doubter at the start who changed his mind about animal magnetism before Mesmer left the castle. That the doctor could induce artificial fever into his patient seemed remarkable enough. The cures Mesmer worked with other patients were too extraordinary to be denied.

Word of his presence in the castle caused a furor in the village and the surrounding hamlets. Peasants, artisans, merchants, and notaries converged on the castle with their wives, hoping for relief from their ailments. So many came that Baron de Horka set aside one room of the castle for them.

One patient who had gone deaf during a thuderstorm received his hearing back when Mesmer held his hands over his ears. Mesmer stroked away the stomach spasm of another, an interesting case because the patient stated his disbelief in animal magnetism and then was healed in spite of himself. His subconscious will prevailed over his conscious doubts.

The most impressive demonstration of Mesmer's healing art resulted from a challenge to him to prove his theory of animal magnetism as a universal fluid flowing from him into his patients. Since he insisted that this fluid could pass through physical objects, Seyfert and some others suggested he prove his point by standing in one room and working his effect on a subject in the adjoining room.

Mesmer demurred, pointing out that the walls of the castle were more than two feet thick—an unacceptable objection since he contended that animal magnetism flowed through the earth itself. Backed into a corner, he agreed to try. Seyfert stood in the doorway between the rooms to see that the conditions were fulfilled. Mesmer pointed at the wall and the man on the other side, made horizontal passes with his hand, and described ovals in the air. The subject followed his gestures by trembling, suffering seizures, and regaining control of himself.

The amazed witnesses agreed that Mesmer did send some kind of ray through the wall. The real explanation would seem to be that the experiment was too crude to prove anything. The subject, motivated by autosuggestion, would have gasped and writhed if Mesmer had done nothing at all. Seyfert kept craning his neck back and forth in the doorway to watch first Mesmer's gestures and then the subject's reactions, and it is likely that the one-to-one correspondence was not as precise as he judged.

Another case impressed Seyfert because it indicated that Mesmer's cures were not only extraordinary, but lasting. The "wizard" brought to an end the chronic chest pains of "a young Jew," who, upon encountering Seyfert a year later, "immediately came up to me and inquired solicitously about Mesmer," the cause, he declared, of his continuing good health after years of suffering.

Mesmer's experience in Hungary increased his reputation. He went on into Germany, where he worked more cures that surprised the physicians. In Bavaria, the elector asked his opinion of Father Johann Gassner, then creating a sensation of his own as a healer who achieved cures through the laying on of hands. Mesmer told the elector that Gassner was getting results with animal magnetism without recognizing or understanding it:

His reputation extended to Vienna, where people held two different opinions of him. One side considered him guilty of imposture and fraud. The other thought he worked miracles through divine intervention. Both sides were wrong. I knew from experience that this man was only a tool of nature. His profession as a priest, reinforced by his native gifts had given him the ability to diagnose recurrent symptoms of certain illnesses although he did not know their causes.

Gassner proved to Mesmer that a human being may be an animal magnet while remaining unaware of his possession of this fundamental force. He may be able to use rough empirical methods while alleging the wrong reasons for his success, talking of the miraculous laying on of hands (Gassner) or the scientific application of magnets (Hell) when all the time he is actually exploiting his personal store of animal magnetism. To know the true cause is to be able to control this force more effectively, to channel it more precisely to the afflicted area of the patient's anatomy.

What about the patient whose illness resists treatment? Mesmer claims to have the explanation for his own failures. He says that all people are not subject to animal magnetism any more than all objects are subject to mineral magnetism. Some are even possessed of a countervailing force that repels animal magnetism. This countervailing force has all the semblance of an *ad hoc* creation pitchforked into the argument for one purpose and no other—to explain the occasional impotence of animal magnetism, Mesmer's inability to effect a cure in some of his cases. By his general theory of the cosmos, no such monster could exist since everything from gravitation to physical objects arises from the behavior of the universal fluid. Logically, he should now look for a more fundamental entity behind both the universal fluid and the countervailing force, giving rise to both. He ignores this point because he is here trying to vindicate his medical practice, explaining his successes and his failures, and so he misses the glaring inconsistency in his cosmology. The countervailing force appears onstage to perform a single function and then departs into the wings while the rest of the play goes forward without it.

To Mesmer it is clear that most people *are* subject to treatment by animal magnetism. He holds that his presumed failures with the universal fluid are usually temporary difficulties caused by ignorance and that the cure will start to work as soon as he has analyzed the degree of animal magnetism involved, or lined up the positive and negative poles properly (these being as real in animal magnetism as in mineral magnetism), or taken account of the moral factors.

With this last point, Mesmer directly confronts psychosomatic medicine. He means that animal magnetism has emotional consequences no less real than its physical consequences, that the emotions affect the body and vice versa, and that the physician must examine the patient's mind and moods before a complete diagnosis is possible.

Physical attraction and repulsion have their analogy in spiritual attraction and repulsion, or sympathy and antipathy. The physician ought to work on both levels. Hence Mesmer's investigation of techniques to influence the feelings of his patients. He did not produce them full-fledged in his Vienna period, but he already understood that the physician confronted by nervous problems should use all the means available to create a rapport between him and his patient (another of Mesmer's anticipations of Freud, who vastly expanded the meaning of rapport).

As the number of his patients grew, Mesmer experimented with various methods of group therapy since he could not give each one his individual attention. He began magnetizing things they all could touch at the same time and benefit from his ministrations indirectly in the manner of Franzl and the sixth cup. This was the point about the baquet, which developed from Horka's bucket into a large tub with several bars protruding from the magnetized water, one for each person in the group.

The number of cures multiplied, some so startling that the beneficiaries believed them to be simply miraculous. Whatever Mesmer may have said privately to these patients, he publicly and officially opposed their religious faith no less resolutely than he opposed the skepticism of the medical profession. He claimed to be following nature, to be obeying the fundamental law of the cosmos, and the last thing he wanted was to be looked upon as another Gassner. He had found a universal cure for functional diseases, and it was as scientific as any partisan of the Age of Reason could wish.

On the other side, angry about the charge of Hell and others that he was nothing more than an ordinary magnetizer, he dropped magnets from his list of aids, though he kept swabs, drugs, and things that, relatively unimportant in themselves, could help to set the mood for animal magnetism. He was probing ever more sensitively into psychosomatic medicine, using autosuggestion and hypnotism and uncovering layers of the mind that would become the field for depth psychology. We can see this, although he could not. Accepting the reality of the psychological factors, he insisted to his dying day that he was dealing in physics. Like Columbus, he never admitted the true nature of his achievement.

In 1776 he visited Bavaria again, once more drawing wide attention because of his success where traditional practitioners were baffled. Returning to Vienna, he found Stoerck and the Faculty of Medicine more united, more adamant, than ever in opposition to him and all his works. Yet he remained optimistic about converting them. It was just a question of making them open their eyes to reality, which they would surely accept as readily as he did.

The chance for such a coup arrived in the person of a young woman whose condition was so pitiful, so puzzling, so obdurate after long treatment that he might now effect the most spectacular cure yet.

CHAPTER 7

The Scandal of the Blind Pianist

Maria Theresa Paradies was a namesake of the empress, whom her father served in the confidential post of private secretary. She was born in 1759, appeared to be a normal child for three years, and then woke up one morning unable to see. Expectations that her blindness would be only temporary proved groundless. She did not regain her sight as suddenly as she had lost it but remained blind for so many years that she learned to live with her affliction. She developed a pleasing personality, showed artistic ability, studied music under the great Viennese teacher Leopold Koželuch, mastered the keyboard, entertained the royal family with her playing when her father brought her to Schönbrunn Palace, and was awarded a pension by the empress in recognition of her talent and as compensation for her disability. She became professional enough to perform in public, where before applauding audiences she made a winsome figure as "the blind pianist."

All during the years since blindness struck so suddenly, Maria Theresa's parents had been consulting the best doctors in Vienna, including those in attendance at the palace, who received orders from the empress to give her godchild all the benefits of medical science available to them. They all failed in their efforts to restore their patient's sight.

Mesmer knew the details of the case because he had seen Maria Theresa Paradies while he was still a medical student, perhaps in a group of future doctors being introduced to live patients at the hospital or the clinic. He had noted her condition and discussed the problem with Stoerck during the ten years and more that the head of the faculty struggled to solve it. Since the optic nerve remained undamaged, Stoerck realized, as did all the physicians, that hysteria was the fundamental reason why Maria Theresa's eyes refused to function. Still, that knowledge did not help him. Confessing himself baffled, he ceased his treatment and added his voice to the medical consensus that declared her incurable.

The Paradieses finally turned as a last hope to the physician they had been warned against, to Dr. Franz Anton Mesmer, the healer who claimed to effect cures when no one else could and who often enough made good his claim. Stoerck, believing that Mesmer could not do any harm to an incurable case and might, for all his unscientific theories, do some good in a practical way, gave his consent. And so the parents took their daughter to the clinic on the Landstrasse.

This patient was for Mesmer the ideal one. She had defeated his respectable opponents, so that if he could cure her, he would be one up on them all. He had long familiarity with her case, much experience in treating psychosomatic illness, and a list of successes where hysteria was the root cause. He justifiably held high hopes for her and for himself as he took her for a patient at the beginning of 1777.

In following the story of Maria Theresa Paradies and Franz Anton Mesmer, one must remember that, just as in the case of Franzl Oesterlin, the information we have comes substantially from Mesmer. He wrote the case history from his point of view, which is a warning to anyone who knows the man and his idiosyncrasies, especially his tendency to construe the silence of others as agreement with himself and tepid acknowledgment as enthusiastic endorsement.

Granted this caveat, the account in his *Memoir* can be accepted as an authentic account of what happened. The combined professionalism and naïveté has an air of verisimilitude to it, and the main facts he presents are consistent with what is known from other sources, of which the principal one is the patient's father.

Mesmer diagnosed the problem in these terms: "It was a complete amaurosis attended by spasms in the eyes. As a consequence, she suffered from deep depression and from obstructions of the spleen and liver, which caused her to go into transports of delirium bad enough to make her fear she was losing her mind."

Maria Theresa's bodily symptoms were the result of a functional problem, more a matter of the nerves than of the eyes, or else Mesmer would never have entertained the possibility of a cure through animal magnetism. His aim, unwavering from the start, was to cure the blindness by eradicating the hysteria behind it.

The first part of the treatment can be followed in a paper written by the father as a testimony to the efficacy of the Mesmerian method and appended to Mesmer's *Memoir*. Paradies had seen his daughter subjected to too many useless and harmful practices in accordance with the limited medical knowledge of the day. Maria Theresa had been through repeated bleedings, purgings, and blisterings. At one time she had been forced to wear a kind of plaster helmet so tight that it caused a continual suppuration from her eyes and made her afraid of suffocating. Attending more to the presumed science than to the real pain, her doctors put her through an agonizing form of electrotherapy. The father describes the harrowing scenes of which he was a witness:

> They used electricity last year. More than three thousand shocks entered her eyes, and she had to endure a hundred at a time. The whole thing proved deleterious to her, resulting in agitation and spasms to the point where numerous bleedings were necessary to save her from utter collapse.

Parents and patient alike were immensely relieved when the new doctor did away with all this. Mesmer judged that the old methods could never work a cure in themselves and that they were only hindrances to the healing flow of animal magnetism. No rapport could be established with the patient when she was being frightened by her physician, and rapport was the first thing they both needed. Releasing her from the fear of peculiar gadgets and painful operations, he began to build up a bond of trust between them such that her will and emotions might be enlisted on the side of the cure. That rapport gained, he explained that nothing would be required except a readiness on her part to receive the animal magnetism he dispensed. Then he started the routine of touching and stroking, with his hands and his wand, in an effort to bring her up to the crisis where her ailment would break and the healing process could commence.

Maria Theresa's eyes were horribly distorted at this time, forced out of their alignment and swollen by the gross ministrations of her doctors. For fear of disappointing her father and mother, all Mesmer would promise was a restoration of her eyes to their normal position, but he later admitted to them that he had from the start believed his methods would bring about a complete cure. Those methods proved astonishingly fast and effective to the distressed, harassed parents who had suffered with their daughter for so long.

Neither Mesmer nor Paradies informs us precisely how the treatment began, but we can imagine it from what we know of his approach in other cases of psychosomatic blindness. He probably began by locating the centers of sensitivity on Maria Theresa's head, cupping his hands above her ears, and bringing his fingertips in a stroking motion from the occiput to the forehead, finally making circular movements with his thumbs around her eyes. As she responded to certain directions, he no doubt repeated them until the reaction became marked enough to suggest that the treatment was working.

Paradies recounts that on the first day Maria Theresa felt her head tilting backward as if some force were pulling it. The spasms in her eyes occurred more frequently. Her body shook. Her arms and legs trembled.

> On the second day, Dr. Mesmer caused an effect very surprising to those who saw it. As he sat beside his patient, he pointed his wand at the reflection of her face in a mirror. Then, as he moved the wand, she moved her head to follow it. She was even able to describe the movements of the wand. The spasms of her eyes increased and decreased notably within and around them, these spasms being followed at times by total quiescence. On the fourth day, she felt real relief and her eyes returned to their normal position. We could see that the left eye was smaller than the right, but the treatment gradually caused them to become the same size.

Maria Theresa was responding to Mesmer's will with an exercise of her own will. Suggestion and autosuggestion were working. She could dimly follow what he was doing with the wand and the mirror, the first intimation her parents had had in fifteen years that she could be responsive to light—that she could actually see something. They were convinced that they had come to the right physician. Both began to spread through Vienna the information that Mesmer had their daughter under his care and was proceeding with a cure.

The symptoms of hysteria began to clear up. The trembling of her limbs ceased. A discharge of green viscous matter relieved an intolerable pressure inside her nose. She felt a pricking along the optic nerve that made her head jerk and suffered recurrent attacks of vertigo. Mesmer interpreted the vertigo as a sign of improvement. Maria Theresa could not adjust to the reports coming in from her eyes, which were sending their nervous impulses to her brain after years during which she had never had to cope with visual perceptions. Her head spun because she was getting well.

Obviously this was part of the truth, and a very significant part. On the other hand, Mesmer might have noticed a danger sign in the vertigo. During her long illness Maria Theresa had naturally wanted to be cured more than anything. Now that something like a cure was approaching, she began to be disturbed by the thought of where it would leave her. She had lived in a world of darkness that seemed natural, the place with which she had come to terms, where she could live comfortably. The world of light was strange and uncomfortable, all the more so as she had to struggle so hard to get into it. Doubt assailed her from time to time. Only her faith in her physician got her past her bad moments.

The general improvement continued. Mesmer had been receiving her at his clinic on a daily basis. He now suggested to her parents that since her newfound sensitivity to light was causing new symptoms, she ought to be where he could keep her under closer observation. They could not disagree with that. Dr. Mesmer was realizing their fondest hopes. This was no time to reject anything he wanted for his patient. With their and her agreement, she moved into his clinic.

There he kept her in a darkened room with a bandage over her eyes in order to subject her by degrees to the perception of light. She felt a variety of stingings, smartings, and other painful sensations in her eyes. Removing the bandage, Mesmer accustomed her to the dim interior of the darkened room and began experimenting with small objects to determine how and what she could see.

White objects were painful to her, obviously because of the glare. He therefore replaced them with black and went ahead with the experiments. By making his patient understand that these new sensations were not subjective or illusory, but cased by things outside her eyes, Mesmer strengthened her confidence in her ability to see the real world. In a short time she could stand sufficient light to differentiate colors. From there she progressed to control of the motor muscles of her eyes, which allowed her to focus on objects according to their distance from her. Paradies continues:

> On February 9, Dr. Mesmer made the first attempt to make her see faces and movements. He used himself for this experiment in the darkened room. The sight of the human face disconcerted her. She thought the nose was ridiculous, and for several days she could not look at it without laughing.

By dint of Mesmer's coaxing, his patient was gaining control of her sight and learning how to coordinate it with her sense of touch. She became curious about and pleased by the things she could see, and she felt the poetry of the starry nighttime sky the first time she looked at it. Future progress under Mesmer's guidance seemed assured. It was mainly a question of his leading her into more sophisticated behavior by teaching her to use her eyes more delicately, to exercise them, and to protect them.

Both her parents continued to speak to their friends about the phenomenal cure their daughter was undergoing. The grateful father sat down and wrote his unsolicited testimonial to the remarkable skill of Dr. Anton Mesmer.

Mesmer gives us the rest of the story himself. That he thought himself vindicated would be an absurd understatement. He considered the Paradies case the *experimentum crucis* of animal magnetism, the final, unanswerable scientific demonstration that his medical theory was right. He had taken Maria Theresa as the patient whose cure would end the opposition in the Vienna Faculty of Medicine, and his judgment seemed validated by the outcome.

He allowed curious visitors, who came in droves, to see his patient and to verify the facts for themselves. He was gratified when a deputation from the faculty arrived, examined Maria Theresa, and apparently withdrew satisfied that Mesmer had succeeded with her illness where all her previous doctors had failed. He was most gratified when Stoerck "told me of his interest in this extraordinary cure, and said he regretted having waited for so long to acknowledge the importance of my discovery."

Never did Mesmer have better reason to believe he had been

convincing. Never did he have better reason to be shocked by incredulity.

It began with Professor Joseph Barth, the ophthalmologist at the university, who no doubt acted out of the envy Mesmer attributes to him. If Maria Theresa was curable, Barth should have cured her. Since he had failed to cure her, he had to argue that Mesmer had not cured her either. Mesmer says Barth based his denial on the patient's confusion in naming objects, a manner of reasoning that would certainly convict the professor of bad faith, for any patient blind from early childhood has to go through the process of identifying all things as if they were new and falls into the mistakes the process entails.

Mesmer's archvillain enters the drama on cue. Professor Jan Ingenhousz was in Vienna, still unfriendly to Mesmer, still publicizing his reservations about animal magnetism. This time Mesmer saw collusion between Ingenhousz, who did not believe in Mesmerian cures as such, and Barth, who did not believe in *this* cure. He says they teamed up to sow doubts in the mind of Herr Paradies, to rouse his suspicion of his daughter's physician, and to persuade him to call the treatment off.

There is a lacuna here in Mesmer's version of the story. He does not account plausibly for Paradies' about-face, which could scarcely have been instigated so simply. Here is a man who has given the physician a warm and unsolicited testimonial based on firsthand knowledge and who now turns on him because a couple of conspirators have been whispering in his ear. The reader is inevitably tempted to believe in a more deep-seated cause and to surmise that for some unexplained reason an antagonism developed between the father and doctor. Perhaps it was something personal—a misunderstanding or a clash of temperaments. Perhaps the father came to resent his daughter's dependence on another man. They might easily have quarreled since Paradies was himself hopelessly neurotic, subject to eruptions of insensate fury breaking into his outward normality. Again, Frau Paradies, who suffered from much the same illness, may have been a prime mover in her husband's unbalanced reaction to the doctor.

Mesmer tells us nothing about any personal conflicts he may have had with the Paradieses. He begins with his conspiracy theory, to which he was susceptible, and then attributes rather paltry interested motives to the father, motives stirred largely by a question of money. The logic is that Paradies began to anticipate serious embarrassment if Maria Theresa was saved from blindness. Her music already suffered from the improvement of her eyes. Partial sight made her nervous at the piano, nervousness made her hit the wrong keys, and the deterioration of her playing made her more nervous. It was a vicious circle from which she could not hope to escape except after long, arduous experience—if then. Meanwhile, she would cease to be the accomplished, petted star of the concert stage with a handsome income of her own. She might lose the pension granted by the empress in consideration of her blindness. She would then become a half-crippled burden on her parents.

Paradies was the kind of man who indulges in self-sophistication when confronted by unpleasant possibilities. He could have been superficially sincere in convincing himself that his daughter would never be happy with her eyesight and that he owed it to her to save her from the physician who was threatening her peace of mind. Mesmer implies, and it was entirely possible, that Paradies acted from contradictory motives: Maria Theresa would not really be saved from blindness by her doctor, so the treatment had no point; she was on the point of having her sight restored by him, so the treatment would deprive her of the favors of the public and the empress. Either way, she should be removed from his care.

The girl objected. Her rapport with her physician was too strong for her to break. She trusted him as the weak trust the strong, as the naïve trust the experienced, as the ill trust their healers. It is likely that an element of eroticism was involved on her side (although certainly not on his). All these factors combined to make her obdurate with her parents when they came to take her home.

Their behavior suggests that she had an added motive: fear of her home life. Frau Paradies came to Mesmer's clinic and demanded that Maria Theresa be handed over, and when he argued against it, the mother went into a neurotic frenzy of stamping and shouting. The spectacle sent the patient into one of her old convulsive attacks, whereupon her mother berated her in strident tones, seized her furiously, and, according to Mesmer, "hurled her headlong against the wall."

When Mesmer rushed forward to lift his now-hysterical patient, the shrieking harridan launched herself at him and had to be pulled away by the members of his staff. A loud, scuffling noise could be heard at the door. The father had arrived, and he was in a paroxysm of rage:

> Herr Paradies, who had been ordered away by one of my servants, came storming into my house waving a sword. Another servant barred the door to the room where we were and struggled to push him away. They finally succeeded in disarming this madman, and he rushed from the house calling down maledictions on me and everybody on the premises.

One need not go beyond this incredible day at the Mesmer ménage to understand the original cause of Maria Theresa's blindness. A young, sensitive, artistic child could hardly have escaped psychological scars at the hands of such a pair. Having been responsible for her illness in the first place, they were now responsible for her relapse back into it.

The Paradies affair quickly became the scandal of Vienna. The parents accused Mesmer of holding their daughter against their will and subjecting her to dangerous experiments. Gossip went further. This was the beginning of the dark suspicions about Messmer and his female patients. Some Viennese considered him a wizard doing strange things in his laboratory. Others considered him a charlatan preying on the credulous. Both these groups speculated on what he was up to with an eighteen-year-old blind girl behind the closed doors of his clinic. That query followed him for the rest of his life, revived in Paris and elsewhere by those who distrusted, or affected to distrust, the doctor's intentions when he helped a hysterical woman from group therapy around his baquet into one of the crisis rooms where they could be alone until the attack passed.

The suspicion was always undeserved. Mesmer was, on all the evidence, interested in women as patients and nothing more. His grand passion was his theory of animal magnetism, something for which he gave up his wife, his home, and his comfortable life in Vienna. We know that he did not corrupt the morals of Maria Theresa Paradies, whose ailment, rather than her person, was his concern. But no one could be sure of that while she remained with him.

The scandal snapped Stoerck's patience, already worn thin with Mesmer's notoriety and the incessant talk about him. Mesmer had, in his usual fashion, exaggerated the belief in the Paradies cure expressed to him by the head of the faculty, whose doubts now returned in full force. Apart from everything else, the incident intruded into Schönbrunn Palace, where Paradies was a private secretary. The empress was scandalized. Hence it happened that Stoerck, writing from the palace on May 2, 1777, ordered Mesmer "to cease this imposture" and release the girl to her parents.

This was not only the unkindest cut of all, but also an impractical demand because Maria Theresa, as a consequence of her parents' violence, was back where she had started, suffering from convulsions, delirium, and blindness. She could not be safely moved. A court physician came to Mesmer's clinic to see for himself and reported back to Stoerck that such was the case.

Paradies, regaining his senses and his cunning, consented to Maria Theresa's remaining with Mesmer during her relapse, at the end of which he plotted, somehow, to resume control of his daughter. Mesmer gradually and painfully recovered the lost ground. As before, he quieted the hysteria by working on her will, stopped the convulsions, and coaxed her successfully into a struggle to see again. At the end of this phase she progressed into sharper visual perceptions, and her health improved so markedly that she could leave the clinic if she wished.

Learning of this, her father got her out of Mesmer's hands by a ruse. He persuaded Mesmer to send her home, and Maria Theresa to come home, by promising that she could return for further treatment when she needed it. That time never came. Paradies kept her at home for good. Not surprisingly, she lapsed back into blindness and never came out of it. Her parents lapsed back into their neurotic attitude toward Mesmer, whom they heatedly denounced for his outrageous treatment of their daughter. It never occurred to them to place *themselves* under his care, which they could have used.

Ordinarily the outcome would have been sheer tragedy for the blind girl. Maria Theresa had a different experience. She got over her dependence on Mesmer, no longer wished to have her sight restored, and returned with relief to the familiar, comfortable world of eternal darkness. One lasting benefit remained with her from her time with Mesmer. He had restored her features to a comely shape. The ugly distortion of her eyes was gone, and it would never return since her parents had no intention of compelling her to accept the leeches, the plaster helmet, or the electric shocks of her earlier doctors.

Maria Theresa's principal motive for accepting her lot was the revival of her musical ability in its full glory. She resumed her piano concerts and went on tours that took her to Paris and London, conquering both capitals in her role of the "blind pianist." In her keyboard technique she displayed the high virtuosity of the true artist. She was so good that Mozart wrote a composition specially for her, the Concerto in B Flat Major, which made no concessions at all to her disability. Mozart, better than anyone else, could discern a performer's ability to dominate the instrument. He knew she could handle anything. He gave her a chance to show it when he handed her this composition.

Maria Theresa introduced the "Paradies Concerto" with éclat in Paris in 1784, at the Tuileries before Louis XVI and Marie Antoinette, who were charmed by the composition and the performer.

When Mozart himself played this concerto in Vienna before an audience including Joseph II, the emperor rose to his feet at the end and called out, "Bravo, Mozart!" It became what it has remained ever since, an indispensable page in the literature for the piano.

Maria Theresa composed music. Although her works lacked the substance to become part of the standard repertoire, they showed a capacity for original musical thinking, and she kept at composition industriously enough to compile a respectable list of songs, pieces for the keyboard, and operas. For a while she taught music to Vienna schoolgirls. She died at the age of sixty-five, in 1824, having lived in the dark since 1777 and her experience with Dr. Mesmer.

By coincidence, Mesmer was in Paris in 1784. They did not meet, and we cannot tell whether either desired a meeting. Maria Theresa might have suffered a nervous attack at an encounter with the physician to whom she had been so close. Mesmer had other things on his mind and certainly did not wish to become entangled with his former patient. Their paths crossed, and they went their separate ways.

Hostile eyes noticed their proximity. Friedrich Melchior Grimm, the German writer who recorded many years of Paris life in his *Correspondance littéraire*, had this to say of Maria Theresa Paradies: "Her ability on the harpsichord, in spite of her total blindness, is the most astonishing thing in the world; but one may well believe that her appearance in Paris at that time surprised Mesmer in a most disagreeable manner."

Mesmer, that is, was supposed to be put out of countenance because this former patient from Vienna arrived on the scene still crippled by the ailment he claimed to have alleviated seven years before. His attitude was actually quite different. He thought his critics were a lot of fools who precisely missed the point—that psychosomatic illnesses may come and go depending on the experience of the sufferer. He knew that the entire case history of the "blind pianist" actually sustained his claim that he was on his way to curing her before the treatment was interrupted. He knew that his temporary restoration of her sight was a notable triumph for his methods of treating hysteria and its consequences, and his only regret was the refusal of her parents to allow him the time to make the cure permanent. The failure was not his fault.

The failure, nevertheless, had driven him from Vienna.

The Paradies affair was an intolerable scandal to Stoerck and his colleagues. Hitherto Mesmer had antagonized them by putting forward odd theories and bizarre claims. Now rumors about his private life were rife in the city. They could not forgive him for leaving himself vulnerable to vulgar gossip. He brought discredit on them all since a member of the Faculty of Medicine should be above suspicion.

Barth was affronted, De Haen furious. Stoerck and Mesmer no longer pretended to be friends. Each man nourished a grievance against the other. Stoerck felt that out of respect for him Mesmer should stop the nonsense; Mesmer felt that Stoerck was letting him down. Stoerck resented Mesmer's going outside the Vienna Faculty for vindication; Mesmer resented Stoerck's making it necessary for him to go outside the faculty. Their mutual feelings turned from cool to cold to icy.

Each time Mesmer expected vindication he found his predicament worse. Every cure merely made him more notorious. He obviously could not work with his medical colleagues after the Paradies imbroglio, so that if he remained in Vienna and continued to

practice medicine, he would do so as a notorious wonder worker
ostracized by the profession. He might well be expelled from the
faculty, the ultimate irony for one whose whole purpose was to win
the approval of his peers.

Vienna having rejected him, he rejected Vienna. There were no
personal ties to keep him in the city, for he and his wife had drifted
apart after six years of rubbing along together in comparative tranquillity.

Maria's attitude was plain enough. She had willingly helped her
husband around his clinic since its foundation, acting as a combination secretary and nurse, receiving patients, applying minor medi-
cation, and keeping their charts. Everything was fine as long as he
remained a fashionable Viennese physician. Everything went
wrong after he became a byword for eccentricity and alienated
their friends. When Mesmer talked about his wife's "stupidity," as
he did in one letter, he meant that she would not see how fitting it
was for him to defy convention and go his own way in the name of
scientific truth.

In the same passage he complained about Maria's "extrava-
gance." Accustomed to affluence, she spent more freely than he
liked of their wealth, much of which derived from her inheritance,
a truth that did not mollify him when he balanced the family accounts. He blamed her for mishandling money while he was in Paris, to which she might have retorted that he had no business stay-
ing in the French capital.

When he left Vienna, he left for good as far as she was concerned, never returning until after her death.

The estrangement of the Mesmers was part of the doctor's new
attitude to human relationships. Musicales, the pleasures of conversation, social functions, medical conferences—all these were secondary in his life. His fixed idea being firmly locked into his mind,
he evaluated other people by their opinion of animal magnetism.
Those who agreed with him were friends, those who disagreed
were enemies, and he categorized the uncommitted among his enemies.

There was only one place for him, the intellectual capital of Europe where novel ideas received a ready welcome. He would go to
Paris.

Obtaining a letter of recommendation from Chancellor von Kaunitz to the Austrian ambassador in Paris, he turned his back on Vienna, made a few stops in Germany and Switzerland, and continued on to France, accompanied by a servant who would be his valet, footman, and coachman. His hopes were high that his luck was about to turn.

CHAPTER 8

Problems in Paris

When Mesmer arrived in the French capital in February, 1778, and established himself in rooms in the Place Vendôme, he did not come as a complete unknown. The intellectuals were aware of him. His reputation had preceded him by way of the scientific, literary, and philosophical journals that kept track of movements of ideas across Europe.

In 1766, the year Mesmer was graduated from medical school, the *Journal encyclopédique* ran a long article on the meaning of the magnetic "fluid" and the question of how it "flows" from the magnet to the magnetized. In 1767 two doctors reported on their successful use of magnets for eye trouble and toothache. In 1771 there was an analysis of magnetism and the nerves. In 1775 Professor Hell of Vienna was cited for his use of magnets to cure a variety of ailments.

In 1776 Mesmer's famous, notorious healing tour caught the attention of this publication:

> There arrived in Munich a short time ago a physician of Swabian origin who cures epilepsy by magnets, which he applies with success to several other maladies without being in the least mysterious about it. This is M. Mesmer. On last November 25 there were assembled in a large room many people suffering from epilepsy. M. Mesmer, in the presence of doctors and surgeons of the city, touched each with his hand impregnated with magnetic power. At the end of five or six minutes each felt the illness accentuated to the highest degree, with very strong convulsions. The patients came to themselves. The physician assured everybody that the seizures would resume, which actually happened a few minutes later. But the malady has not returned since then. The Elector of Bavaria wanted to witness this cure, which succeeded perfectly. M. Mesmer healed in this simple manner all sorts of nervous illnesses.

Also in 1776, the *Journal* reprinted Mesmer himself, a passage from a letter responding to those who asked for an explanation of his methods. Liking nothing better than such a request, Mesmer promised to speak "with my customary candor. I have no secrets where the good of humanity is the question, and I have never refused anyone my counsel." After describing the many objects he had magnetized for the propagation of animal magnetism, he added the advice: "In following these rules, one must not fear any symptoms, even convulsions. One must, on the contrary, regard them as salutary effects of the magnets."

The favorable tone of the *Journal* did not endure. Only a month after Mesmer arrived in Paris, an extract was printed from a letter written by Hell in 1777. This extract terms Mesmer ignorant of science, compares him to Gassner, mentions the "imposture" of the Paradies case, and warns about his throwing patients into "horrible convulsions and frightful agony." The passage concludes contemptuously: "M. Mesmer's reputation is making a lot of noise elsewhere; but in Vienna it speaks so softly that one can scarcely hear it."

Mesmer believed this Hell screed was selected at this moment to discredit him, a fair enough verdict since, just as he wrote in the periodicals in his own defense, so did his enemies pursue him in the same publications. Harsh judgments on him were common in the French press.

Undaunted, he launched his Paris campaign with his habitual energy and optimism.

His strategy was to seek scientific vindication rather than medical acceptance. He had given up on the doctors, feeling that his Vienna failure might be repeated if he asked the physicians of Paris for a different verdict. He had decided to approach the scientists, the physicists, and to pitch everything on the truth of his cosmological theory, on the reality of the universal fluid extending across the cosmos, penetrating all things, and coming to a focus in animal magnets such as himself. Once the physicists agreed with him on the *existence* of animal magnetism, the physicians would be compelled to agree with him about the cures he worked *through* animal magnetism.

To begin by healing patients and then to infer the reason for success were to attack the problem the wrong way around. The cause should precede the effect in logic as in fact. When urged by scientists to show the Parisians some striking cures first, he explained why he could not take their advice. His *Short History of Animal Magnetism* (1782) recalls that:

> I flatly rejected this method of persuasion because experience had taught me how little the most remarkable cures had done to vindicate my cause in Vienna. I added that the actual evidence of their own senses ought to enable all witnesses, especially scientists who are less likely than others to be deceived, to appreciate the worth of experiments such as mine. "My principal object," I pointed out, "is to prove the existence of a physical agent never before observed, and not to rouse against my discovery a cabal of medical men whose personal interests would necessarily lead them to oppose both my cause and myself. It is as a scientist, not as a physician, that I appeal to you men of science, asking you to examine the natural phenomena and then render a verdict on my system."

Mesmer thought that the scientific facts carried their own validity, while the medical facts did not. There was too much room in medicine for stupidity and hypocrisy. The most remarkable cures (Franzl Oesterlin, Maria Theresa Paradies) could be attributed by skeptics (Stoerck, Ingenhousz) to familiar causes or chance or a wrong diagnosis, to anything, that is, except animal magnetism. Mesmer was determined to avoid a repetition of his Vienna fiasco by setting aside his old type of medical demonstration in favor of scientific experiment:

> For example, if the touch of my hand causes a subject to feel pain, and if I can move this pain from spot to spot by moving my hand; if as I please I can move it from the head to the chest, from the chest to the abdomen, and then from the abdomen back to the chest, and from the chest to the head—then nothing except gross stupidity or wicked malice can induce the observer to deny who is causing these sensations. So, I lay it down as an undeniable axiom when I say that a scientist can be as convinced in one hour of the truth of my discovery as a country bumpkin in Switzerland after a treatment lasting for months.

It was, then, primarily as a scientist that Mesmer came to Paris. He presented his letter of recommendation from Kaunitz to Count

Florimund Mercy d'Argenteau, the Austrian ambassador to France, who opened a few doors for him but did not go out of his way to patronize a man whose notoriety had preceded him to the French capital. Mesmer made his way on his own.

As he knew, Paris was susceptible to ideas. The two great men of ideas, Voltaire and Rousseau, died in that year of 1778, leaving two armies of disciples to disseminate their principles. Diderot had recently published the final volume of the great *Encyclopédie,* the doorway to knowledge for educated Frenchmen and Europeans. Laplace was working on the origin of the solar system, Buffon on natural history, Lavoisier on chemistry, Lagrange on algebraic equations. Fashionable ladies dabbled in electricity, the rage ever since Franklin's famous kite. Galvani would soon draw attention to "animal electricity" by showing that a dead frog's leg will move convulsively when touched by an electrical current. All things seemed possible to science. Newton was the god of the time and place.

Mesmer, as scientific and Newtonian as anyone, in his own mind, entered the Parisian milieu as one who belonged there by right. He never was accepted on that basis. Worse, he appealed to the opposite mentality, also prevalent in Paris. The eighteenth century, the self-proclaimed Age of Reason, followed a strong bias toward mysticism. The Rosicrucians and other secret societies had found a home in the city on the Seine. Emanuel Swedenborg's writings on the occult sciences were read by the populace and the aristocracy. Fanatics and fools created a climate of credulity exploited by clever rogues. Charms and elixirs were sold by the ounce and the dram.

Mesmer's reputation, according to some reports from Vienna, fitted into this background of mystical lore and miraculous cures. The occultists had heard that he was one of them, and he would have attracted an avid public if he had set up in business as a seer, magician, faith healer, or alchemist.

Mesmer could have shrugged this off as so much irrelevant nonsense except for his awareness that men of science and medicine had heard the same reports and knew that the suspicion of occultism followed him around like a shadow. Echoes of the Vienna quarrels reached them through newspapers, journals, and private letters of one doctor to another. Professionals tend to be hostile to any free lances wandering around unsupervised, performing their functions in an unorthodox manner and terming their methods outmoded. Such was Franz Anton Mesmer in 1778. Attacks on Mesmer continued to come out of Vienna after he left, terming him a dangerous quack against whom the medical profession everywhere should be warned. The physicians of Paris considered themselves warned and were on their guard.

Since Mesmer's whole purpose was to avoid being judged by this mentality, so narrow and bigoted in his view, so constrained by professional jealousy, he tried to evade it by not taking patients in Paris. The public refused to let him off so easily. His reputation for effecting extraordinary cures had the same effect here as everywhere else—the ill found him out, flocked around him, and begged to be healed.

Mesmer was too much of a physician to send them away. We know from his writings that he felt a humane desire to alleviate pain and cure disease and that the persistence with which he promoted his system came from that desire at least as much as from personal ambition. His combativeness sprang in part from his anger at his opponents for withholding a great balm from suffering humanity. He therefore accepted patients at his Place Vendôme quarters, even though he feared his success would add to his notoriety without making him acceptable in the quarters where he wanted above all to be accepted.

He concentrated his attention at first on the French Academy of Sciences. The president of the academy, Charles Leroy, was both a chemist and a physician, a combination that augured well for one who represented a combination of physics and physiology (as Mesmer considered animal magnetism to be). Mesmer lost no time in making his acquaintance. Leroy was judiciously restrained. Mesmer's universal fluid might be worth looking into—the term "fluid" was common enough in scientific parlance, used for all kinds of physical phenomena not yet understood—but the question of evidence remained to be answered.

The question was all that Mesmer wanted of Leroy. He promised to supply the answer if granted the proper forum, and Leroy arranged a meeting at the academy.

Mesmer determined to make a good impression when the day came: "I was punctual. I got there early enough to see each member as he came in." He had his written statement in his pocket, an explanation of animal magnetism in scientific terms, but he never got a chance to deliver it because the academicians were too disorderly to listen to him. Whether or not they were quite as bad as he says, a majority of them certainly came to the session with closed minds, holding animal magnetism to be a product of Mesmer's imagination and outside the realm of science. It is not improbable that some were uncivil to him. He says they were even uncivil to the president of the academy. The scene cannot be reconstructed from other sources. We have to take Mesmer's word that he would have left if Leroy had not persuaded him to wait until quiet fell over the room, which happened only after most of the members had left in derision, a dozen or so remaining to pay attention, such as it was, to Mesmer.

These academicians were interested only in seeing him perform a cure before their very eyes, just the thing he wanted to put off until the scientific issue was settled, and in any case he could not feel at his best on a moment's notice with a strange patient before a group of smiling, winking unbelievers.

The patient presented to him suffered from asthma. Mesmer's fumbling efforts caused the rest of the scoffers to drift off, convinced that Mesmer was, as they had heard, a charlatan. Their disappearance relieved the tension:

> I got the impression that M. A— felt more at ease after the departure of some of these men. We were now only five, including M. Leroy, M. A— and myself. I suggested some other experiments to them. They agreed. I therefore bandaged the eyes of M. A— and made a number of passes under his nose, and he smelled the odor of sulphur or ceased to smell it as I directed. Having controlled the sense of smell, I also controlled his sense of taste by offering him a cup of water, which gave him, at my will, the taste of different flavors.

Mesmer had intended to found his case at least partly on his ability to rouse sensory responses to animal magnetism, and this demonstration seemed evidential to him. The last observers went away skeptical, perhaps because of anti-Mesmer prepossessions, but also because olfactory and gustatory perceptions were too intangible, too evanescent, to sustain a broad theory of scientific medicine.

Mesmer's account of this session at the Academy of Sciences is one-sided, shot through with the disappointment that bit into his soul as he made his way back to the Place Vendôme. His acidulous nature asserted itself when he heard that Leroy accounted his efforts at the Academy a failure:

> I encountered M. Leroy at the home of M. de Maillebois, and I said quite frankly that he had taken advantage of me, a foreigner and friendless, and allowed me to be the object of the impertinent laughter of his colleagues. In my just indignation I did not scruple to state my low opinion of one who, having taken up the cause of truth, disgracefully retreated at the first opportunity.

The old Mesmer, the Mesmer of Vienna—of the Hell, Ingenhousz, and Stoerck disputes—was already emerging in Paris. He *would* make enemies and start feuds. He owed a gread deal to Leroy for presenting him at the academy, and Leroy, by Mesmer's testimony, could not be held responsible for the outcome. But Mesmer did not convince Leroy of the truth of animal magnetism, and Leroy admitted it, and so Leroy must be censured.

The president of the academy was too much of a gentleman to quarrel. Mesmer, in a moment of insight, says that "French urbanity" smoothed the matter over. Leroy remained amicable enough to attend a later meeting at Mesmer's lodging, even bringing his wife and some friends to see a demonstration. This meeting left both sides equally dissatisfied. Mesmer caused the limbs of a dropsy patient to swell and diminish at his touch. Still:

> I had on earlier occasions heard the opinion stated in a vague way that imagination was the cause of some of those effects—which no one would think of denying. But it was new to me to hear imagination alleged as the cause of phenomena as remarkable as those I had just elicited. I heard this preposterous notion from M. Leroy himself.

At this point Leroy decided it was time to withdraw tactfully. Realizing that he was patronizing a Tatar who would be satisfied with nothing less than endorsement of the animal magnetism theory, he cut the ties between them. He left unanswered Mesmer's last letter requesting, with incredible naïveté in the light of Mesmer's language to him, another Leroy-supported investigation of Mesmerism.

Having failed with the Academy of Sciences, Mesmer perforce fell back on medical cures as the next best thing. He approached, not the Paris Faculty of Medicine, which resembled too much the Vienna faculty that had caused him so much trouble, but the Royal Society of Medicine, a new organization presumably more open to novelties than the traditional and orthodox corporation of physicians.

The leaders of the Royal Society of Medicine, although dubious about Mesmer, deputed two members, Antoine Mauduit and Charles Andry, to visit him, examine his clinic and his cures, and report back on what they found. Mesmer chose to exhibit a case of epilepsy, a young woman, identified as Mlle. L., who was subject to sudden, violent, repeated convulsions. He also added a number of patients suffering from less severe nervous ailments.

The general pattern of his practical art was this. He and his patient sat opposite each other in chairs arranged to bring their right and left sides into alignment. Placing his hands on the patient's shoulders, Mesmer paused momentarily before running his hands down the arms to the fingertips; then he held the thumbs momentarily before repeating the process. The purpose, as with Baron de Horka, was to set up a flow of animal magnetism into the extremities. The gasping, palpitations, or convulsions of the patient proved to Mesmer that he had made a triumphant demonstration.

For Mauduit and Andry, it was an outlandish spectacle unworthy of the medical profession. The stroking seemed to them absurd window dressing, useless at best and immoral at worst.

As for the case of Mlle. L. and her epilepsy, it was Mesmer's bad luck that she had been in the care of Mauduit, who had subjected her to a painful and fruitless round of electrotherapy. The French physician was annoyed to find her in the clinic of the notorious Viennese. Naturally he could see nothing of particular interest in Mlle. L. or in Mesmer's success in controlling her epileptic fits. Nor could Andry, the two being of one opinion about medical exhibitions such as this. Stubbornly negative, they raised all the usual objections to Mesmerian cures, including the possibility that some ailments were feigned, that so-called patients were only pretending to be epileptic, paralyzed, paralytic, blind, or deaf.

The Mauduit-Andry reaction incensed Mesmer when he considered how unfavorable to him the pair would be in reporting to the Royal Society of Medicine. He decided to appeal directly to the society in his own behalf.

He made his appeal from Créteil, a town outside Paris to which he had moved on May 1, 1778. He had to have a bigger clinic than the Place Vendôme suite permitted. The number of the ill overflowed his apartment, he lacked special rooms for lingering and critical cases, his staff had grown proportionately, and he therefore took a house at Créteil in the country. Here he lived amid his patients, followed individual illnesses that called for his personal attention, and developed group therapy for minor cases and the convalescent.

He perfected the baquet into a large wooden tub lined in various ways, but typically with bottles of magnetic water in concentric circles around the axis, pointing outward like spokes in a wheel, submerged in water containing magnetized bits of metal, stone, glass, et cetera. The magnetism was, of course, animal magnetism, and Mesmer himself magnetized each item by touching or pointing at it. The baquet had iron rods protruding from the tub, one for each patient to press against the afflicted part of his anatomy. At the same time, the group around the tub set up a "current" by holding hands so that each might benefit from all the animal magnetism radiating from the tub.

A phenomenal number of patients regained their health at Mesmer's baquet. Virtually all the categories of nervous disorders, and many physiological problems only remotely affected by the nerves, are listed by Mesmer, his colleagues, and his patients among the cures at Créteil.

Several extremely ill individuals, who had come to Mesmer in desperation and who had found their faith in him justified by the results, agreed to assist his campaign for recognition. They signed formal certificates about their apparently incurable illnesses—blindness, paralysis, palsy—and about their miraculous recovery at Mesmer's clinic.

With these testimonials in hand, Mesmer opened a correspondence with Félix Vicq-d'Azyr, secretary of the Royal Society of Medicine. Vicq-d'Azyr was one of the great secretaries who guided the learned organizations of the eighteenth century to their prominent place in the intellectual history of Europe. He wrote on biology, comparative anatomy, and epidemics, coaxed papers from specialists in all departments of medicine, scheduled lectures and conferences, and maintained a voluminous correspondence. It was said of him that he broadened the interests of the royal society to the point where it became a veritable academy.

This was the savant to whom Mesmer dispatched his testimonials, enclosing a covering letter in which he requested that they be made available to the members of the society who had not witnessed his cures and might be imposed upon by the biased account of the pair who had been to his clinic. Vicq-d'Azyr sent the certificates back unopened, explaining that his colleagues could not venture an opinion about cases unfamiliar to them.

Most men would have accepted the rebuff. Mesmer was not that timid. He returned the certificates to the society and waited expectantly for a more satisfying reply. Hearing nothing for three months (May–August), he allowed the meaning of the silence to elude him. He wrote "To M. Vicq-d'Azyr, Secretary of the Royal Society of Medicine of Paris. Créteil, August 20, 1778":

> Assuming that the members of your learned society have received, through your hands, my communication of last May 12, I am taking this opportunity to invite your committee to come and see for themselves the results of my methods. I will be especially indebted to you if you will let me know the day and hour they choose, so that they will find me prepared to receive them with all due respect.

Vicq-d'Azyr sent a statement that the society could not act on the request. Mesmer sent a reminder that he would be accommodating when the society decided to act. The secretary's replies, like his temper, were growing shorter. Experiencing Mesmer's famed persistence, he struggled to disengage himself from the clinging embraces of a suitor who refused to believe that the answer could really be "No!" He must have shuddered every time he saw a letter from Mesmer in the mail on his desk.

The correspondence between Mesmer and Vicq-d'Azyr is one of the more entertaining things in the history of Mesmerism. Mesmer, who should have realized he would never get an affirmative answer from Vicq-d'Azyr, believed in his customary fashion that anything less than outright hostility should be interpreted to mean at least partial endorsement. He read encouragement between the lines where Vicq-d'Azyr had in actual fact written nothing.

Their correspondence came down to a final curt note from the secretary: "I have submitted your letter of the 20th to the society. This organization, not having examined the cases treated by you, cannot give an opinion on the subject."

That *did* end the affair. Even Mesmer at his most sanguine could not miss the implication. The Royal Society of Medicine was lost to the cause of Mesmerism, and Mesmer bowed to the reality when it finally came home to him.

He had consolations to fall back on. A number of Parisian doctors visited his clinic of their own volition during the Créteil period, drawn out of curiosity, wishing to see for themselves what the uproar was all about. Most went away disenchanted for the usual reasons, but a few agreed that Mesmer was on to something worth pursuing. This crack in the wall of opposition strengthened Mesmer in his conviction that it must come tumbling down someday.

His great catch among these physicians became a totally convinced believer in animal magnetism, a disciple of Mesmer, and a practitioner of Mesmerism. Charles Deslon was private physician to the Comte d'Artois, brother of King Louis XVI and destined to rule France for six years in the nineteenth century as Charles X. Deslon therefore ranked very high in the French medical profession. He brought distinction to any cause with which he associated himself. His value to the cause of Mesmerism could hardly be overestimated.

Besides, he was a converted skeptic, jarred out of his doubts when he saw the manner in which Mesmer controlled epileptic convulsions. He never lost his trust in animal magnetism after that. He learned the method, had himself magnetized, served as an assistant to Mesmer, and established his own clinic.

The parallel with psychoanalysis again imposes itself. Anton Mesmer was to Charles Deslon what Sigmund Freud would be to Carl Jung, even down to the fact that each master eventually quarreled with this, the ablest of his followers.

Deslon belonged to the Paris Faculty of Medicine. Spurred by the enthusiasm of the convert, he suggested to Mesmer that they take the case for animal magnetism to the faculty, which he thought would be receptive since the members must surely see the truth as clearly as he did. Mesmer naturally agreed. He was uncomfortable about being under the judgment of another faculty of medicine, but this seemed the best strategy now open to him.

Before the meeting, Mesmer moved again because Créteil, for all its advantages, was too far from Paris to be convenient. He found a more satisfactory place, the Hôtel Bullion in Paris on the rue Coq Héron, in an area countrified enough to provide woods and a nearby lake but also easily available to his patients.

At Deslon's invitation, a dozen members of the Faculty of Medicine attended the clinic in the Hôtel Bullion to learn what they could of animal magnetism. This time Mesmer made certain of not being shunted from science to medicine before he was ready. He read his *Memoir* to the group, stressing the reality of the universal fluid behind the cures that had made his reputation in Vienna. The session did not go at all well. He could not budge his listeners from their medical orthodoxy.

Nevertheless, three of the physicians agreed to watch a series of treatments at the Mesmer clinic. The trio owned distinguished names in the French medical profession—Alexandre Bertrand, Jean Mallöet, Armand Sollier—and Mesmer moved heaven and earth to gain a favorable report from them. As usual there were a number of extremely difficult cases under his care, so that he had his object lessons ready to hand when the examiners arrived. During the next two months he and Deslon produced what they considered ironclad proof of their doctrine. They made the paralytic walk, the blind see, the deaf hear, the neurotic recover their equilibrium.

With maddening recalcitrance, the men from the faculty remained cold to everything Mesmer urged on them. They argued that some healings were only partial, that others might be feigned, that patently effective cures could be the result of nature acting on illnesses, and that they would be unprofessional if they validated cases they had not seen from the start. Mesmer, verging on desperation, asked what would satisfy them. They suggested selecting some cases themselves for him to treat, Mesmer agreed, and then they announced their inability to find the type of patient they needed for the experiment.

Bertrand, Mallöet, and Sollier had only this to say at the end: "The facts are undoubtedly amazing, but they are inconclusive." How often had Mesmer heard that!

The Paris Faculty of Medicine, like the Royal Society of Medicine and the French Academy of Sciences, was lost to the cause of Mesmerism. What could Mesmer do now? He could do what he had done before. Believing that old-fashioned professionals were quibbling with him, he appealed away from the bureaucracy to a wider public. He published his *Memoir,* to which he subjoined twenty-seven propositions of the first importance for his theory of animal magnetism. To wit:

1. There is a mutual influence between heavenly bodies, the earth and living things.

2. A universally distributed fluid, so continuous as to admit of no vacuum anywhere, rarefied beyond all comparison, and by nature able to receive, propagate and communicate all motion—this is the medium of the influence.

3. This mutual influence obeys mechanical laws that have not as yet been explained.

4. This mutual influence causes alternate effects, which we may consider a kind of ebb and flow.

5. This ebb and flow is more or less general, more or less particular, more or less compound, according to the causes that determine it.

6. Through this agent (the most universal we find in nature), the heavenly bodies, the earth and the parts that compose it mutually influence one another.

7. All the properties of matter and of living organisms depend on this agent.

8. The animal body reacts to the alternate effects of this agent, which by entering the substance of the nerves affects them immediately.

9. Certain properties analogous to those of the magnet reveal themselves, especially in the human body. It is possible to distinguish different and opposite poles that may be changed, linked, destroyed or reinforced. Even the declination phenomenon can be observed.

10. This property of the human body, which makes it responsive to the influence of the heavenly bodies, and to the reciprocal action of the bodies around it, made me, in view of the analogy with the magnet, call it *animal magnetism.*

11. The action and the properties of animal magnetism can be communicated to other animate and inanimate bodies. These differ in the degree of their susceptibility to it.

12. The action and the properties can be reinforced and propagated by the same bodies.

13. Experience shows a diffusion of matter so subtle that it penetrates all other bodies, apparently without any loss of potency.

14. Its action takes place at a distance, without the need of any intermediate object.

15. It is like light in that it can be reinforced and reflected by mirrors.

16. It can be communicated, propagated and reinforced by the action of sound.

17. This magnetic property can be accumulated, concentrated, and transported from one place to another.

18. I have remarked that not all animate bodies are equally susceptible to it. Some exist, although they are rare, that have properties so opposed as to destroy by their very presence every effect of animal magnetism in other bodies.

19. This contrary property also penetrates all bodies. It too can be communicated, propagated, accumulated, concentrated, transported, reflected by mirrors, and propagated by sound. This property is not merely a negation of animal magnetism but a positive and opposite power.

20. The magnet, natural or artificial, is, like other bodies, susceptible both to animal magnetism and to its contrary, without in either case suffering any alteration in its effect on iron or the needle—which proves that the principle of *animal magnetism* is essentially different from that of *mineral magnetism.*

21. This system will produce new explanations of the nature of fire and light, of the theory of gravitation, of ebb and flow in nature, of the magnet and of electricity.

22. It will show that the magnet and electricity only have, as far as illness is concerned, properties common to many other natural agents and that if some useful results have been obtained from their use, these are due to animal magnetism.

23. We can see from the facts that this principle, in accordance with the practical rules I shall set forth, can cure nervous ailments directly and other ailments indirectly.

24. Relying on its aid, the physician learns the proper use of medicines. He strengthens their action and causes and directs beneficial crises in such a manner as to keep control of them.

25. In making my method public, I will demonstrate by a new theory of disease the universal effectiveness of the principle I employ to combat it.

26. Basing himself on this knowledge, the physician will be able to diagnose with certainty the origin, nature, and progress of diseases, even the most complicated. He will prevent them from becoming worse and devise a cure without ever exposing the patient to dangerous or disagreeable consequences regardless of age, temperament, or

sex. Women, even in pregnancy and at the time of delivery, will profit from the same advantages.

27. To conclude, this doctrine will make it possible for the physician to diagnose the health of each individual and to shield him from the illnesses to which he may be exposed. The art of healing will then reach its ultimate perfection.

These propositions are essentially the ideas of Mesmer's doctoral dissertation rendered more complete and systematic by his scientific studies and applied more precisely to medicine through knowledge gained in his medical practice.

The first seven amount to a summary of one section of *The Influence of the Planets on the Human Body,* except that the thought is pushed beyond mere references to Newton and the theory of gravitation. Mesmer is now dogmatic about his universal fluid's being the cause of the properties of bodies and their mutual attraction in obedience to Newton's equation. Number 3 gave him much trouble, for it was taken to be a confession of ignorance illegitimate in one pontificating about the most fundamental substance in the universe.

The next three present his reasons for dropping the phrase "animal gravitation" in favor of "animal magnetism." The change in terminology is really no help. Since his universal fluid acts on both animate and inanimate bodies, it cannot be properly defined by the adjective "animal," no matter what the noun. He would have done better to use "cosmic magnetism," although if this phrase occurred to him, he might have shied away from it as sounding too occult. Number 9 never enjoyed much success, the existence of animal magnetic poles in the human body being unproved and unprovable.

The series 11–17 returns to the physics of the universal fluid. Number 12 is important because it contains the germ of the "animal magnet" concept, which Mesmer, despite his not saying so here, applies mainly to himself—he is one of the bodies that can reinforce and propagate animal magnetism. Number 14 means that animal magnetism exists everywhere, not that it acts at a distance across a vacuum, the possibility of which is expressly denied (number two). When Mesmer came to Number 15, he must have had in mind the apparent verification of his theory when Maria Theresa Paradies followed the movement of his wand, reacting to the animal magnetism that flowed from him to the mirror and was reflected back into her eyes.

Next, Mesmer introduces the great contradiction in his system. If the universal fluid is responsible for all the properties of bodies (number seven), then no other physical agent can exist, let alone counteract the operation of the universal fluid (18–19). He still does not see this problem. He never did see it.

After differentiating animal magnetism and mineral magnetism (20), he makes grandiose predictions about animal magnetism revolutionizing physics (21–22), and then, following up the hint in Number 8, promises to revolutionize medicine (23–27). Number 23 is not justified within the system. If the universal fluid penetrates the human body, there is no discernible reason why it should not act directly on all the fibers and fluids instead of being restricted to indirect action through the nerves. No doubt Mesmer had the Cartesian theory of animal spirits in mind when he set down this proposition, but it is also possible to see his practice affecting his abstract thought. His cures were of nervous illnesses or those connected indirectly with the nerves, and so he assumed that his universal fluid touched the nervous system directly, the rest of the body indirectly. This was a fallacy in his logic. His premises implied that there is one illness and one cure, and he drew the implication later in his career.

The twenty-seven propositions resisted all attempts to make sense of them as a system. That is why Mesmer fought a losing battle when he asked for their acceptance en bloc. Only the most credulous disciple could bow his head and murmur "credo" in good faith.

The history of ideas has its tragic conflicts. This was one of them. Many observers who believed there was something in Mesmerism could not see what it was because Mesmer obscured their view by throwing up a smoke screen of baffling theories. Where he stirred interest among scientists, they were the nondogmatists who were not willing to deny his universal fluid categorically for fear that it might someday rank as an accepted reality with mineral magnetism, electricity, and gravitation. The best Mesmer could get from them—and they were a tiny minority—was an acknowledgment of the possibility that his central idea would be retained in some form.

The medical men, on the other hand, might be impressed by his cures, but they in general could not believe in animal magnetism leaping across the space between Mesmer and his patients. Something was going on that called for explanation, but Mesmer's explanation explained nothing for them.

Thus, Mesmer was left with his faithful Mesmerians, who agreed with him on virtually everything. He could let his acrimony melt in the warmth of their adulation. Yet they led him into hopes doomed to be disappointed. Their faith hardened his *idée fixe,* for he cherished the illusion that they might prove to be a model for all the learned world and that if only he did not lose his single-minded intensity or allow his energy to flag, he must one day be fully vindicated.

His resilience was born of that belief. Acerbic and even insulting after every defeat, he always recovered his equanimity and began a fresh campaign for his system, mounting an attack on the nearest individual or group that seemed most promising.

The learned world failed him. Physics was *not* revolutionized by the use of animal magnetism as a working hypothesis, and it soon ceased to be credible to scientists. Finally, when Mesmerism did revolutionize psychology and psychosomatic medicine, this development proceeded only by getting rid of animal magnetism.

Mesmer was wrong and even wrongheaded in charging bias against those who refused to give him an endorsement. He was making an impossible intellectual demand in asking them to see the unity of his theory and practice, for that unity was a mirage of his own imagining. Different theories were possible of why his healing art worked. As yet, no one had a theory that explained the facts.

The facts continued to be sufficiently startling. Mesmer expanded the practical side of his system on a larger scale than ever before, handled a multitude of patients, continued to achieve success where the orthodox doctors had failed, and became the talk of Paris.

CHAPTER 9

Mesmerism: The Crisis

Some of the most fashionable of the fashionable Parisians made their way to Mesmer's establishment during the years 1778–85. The Princesse de Lamballe, intimate confidante of Marie Antoinette, came to have an ulcer treated. Mesmer did not cause the ulcer to disappear, but he did give the princesse sufficient relief to make her one of his fervid partisans. The Comtesse de la Malmaison suffered from paralysis from the waist down after taking a spill out of her carriage. As so often in Mesmer's career, this patient had been a patient of a rival, for the contesse had been treated by Leroy. She went in despair to Mesmer, recovered her health, and wrote one of the testimonials he tried to force on the Royal Society of Medicine. The Duchesse de Chaulnes suffered from nervous problems brought on by her husband's coldness and neglect, and from Mesmer she received the psychological stability to endure her marital misfortunes. The rich and the influential passed one another in their carriages before Mesmer's door.

Some of the lowliest Parisians passed one another on foot. Peasants, tradesmen, cobblers, innkeepers, scullery maids—they rubbed elbows with their betters, metaphorically speaking at least, in Mesmer's clinic. They received his attention as fully as anyone else. He did not neglect them for this duke or that duchess. Always the healer looking to cure the illness before him regardless of the class of the person suffering from it, he opened his clinic to one and all, something he could do because he offset the inability of the poor to pay by charging large fees of those who could afford it.

When Mesmer took a patient, his first concern was to determine whether the ailment was organic or functional. If it was organic, the result of physical damage to the tissue, he considered it, following Proposition 23, beyond the aid of animal magnetism. If it was functional, a physiological disorder affected by the nerves, it fell within the class of diseases he felt uniquely qualified to handle with his therapeutic technique. Anyone suffering from a psychosomatic ailment could rely on him, not only as a physician committed to the art of healing, but also as the discoverer of animal magnetism anxious to validate his discovery through new cures and new patients willing to declare publicly what they owed to him.

Having made his diagnosis in a given case, Mesmer laid out a regimen designed to intensify the illness to an extreme limit, from which point it would suddenly and swiftly begin to recede. This was the crisis of Mesmerism.

Its necessity followed from Mesmer's physiological theory. Health is the result of the organs acting properly on the fibers and the liquids of the body—the blood, secretions, and so on. Now the organs act properly when influenced by animal magnetism, by the universal fluid of the cosmos flowing into them through the nerves. Mesmer states that magnetism is to the bodily organs as the wind is to the windmill, an apt figure of speech suggesting the need for motive power in each case.

If the wind ceases to blow, the sails of the windmill stop turning, the milling process comes to a halt, and should the cessation continue long enough, the windmill may fall into disrepair or even ruin. The salvation of the miller comes when the wind begins to blow again, making the machinery of the windmill work again. Just so for the psychosomatic illnesses, where the salvation is to send animal magnetism streaming into the nervous system until the organs begin to function as they should.

Again, a greater effort is required to start a windmill after it has stopped than to keep it going, especially if disrepair has set in. The same is true of the psychosomatic illnesses. When animal magnetism ceases to course freely through the nervous system, the organs begin to malfunction and the whole physiology slows down. Fluids become stagnant and viscous and begin to block the blood vessels and other canals of the body. Arteries harden, joints become stiff, and the symptoms of familiar ailments appear. The symptoms become worse because the organs grow weaker as the obstructions grow larger and vice versa. Mesmer thought the organs then must be galvanized into a greater effort than ever before to push the fluids through the natural channels, and it is animal magnetism that galvanizes them.

This analysis led Mesmer to the belief that the crisis could not be avoided in any case of psychosomatic illness, and his practice convinced him that his major cures always in fact followed a crisis—the catalepsy of Franzl Oesterlin, the eye spasms of Maria Theresa Paradies.

Mesmer's methods created one big difficulty for certain patients, who withdrew when they realized where he was leading them. Like Baron de Horka, they were more afraid of the Mesmerian crisis than of the disease. They preferred nervous trembling or occasional nausea to delirium or convulsions. Mesmer recalls one patient who suffered from nervous pains in the head: "He was very uneasy for fear that the spasms I had caused might last fifteen days as usual. He again asked me anxiously if I could release him from the problem I had created for him. I said I could, and succeeded completely in a few minutes."

This was a comparatively unimportant ailment because it was tolerable to the sufferer. The most interesting cases were the serious ones in which patients felt that anything Mesmer might visit on them would be preferable to the state they were in. They underwent crises, always painful, often dramatic, sometimes terrifying, at the clinic. His descriptions of those he cured include the following typical scenes.

An asthmatic patient: "At a distance of four or five paces, I pointed my wand at his chest. His breathing immediately stopped, and he would have fainted if I had not ceased at his request."

A paralytic patient: "As soon as I pointed my wand at her left side, Mlle. Belancourt staggered and fell to the floor in violent convulsions."

A neuralgic patient: "When I pointed my wand at him, this caused him to tremble wildly; his face became flushed; he appeared about to suffocate; he perspired profusely; he fainted and fell back on the sofa unconscious."

Mesmer reports such incidents with the cool professionalism of any doctor prescribing a painful remedy for a patient. The convulsions and other psychosomatic manifestations were part of the healing process, and far from being disturbed, he welcomed them, displayed them openly and insistently to visitors, and described them clinically in quiet triumph in the pages of his writings. They ranked among his proofs positive of the curative properties of animal magnetism.

They made him, nonetheless, notorious. Most witnesses did not take kindly to the emotional outbursts at the clinic. Hostile observers condemned Mesmer for encouraging such things, declared them to be harmful, and even suggested that the authorities put an end to the proceedings if Mesmer refused.

Among the most hostile, and certainly the most dangerous, to him were members of the two royal commissions who investigated Mesmerism in 1784 (we will see them at work in a later chapter). They were dealing with Deslon's clinic, but Deslon was strictly Mesmerian in his use of the crisis, and the inquisitors lumped the two magnetizers together. According to their report, they were astonished and appalled by the sight of patients going suddenly into agonizing physical contortions. "These convulsions," they reported, "are extraordinary for their number, their duration, and their force." The report went on:

> These convulsions are marked by violent, involuntary movements of the limbs and the whole body, by constriction of the throat, by throbbing in the chest and nausea in the stomach, by rapid blinking and crossed eyes, by piercing cries, tears, hiccups and uncontrollable laughter. These are preceded or followed by a state of languor and daydreams, a type of abatement or even slumber. The slightest sudden sound causes a startled shuddering; and it has been observed that a change of tone or beat in music played on the piano influences the ill, so that a rapid composition agitates them and throws them back into convulsions.

The Mesmerian crisis appeared grotesque to the commissioners, and yet they admitted the reality of the cures that followed it. No one could get around the testimony of the patients who insisted on the method's unique healing capacity as far as they were themselves concerned. Thus Charles du Hussay, an army officer who wrote one of the testimonials dispatched by Mesmer to the Royal Society of Medicine, declared that he came to the doctor with a whole set of interconnected ailments—fever, nervous trembling, protruding eyes, partial paralysis. "In short," he wrote, "my gait was that of an elderly drunkard, not that of a man of forty." After treatment by the physician from Vienna:

> I know nothing of the means used by Dr. Mesmer. However, I can say in all candor that, without treating me with drugs or any other

remedy than what he calls animal magnetism, he caused me to feel powerful sensations from head to foot. I went into a crisis marked by a cold so intense that my body seemed to be turning to ice. Then I felt an intense heat causing much fetid sweating, so much that my mattress was soaked through. This crisis lasted more than a month. Since then, I have rapidly recovered. Four months later, I can stand erect and stable on my feet. My head is steady. I have regained the use of my tongue and can speak as intelligibly as anybody. My nose, eyes and cheeks have resumed their natural consistency. My color is that of a man of my age in good health. I breathe freely. My chest has expanded. I am not suffering any pain. My legs are steady and strong, and I can walk rapidly and easily. I have an excellent digestion and appetite. In short, I am entirely free from all my infirmities.

This crisis occurred while Mesmer was giving Hussay individual treatment. Crises of the type described by the commissioners' report occurred in the midst of group therapy and tended to be the most violent of all because mass emotion reinforced personal feeling. Mesmer maintained crisis rooms for the patients who went into delirium, convulsions, or other nervous eruptions that necessitated their removal from the group. Each crisis room was padded to prevent the afflicted from hurting themselves in their convulsive thrashing about. Here Mesmer or members of his staff gave each personalized attention.

Since the majority of his patients were women, Parisian wit found a titillating subject for lampoons, cartoons, and satirical verse about what went on in the crisis rooms. Sober investigators were disturbed by the fact that Mesmer sat face to face and knee to knee with a patient and then proceeded to alleviate the crisis by appropriate touching and stroking.

The simple answer to the innuendos is that no record exists of a jealous husband in Mesmer's career. His enemies—and he made many enemies—used all the arguments against him that were available to them. They got Mesmerism condemned for various reasons, but never by accusing its founder of violating medical ethics or the trust of his patients.

The Mesmerian crisis was a difficult problem for the experts because the concept of a crisis as the way from disease to health was standard in the medical profession, a commonplace since Hippocrates and Galen. Mesmer had learned to watch for the culmination and then the break in fevers and other illnesses while studying medicine in Vienna. The question, therefore, was whether the conditions provoked by the practitioner of animal magnetism could be considered a valid subdivision of the medical crisis.

In the end, neither Mesmer nor his enemies would concede that it could. They agreed on its uniqueness without agreeing about what made it unique or whether it was good or bad.

Was it really a good thing to throw patients into immensely painful contortions, thereby reinforcing the malady of which they were desperate to be cured? Mesmer answers the challenge by differentiating between "symptomatic symptoms" and "critical symptoms."

Symptomatic symptoms are those the patient shows when he arrives for treatment—in this case, the convulsions resulting from some profound nervous illness and its physiological consequences. Of course, these convulsions are not desirable. The whole point is to get rid of them.

Critical symptoms, on the contrary, Mesmer said, are caused, not by the illness, but by animal magnetism coursing through the nervous system and galvanizing the organs into more strenuous efforts to overcome the obstructions causing the illness. Sometimes the shock is enough to throw the patient into convulsions, but only a grossly incompetent diagnosis by the doctor will judge these to be undesirable. They are precisely what is needed. When the convulsions cease to be symptomatic symptoms and become critical symptoms, then the patient is on the road to being cured. Neither the doctor nor the patient should be discouraged when convulsions increase in violence and come more frequently but should consider this the best possible sign that the treatment is working.

If a violent crisis did not take place, Mesmer explained that the illness was not severe enough to make one necessary—the obstructions in the bodily canals were comparatively trivial and easily overcome by a small infusion of animal magnetism. However, he never discarded his belief that *some* crisis must necessarily occur. He rejected the diagnoses of those Mesmerians who claimed they were working cures with animal magnetism without provoking critical symptoms in their patients. He thought that such symptoms, however mild or difficult to discern, would invariably be found if the search was sufficiently exhaustive.

It was not just a fact of his medical experience or a listing of cases where he recorded critical symptoms. It was a matter of basic physics, the Newtonian physics of Mesmer's *Influence of the Planets on the*

Human Body. If the universal fluid flowed from the magnetizer into the subject in doses powerful enough to start defective physiological machinery working again, then the subject *had* to be severely affected. The action *had* to be followed by a reaction just as Newton said of all mutually interacting objects. An electrical machine shakes when you start it and then settles down to its proper uniform movement. The body does the same thing when triggered into action by animal magnetism.

Mesmer's doctoral dissertation had compared the "tides" in the physiology to those on the earth and through the universe. These tides also implied the Mesmerian crisis. When the moon pulls the surface of the sea in one direction, the water gains an inertia that causes it to pound farther up the beach than lunar gravitation alone would carry it. The surf reaches a high-water mark, pauses, and then recedes as the tide changes, repeating the process again and again to keep pace with changes in the alignment of the earth and the moon. This is the ebb-and-flow effect. Similarly, the universal fluid gains inertia and courses through the nervous system and the bloodstream farther than is needed for the cure—the magnetizer, no more than the moon, can draw a fine line to delimit the headlong plunge of the tide. This too is the ebb-and-flow effect. The limit of the flow is the limit of the crisis. The ebb is the recession from illness toward health.

Mesmer's logic was sound, granted his premise. When the premise was denied, the logic collapsed. If no universal fluid is involved and if nothing physical passes from the magnetizer into the subject, then Mesmer's inferred action does not occur and no reaction is implied. This position was taken by those who said the phenomena of Mesmerism were psychological rather than physical, who attributed the cures to suggestion and imagination rather than to animal magnetism.

Either logic might be invoked to explain the cures. Either logic might be invoked to explain the failures. According to the Mesmerians of the opposite school, the magnetizer failed because he had a refractory subject, one who was too strong-willed to permit his imagination to be controlled in the interest of the cure. For Mesmer, the countervailing force of his Propositions 18–19 occupied the subject's body, preventing the cure by blocking the flow of animal magnetism.

Suggestion and imagination, will and emotions—all had a place in Mesmer's theory of medicine, but only as subsidiary factors. They could open the valves, so to speak, and admit animal magnetism into the nervous system. They could close the valves and keep it out. That was why the physician had to be so careful to establish rapport with the patient at the start of the treatment and why he had to sustain the mood of confidence throughout, the patient's faith in the cure being an ingredient of the cure. When so much has been admitted, even insisted upon, the *vera causa* of the healing process is animal magnetism. The psychological factors may help or hinder the physics of healing, but the physics remains basic. Control the tidal waves entering the physiology from outside the body, and you control the illness.

This being so, Mesmer clung to his concept of the crisis. Mesmerism meant for him reinforcing and guiding the illness to a decisive breaking point when the universal fluid flowed to its maximum limit and, before ebbing, forced the most stricken people to experience their worst symptoms in a violent, shattering way. Technically, the symptomatic symptoms gave way to the critical symptoms.

Mesmer could not promise his patients anything less than this. Grimm, writing of Deslon but including Mesmer in his thought, commented sardonically that men and women went to them "to have convulsions at ten louis per month."

CHAPTER 10

Mesmerism: The Trance

The use of animal magnetism to induce the Mesmerian crisis was part of Mesmer's therapeutic technique from the beginning because the two were logically connected as cause and effect. Mesmer could not foresee certain by-products of the technique, things without any logical necessity that he stumbled on along the way and assimilated into his system because they were simply factual.

Much the most significant of the unexpected discoveries was Mesmer's ability to throw subjects into a state between sleep and wakefulness so that they could and would obey commands even though their faculties had stopped functioning in the normal manner. This was the trance of Mesmerism.

Although not part of his original vision, the trance grew in importance until it overshadowed everything else and became the essential phenomenon of the system. This is what "Mesmerism" came to mean. The verb "to mesmerize" entered the language of the West as a synonym for "to throw into a trance."

Mesmer learned how to control the phenomenon while guiding Franzl Oesterlin toward a crisis in her convulsive hysteria. Having found that he could send her into a trance by pointing at her and that the trance was part of the healing process, he followed up this lead in his subsequent cases, eventually becoming a consummate master able to cause paralysis, drowsiness, sleep, and semiconscious states in his patients.

Mesmer understood full well that his will dominated the will of the patient, the cure coming about partly because he made the patient will the cure. He saw, moreover, that the subject in a trance could obey his commands because something deeper than ordinary consciousness was at work. He did not at once grasp the concept of the unconscious mind or realize that he was probing into deeply hidden parts of the psyche. Only after Mesmerism developed along unexpected lines, in his own hands and in those of his followers, did he comprehend the meaning of the trance.

Years later he wrote: "Sleep is not a negative condition or simply the absence of wakefulness . . . the human faculties are not always quiescent but are actually as active as during wakefulness." By then he realized what he had been doing with his patients—he had been putting them into a special kind of sleep and then making them use their faculties in a special way. Today we would say that he had discovered controlled hypnotism.

Hypnotic phenomena, of course, were as old as humanity. Countless records existed of men and women who had gone through long, involved experiences, who had performed complicated acts often involving much exertion and considerable moving around, without remembering anything afterward. Sometimes the thing occurred spontaneously, to the consternation of witnesses. A multitude of oracles, seers, swamis, and faith healers had learned how to arouse odd or morbid psychological manifestations, and the annals of religion and medicine were filled with actions inexplicable by the actors, from seeing visions to talking gibberish. Nor was it all past history. Paris had seen, within living memory, the Convulsionaries of St. Médard.

François de Pâris, a deacon reputed to be a saint, died in 1727 and was buried in the cemetery of St. Médard. Reports of healing miracles at his tomb caused mob scenes in which believers went into trances and showed all the signs of mass hysteria. They babbled as if in their sleep, uttered wild prophecies, danced and cavorted, and fell down in the fits that caught most attention and gave them their title. The Convulsionaries of St. Médard had petered out before Mesmer's arrival in Paris, but there were occultists around who could make people do strange things while their minds were in the twilight zone between consciousness and unconsciousness.

Mesmer's distinction was to make a science of hypnotism. This was no orgy of indiscriminate acts, but rather the controlled response of patients to their physician.

The trance was for Mesmer one way to bring on the crisis. The patient might lose consciousness or not. If consciousness remained, one or all of the five senses might lapse. Convulsions or catalepsy might supervene. The experience could be painful or pleasant, and one type generated a passionate desire on the part of the subject for its continuance—namely, the erotic trance. The examiners at Deslon's clinic commented specifically on the diminished resistance of the patient moving into the erotic trance:

> When this type of crisis is developing, the face becomes flushed by degrees, the eye becomes ardent, and this is the signal by which nature announces the arrival of physical desire. One sees the woman lower her head and cover her eyes with her hands; her natural modesty awakens automatically and makes her wish to hide. However, the crisis grows and her eyes become disturbed, an unequivocal sign of the total disorder of the senses. This disorder may not be experienced by the woman suffering from it, but it does not escape the notice of doctors. After this sign manifests itself, the eyelids become moist; respiration is short and spasmodic; and the breast rises and falls tumultuously; tremors begin along with precipitate and brusque movements of the limbs or the entire body. With the most balanced and sensible women, the final stage, the end of the gentlest emotions, is often a bodily spasm. Languor and quiescence follow this stage, a sort of sleep of the senses, a necessary repose after such extreme agitation.

We do not have so complete a report on Mesmer's clinic, but the commissioners explicitly reported that his practice was the same as Deslon's with the same kinds of patients and cures. Mesmer, therefore, must be credited with having taught Deslon how to handle such cases and how to meet the dangers of the erotic trance by appointing only trained and disciplined men of the highest integrity as assistants.

The criticism that other practitioners of Mesmerism might not be so careful or honorable could not, in the nature of the case, be refuted. But then neither could the rejoinder that Mesmerism was bound to spread, so that the real responsibility of the authorities was to endorse the practitioners who were genuine and suppress those who were not.

And it did spread with remarkable speed. The first person to exploit the trance in its most celebrated form was another follower of Mesmer, the Marquis de Puységur, who practiced the art at the family estate in Busancy near Soissons. Puységur was an aristocrat with a social conscience and an amateur's interest in science. Having learned Mesmerism from Mesmer, he began to use animal magnetism to cure the illnesses of the people in his area. Touching, stroking, and pointing, employing magnetized objects in group therapy, he cleared up a number of chronic ailments. His baquet was a magnetized tree with ropes dangling from the branches. His patients each seized a rope and communally absorbed animal magnetism in a bucolic scene of mass healing. Puységur also gave individualized attention to those who needed it, and quite abruptly, he had a remarkable experience:

> These small successes tempted me to try to aid a peasant, a man of twenty-three, bedridden with pneumonia for four days. I went to see him this past Tuesday, the fourth of the month, at eight in the evening. The fever was making him weaker. After helping him up, I magnetized him. To my surprise, at the end of a quarter of an hour he quietly fell asleep in my arms—without convulsions or pain! I continued the treatment and he began to tremble. He spoke frankly about his private affairs. When I saw his thoughts were having a bad effect on him, I stopped them and tried to make him think of more pleasant things. It did not cost me much effort to achieve this. He imagined himself winning a prize, dancing at a fete, and so forth. I encouraged these images.

Puységur had induced a hypnotic trance in which the subject could hear his words and respond sensibly to them without remembering a thing about it when he came out of the trance. The change in this man under hypnosis appeared inexplicable:

> When he enters the magnetic state, he is no longer an ignorant peasant who can scarcely speak a word in response to a question. He is a different being whom I do not know how to identify. . . . When somebody else enters the room, he sees that person *if I wish him to*. He speaks to that person, saying the things *I wish him to say*, not necessarily word for word, but substantially the same.

This is the first full description of what Puységur called somnambulism, a rather mistaken term since it means sleepwalking of the familiar type, while he was referring to activities carried out by the subject during curtailed consciousness and under the orders, or at least with the consent, of the one who induced the condition. The later term "hypnosis," meaning nervous sleep, was more accurate and for that reason supplanted "somnambulism" as well as "mesmerism."

What Puységur added to Mesmer's discovery was a nonconvulsive form of the Mesmerian trance. The subject went to sleep and then did ordinary things as if he were awake—answering questions, making suggestions, reporting coherent and objectively verifiable events. He was hypnotically blind at the time. Objects right before his eyes did not exist for him if the hypnotist said they were not there. When he awoke, he recalled what the hypnotist instructed him to recall. And the condition lasted as long as the hypnotist made it last. It was full-blown hypnosis, the kind of thing that is common coin in psychology today but was received with incredulity when Puységur published his book on animal magnetism.

Puységur advanced the art and science begun by Mesmer of investigating springs of human action too far down into the psyche for the individual to be aware of them. Puységur's somnambulists could recall events in their early lives, even in young childhood, that seemed to have been forgotten forever. These memories clearly reposed in some kind of "pool" from which they could be drawn under the right conditions. The somnambulists were able to describe their motives in a manner beyond their powers while awake, permitting Puységur to perceive rationality behind apparently irrational behavior. This activity could be triggered in some inexplicable way when the ordinary sense perceptions and thought processes lapsed.

The subject being "asleep," something more than normal mental acts was occurring, something allied to dreaming, which can also dredge up old memories and reveal hidden desires. One difference between natural somnambulism and artificial somnambulism was Puységur's ability to guide the ideas of his subjects toward a state of mind that constituted a purge of the nerves and emotions. He gave Mesmerism a new technique for working cures.

In modern terminology, Mesmer and Puységur were probing into the unconscious. They were working in depth psychology and dynamic psychiatry. They were pioneers in the art of mental healing, pathfinders in the trek toward multilevel studies of personality in the nineteenth and twentieth centuries when the magisterial names would be Charcot and Bernheim, Freud and Jung.

The explanation Mesmer put forward to account for somnambulism was that an inner sense then functions as a sixth sense, a faculty that can operate independently when the five outer senses have gone into abeyance. The inner sense can cause ordinary sleepers to have subjective dreams without recourse to other means of communications, and it can give the somnambulist perceptions of the objective world solely through the animal magnetism flowing into it through the nervous system. This thought, when Mesmer had pondered it long enough, gave rise to the fantastic occult speculations of his later years.

Here Mesmer walked into a blind alley, and he persuaded the Fluidists of Mesmerism to follow him—those who agreed that the trance could be explained by the universal fluid or animal magnetism. The Animists of Mesmerism took the opposite way, which, although muddied by the extravagances of spiritualism, eventually opened up into a broad highway into modern psychology. They denied the reality of animal magnetism, or at least that it had any function in the trance, which they attributed to suggestion and imagination, psychological causes contrasting with the physics of Mesmer. They stripped the husk from the kernel of Mesmerism, which grew and flourished as physicians investigated those areas of the psyche where the will, mysteriously no doubt but still undeniably, imposes itself on mind and body, on perceptions, beliefs, emotions, nerves, blood pressure, and organic physiology.

Mesmerism with animal magnetism is an interesting fallacy in the history of science. Mesmerism without animal magnetism is hypnosis.

Arrival at the truth took time, and there were halfway houses where one or another mesmerizer paused en route. Puységur built one. The marquis was a convinced Fluidist, but his study of practical Mesmerism caused him to abandon the Mesmerian crisis. He found that his patients did not have to experience delirium or convulsions to be cured. They could be put through a regimen of psychosomatic healing, or induced into a trance, without passing through the unnerving critical symptoms that Mesmer considered necessary.

Mesmer had seen patients recoil from the painful climax he planned for them, but he would not change a course laid out by nature and the laws of Newtonian physics. Puységur was too much of a realist to let abstract reasoning stand in his way. He was dealing with the peasantry of Busancy, ignorant men and women who frequently lacked the morale to steel themselves for the crisis. When the ill needed help and animal magnetism was an obstacle, he simply moved it out of his way and forgot about it for the time being.

Puységur took for his motto *Croyez et Voulez* ("Believe and Will"), a clear indication that he understood the extent to which he was dealing with imagination and volition. If he had dropped animal magnetism altogether and joined the Animists, he would have made the breakthrough into pure hypnosis.

With Deslon, Puységur, and others carrying on in their individual ways and Mesmer himself promoting Mesmerism with as much pertinacity as ever, there was no end to the gossip about it. The trance became a favorite subject of the satirists. There were burlesques of the magnetizer pointing his fingers from which rays of animal magnetism darted toward the subject and held him mesmerized. The mesmerizer appeared on the Paris stage in uproarious farces where the big scene showed him throwing victims into wide-eyed, slack-jawed, paralyzed trances. He was a magician or a charlatan, a confidence man or an extortionist mulcting the gullible by threatening them with devastating infusions of animal magnetism.

If we move forward to the year 1790, we find Mozart introducing his old friend, Dr. Mesmer, to opera audiences in *Così fan tutte*. When Despina draws the magnet from under her robe and waves it in the faces of the tenor and the bass, she mesmerizes them.

During the nineteenth century the trance induced by Mesmerism became a staple of the vaudeville show, one of the acts sandwiched somewhere between the clowns, dancers, pantomimists, prestidigitators, and performing dogs. The mesmerist would invite a volunteer onstage, put him into a trance with a beady-eyed look and some mysterious passes, and then cause the audience to gasp or laugh by getting him to carry out remarkable muscular feats or make a spectacle of himself. The act was not invariably rehearsed in advance. Some people have the gift of a dominant will, and some are weak-willed, and that is sufficient to explain many of the mesmerizers who featured in playbills from Germany to California.

The Mesmerian trance provided the spark for a thousand melodramas, one of which holds its place as a minor literary masterpiece—George du Maurier's Victorian novel *Trilby,* which shocked

London and New York because it portrayed low life in Paris, made its heroine an artists' model, and presented a villainous character whose name is a common noun standing for one who holds another in his power. Two of the novel's early scenes introduced the villain and the mystery.

Svengali told her to sit down on the divan, and sat opposite to her, and bade her look him well in the white of the eyes.

"Recartez-moi pien tans le planc tes yeux."

Then he made little passes and counterpasses on her forehead and temples and down her cheek and neck. Soon her eyes closed and her face grew placid. After a while, a quarter of an hour perhaps, he asked her if she suffered still.

"Oh! presque plus de tout, Monsieur—c'est le ciel."

In a few minutes more he asked the Laird if he knew German.

"Just enough to understand," said the Laird (who had spent a year in Dusseldorf), and Svengali said to him in German: "See, she sleeps not, but she shall not open her eyes. Ask her."

"Are you asleep, Miss Trilby?" asked the Laird.

"No."

"Then open your eyes and look at me."

She strained to open her eyes, but could not, and said so.

Then Svengali said, again in German, "She shall not open her mouth. Ask her."

"Why couldn't you open your eyes, Miss Trilby?"

She strained to open her mouth and speak, but in vain.

"She shall not rise from the divan. Ask her."

But Trilby was spellbound, and could not move.

"I will now set her free," said Svengali.

And lo! She got up and waved her arms, and cried, "Vive la Prusse! me v'la guerie!" and in her gratitude she kissed Svengali's hand; and he leered, and showed his big brown teeth and the yellow whites at the top of his big black eyes, and drew his breath in with a hiss.

"He's a rum 'un, ain't he?" said Trilby. "He reminds me of a big hungry spider, and makes me feel like a fly! But he's cured my pain! he's cured my pain! Ah! you don't know what my pain is when it comes!"

"I wouldn't have much to do with him, all the same!" said the Laird. "I'd sooner have any pain than have it cured in that unnatural way, and by such a man as that! He's a bad fellow, Svengali—I'm sure of it! He mesmerized you; that's what it is—mesmerism! I've often heard of it, but never seen it done before. They get you into their power, and just make you do any blessed thing they please—lie, murder, steal—anything! and kill yourself into the bargain when they've done with you! It's just too terrible to think of!"

The author adds: "Cold shivers went down Trilby's back as she listened." He fails to note, however, that somebody had been telling the Laird tall tales about Mesmerism.

Chapter 11

Mesmerism: The Séance

Since Mesmer recognized the part suggestion and imagination play in the healing process and since he understood the influence of the surroundings on both, he took great pains to provide his patients with a setting in which they could be persuaded to submit to his technique. His whole purpose was to establish rapport with them, to gain their confidence and trust, and then, their nerves being now receptive, to introduce doses of animal magnetism into their bodies.

Mesmer laid out his clinic as meticulously as if he were stage managing a play. Only when he had the right conditions around him was he ready for the day's session. This was the séance of Mesmerism.

It began in a large room where dozens of patients could be taken care of at the same time in individualized and group therapy. The room at the Hôtel Bullion was an opulent, spacious one in which previous residents had entertained the *beau monde* of Paris. It had a lofty ceiling, inlaid floors, paneled walls, full-length mirrors, and oriel windows. The furnishings were in the best Louis Quinze style, from the artwork on the walls and tables to the chairs in which the patients sat while they were being magnetized.

Mesmer needed this elegant setting. The aristocrats who came to the clinic would feel at ease in the type of room familiar to them, while the poor would feel that they were being lifted by Dr. Mesmer above the hard or sordid lives they led. In either case, the setting aided the cure.

During the séance Mesmer kept the doors and windows closed. Heavy drapes allowed only a dim light and no noise to filter in from the outside. The atmosphere was warm and oppressive, causing labored breathing conducive to emotional excitement. Silence

125

reigned except for whispers between patients and doctors (Mesmer or his assistants) in the give-and-take of diagnosis, treatment, and prescription. One cardinal exception—the sound of a piano or glass harmonica came from a corner of the room. Mesmer had learned from his Viennese teachers about the healing properties of music; he had stated in Proposition 16 of his *Memoir* that animal magnetism "can be communicated, propagated, and reinforced by sound," and he combined the two ideas by placing instruments where his patients could hear and be moved by them.

How far he still played for his own satisfaction is a matter of conjecture. It is pleasant to imagine him visiting the clinic after hours when his patients were gone and night had fallen, sitting down at the piano, running his fingers over the keys, and delighting himself with a bit of Gluck, Haydn, or Mozart—the melodies of the masters filling the big, empty, murky room, flowing over the array of Mesmerian apparatus.

He was not interested in melody as such when he placed musical instruments in the clinic. They were indispensable to his medical practice, swaying, disturbing, calming the ill. Stormy music helped bring on the Mesmerian crisis, and soft music helped allay it. The musician shifted from one to the other at a signal from Mesmer or an assistant. One of Mesmer's followers, Caullet de Vaumorel, testified to the exquisite sensitivity with which the mood of the patients changed as the mood of the music changed.

There were four baquets in the large room, three for those who could pay and one for the indigent. As the patients arrived, they were examined, given whatever preliminary treatment Mesmer considered necessary, and escorted by his assistants to their places around one or other of the baquets. They took hold of the protruding bars leading up from the magnetized water, touched the ends to their ailing bodies, held hands to set up a "current" of animal magnetism, and waited for the healing process to begin.

Mesmer presided. He maintained the proper presence for the occasion, the "bedside manner" of the Mesmerian séance, appearing in a powdered wig with a coat and breeches of purple silk, ruffles of lace at his wrists, shining buckled shoes on his feet. In his right hand he carried a wand, usually of wrought iron. Moving through the room from baquet to baquet, from patient to patient, he kept an eye on how each was progressing. At one moment he would whisper a word of advice, at another he would give instructions to an assistant.

He stared fixedly into the eyes of this patient, made passes with his hand before the face of that one, ignored the other, taking his cue in each case from the state of the subject at the particular moment. When he judged the moment ripe for any patient, he would inject his animal magnetism directly by touching or stroking, or he might simply point the wand from a distance of several feet.

Within a short space of time, the phenomena of Mesmerism began to manifest themselves at the séance. Depending on how far advanced their treatment was, individuals gasped, blinked, shuddered, twitched, hiccuped, felt better or worse, went into the trance or the crisis. Ecstatically the lame walked and the deaf heard. Paralysis deepened for some, but not despair since Mesmer had predicted this as the prelude to the cure. Those heading for their crises would suddenly scream, fall back, and go into catalepsy or convulsions. Mesmer's assistants promptly came to their aid, giving treatment on the spot or helping the worst cases into the padded crisis rooms to be stroked, hypnotized, or otherwise guided through the crisis into a state of quiescence.

Such were the scenes to which visitors to Mesmer's clinic were treated. A minority of professional physicians (Deslon, Vaumorel) agreed that the séance was a legitimate part of Mesmerism. Some magnetizers (Puységur) dispensed with most of the trappings, holding that better results could be achieved in a bright, cheerful, informal atmosphere. The common run of unprofessional observers who came out of curiosity tended to be skeptical about the whole thing, judging it to be either well-intended nonsense or else outright fraud.

Grimm wrote of Mesmer in September, 1780: "He has had the honor of finding the most enthusiastic admirers, the most opinionated opponents, and patients the most submissive or credulous." The irony behind the words sprang from the writer's total disbelief in Mesmerism and the knowledge that the philosophers with whom he mingled shared his attitude.

Another famous name had something to say on the subject. Madame Du Barry, mistress of the late king, living in retirement in the country, had a brush with Mesmerism for want of something better to do with her time. She says, addressing a friend:

Women chiefly became enthusiastic about this medicine dealing in sympathetic emotions, mysterious contacts, prophetic sleep, etc., etc. For myself, I sought distractions although not remedies in this new temple of health. I was intrigued like others by these wonder-working baquets, these crisis rooms so carefully padded, and all the bizarre apparatus· of mesmerism. You have known adepts who would burn themselves for the cause, and furious opponents who would willingly burn them. . . .Madame de Forcalquier, whose ardent imagination always believes fantastic things, was the first who preached animal magnetism and somnambulism to me. She didn't have much difficulty turning my wits and making me see and believe. We became fervent neophytes in a brief time; I set up in my house a magnetic apparatus, which several of the initiated directed by turns for one hundred louis. M. Mesmer had spoken so often of being disinterested that it seemed strange to me that he would demand so large a sum to make available a means of serving humanity; but the enthusiasts recommended my agreeing as long as magnetism was in vogue.

Madame Du Barry held séances at Louvenciennes, her country retreat, using the baquet with its magnetized water and Mesmerians there to show her and her guests how to use it. No extraordinary cures occurred. The aging adventuress, bored and cynical, was not the best material for Mesmerism to work on, nor did she provide the optimum atmosphere for the séances, certainly not the solemnity Mesmer postulated as a condition of success. She cannot have ever been as complete a believer as the passage suggests—she habitually dramatized events when she looked back at them. The truth seems to be that she was genuinely curious about Mesmerism, gave it a whirl in the hope of finding it piquant, and dropped it when the novelty wore off. Her experience is worth noting because of the person she was and the past she had. Mesmerism cannot have been tried in a more unlikely spot than the living room of Madame Du Barry at Louvenciennes.

Another exception to the rule that women succumbed to Mesmerism was Elisabeth Vigée-Lebrun, one of the best portrait painters of the period, who visited Mesmer himself. The first part of her reminiscence is not without humor:

I had heard endless talk about this notorious charlatan, and I therefore was curious enough to visit one of the meetings he calls "séances" in order to judge his chicanery for myself. When I entered the first room where the devotees of animal magnetism were congregated, I saw many people standing around a large tub. Most of the men and women were holding hands to form a chain. My first impulse was to join the chain, but then I noticed that the man who would be next to me was scruffy. I don't have to tell you how quickly I pulled my hand away and moved on.

The nearness of the unwashed multitude made a bad impression on Madame Vigée-Lebrun at the start of her visit to Mesmer's clinic, and her impressions got no better when she finally saw the master himself in the midst of his ministrations:

As I crossed the room, Mesmer's minions pointed small iron wands at me from every side, which really irritated me. Having visited the various rooms, all packed with the ill or the curious, I was about to leave when I saw a tall, young, rather attractive girl emerging from a nearby room with Mesmer holding her hand. She was dishevelled and seemed delirious, but she took great care to keep her eyes shut. A crowd at once surrounded them. "She is inspired," Mesmer declared. "She knows everything even though she is fast asleep." Then he told her to sit down, seated himself in front of her, and after taking both of her hands asked her what time it was. I saw clearly how he kept his feet on those of this pretended oracle, which made it easy for him to let her know the hour and even the minute. No wonder the girl's replies were so precise that they agreed with the watches of the assistants.

A witness as beguiling as this one ought not to be interrogated for the truth value of her report. All that is needed after the above passage is the conclusion in which she passes a final judgment on Mesmerism:

Today, when tubs and small iron wands have vanished, it is still possible to find people who are persuaded that one woman or another, frequently illiterate, put to sleep by a magnetizer, can not only tell the time of day but also guess what illness you are suffering from and prescribe the right treatment for it. I hope these somnambulist sibyls do some good to those who consult them. For myself, when I am ill I would rather call in a knowledgeable, wide-awake doctor.

There speaks the no-nonsense French middle-class mentality, joining in its instinctive distaste for the Mesmerian séance the wits who considered themselves too intelligent for Dr. Mesmer. They all knew too much about wizards and charlatans and purveyors of sorcery to be taken in. They had seen Saint-Germain and Casanova pass through Paris, and the star of Cagliostro was just rising.

The Comte de Saint-Germain awarded himself that title, concealing his real name and origin so successfully that to this day no one can say for sure who he was. Wandering around Europe, taking whatever he could wherever he could, he left behind him both unpaid debts and a reputation for being able to speak to the dead and restore youth through an elixir he had concocted. In Paris he imposed on the credulity of no less a personage than Louis XV, after interesting Madame de Pompadour in the elixir of youth. The king gave him a pension and a laboratory for alchemical experiments that, if they actually turned lead into gold, might balance the kindgdom's budget overnight. Saint-Germain rattled his retorts and filled the laboratory with sulfurous fumes and never produced an ounce of gold. Too many people close to the king saw through the fraud. Eventually His Majesty, too, was convinced he had made a mistake. Shortly thereafter, the magician was on his travels again. He died in Germany in 1784, a fact known in Paris while Mesmer was there.

Giovanni Giacomo Casanova is remembered today as an inordinate lecher and a fine writer who put a set of memoirs into the classics of that literary genre. To the eighteenth century he was another wandering occultist. In France he made the Marquise d'Urfé his principal victim, an easy enough achievement since she was the eternal ideal of the confidence man, the victim who insists on being fooled and fleeced. Wishing to speak to the spirits of the nether world, convinced that Casanova's "familiar" was a sure medium, she eagerly pressed money on him to overcome his scruples. He imposed on the superstitions of the marquise, profited handsomely, and fled from France one jump ahead of the law, scarcely hoping to find so easy a mark again. He visited Paris briefly in 1783 and met Benjamin Franklin, but not Mesmer.

Count Cagliostro outshone all the charlatans, if "outshone" is the correct word for a corrupt adventurer. Originally Giuseppe Balsamo from Palermo, he became Count Alessandro Cagliostro for the benefit of deluded individuals who succumbed readily to an artistocratic name and title. Apparently Cagliostro enjoyed some genuine success as a faith healer, using a piercing glance, a sensitive touch, and an air of possessing uncanny gifts to persuade his patients to heal themselves. Sedulously cultivating the belief that he could, like Faust, summon beings from the nether world, he appeared in France, set up in business as a professional magician, and founded the Council of Egyptian Masonry.

Cagliostro was a confidence man who created the proper mood for his patrons. He often greeted the simpleminded in flowing robes and a tall turban in dimly lighted chambers where incense hung in the air. He seems to have perfected the crystal ball technique, which would from then on enjoy the eternal youth he promised his patrons. Cupping his hands around his prop, gazing solemnly into its depths, he saw visions, reported prophecies, and uttered mystic phrases in tongues from the ancient East or the Inferno. This may seem the cliché of clichés today, but it was the most up-to-date occultism available when Count Cagliostro ran the séance.

Where crude deception was out of the question, Cagliostro could be an engaging, amusing companion and a shrewd observer of men and events. He warned his chief patron, Cardinal de Rohan, against the conspirators of the Diamond Necklace affair. The cardinal was taken in by the pretenders, Marc and Jeanne de La Motte, who led him to believe that Marie Antoinette wanted him to buy a diamond necklace for her. They even arranged a presumed meeting between the cardinal and the queen by night, in a garden, at a distance. Rohan went ahead and bought the necklace, against the advice of Cagliostro, who said that Marie Antoinette would never be party to such an arrangement, so that she must have been impersonated by someone else at the meeting—which turned out to be true.

Ironically, Cagliostro, who for once was not in on the confidence game, but rather tried to alert the victim, did time in the Bastille and had to leave France in 1786, the year after Rohan's downfall, the year after Mesmer abandoned the French capital.

Paris had, in the 1780s, a regiment of mountebanks, sorcerers, conjurers, and imposters who trailed along behind the leaders, and it was inevitable that Mesmer should be numbered among them.

Animal magnetism seemed to be an occult cosmic power closely related to the preternatural celestial influences of which the Swedenborgians talked bemusedly; its healing capacity resembled the alchemists' elixir of life. The screaming, fainting, and sudden cures in the clinic were thought to be those of miraculous faith healing—Mesmer's patients were explicitly compared to the Convulsionaries of St. Médard. The baquet, oddly put together, having astounding claims made for it, looked like a contrived machine that might have come out of Saint-Germain's laboratory. If Casanova made money from his art, well, so did Mesmer. As for the séance, where was the difference between Cagliostro and his crystal ball, Mesmer and his wand?

The difference got lost in the torrent of anti-Mesmer writing, but it was perfectly plain all the time. Mesmer did not affect a mysterious air, as did Saint-Germain, Casanova, and Cagliostro. He persistently appealed to some of the most intelligent men in Paris to visit his institution, and to those who accepted his invitation he gave the fullest, most candid explanation of his aims, methods, and results. The knaves claimed occult powers, which Mesmer disclaimed precisely because they contradicted his actual achievement, which was so far from being personal that he wanted all physicians to adopt it. The dim lights, the music, the wand, and the rest of the paraphernalia, rather than being stage properties to deceive the gullible, were there to set the mood for his patients, something professional medical men could understand, whether they agreed with the wand or not, because they understood the relationship between mood and cure.

It was a hard fate for Mesmer to be proclaimed an occultist at a time when he considered occultism the worst enemy of his type of medicine. He resented his fate, becoming more disappointed and embittered as the scientific acclaim he craved eluded him. Like so many pioneers abused in their own time, he was not present to enjoy his vindication when it finally came.

We know he was no Cagliostro. A better, although still inexact, comparison can be drawn. Mesmer is the Wizard from Vienna in the sense that Edison is the Wizard of Menlo Park.

CHAPTER 12

A Letter to Marie Antoinette

All of Mesmer's successes as a physician and expert in abnormal psychology left him dissatisfied with his lot. He was human enough to appreciate the laudatory appraisals of his work by his patients, assistants, and friends; he was humane enough to rejoice with the ill when they felt their pain vanishing and recovered the use of their limbs or senses in his clinic; he was gratified as a pure truth seeker that the enormous accumulation of evidence in his medical files gave him every reason to believe in, and no reason to doubt, the validity of his system. But that did not compensate for his rejection by the scientific and medical corporations of Paris. He would try again for official recognition, but immediately after publishing his *Memoir* in 1779, he concentrated his attention on his patients and their problems.

He could afford a breathing spell because his principal colleague stepped forward as a defender of the Mesmerian faith.

Charles Deslon was everything Mesmer could have hoped for in a disciple—a hard worker, a true believer, and a propagandist with influence in quarters where the master was *persona non grata*. He had a pleasing personality, graceful manner, and lively intelligence. Originally one of the bright young men of French medicine just after his graduation from medical school, he had made his mark in the profession, risen to a distinguished place on the faculty, and assembled a choice collection of patients from the aristocracy before becoming private physician to the Comte d'Artois.

Deslon's conversion to Mesmerism gave the doctrine respectability among people who otherwise would not have accorded it a moment's consideration. He admired Mesmer, deferred to him as the originator, and felt committed to promoting Mesmerism to the limit of his ability and influence. Moreover, the age differential between them was the optimum one for such an association—Mesmer forty-five, Deslon twenty-nine—so that they could be active partners, carrying on their work in unison, with no question about who was the senior partner. Deslon, quintessentially French, equable, willing to look for compromises and accommodations, complemented Mesmer, the foreigner, with his personal intensity, irascible temper, inclination to suspect collusions and conspiracies, and innate feeling that the outraged indignation of the just and the honorable (himself) should be allowed to find an outlet in blunt language, no matter who the party of the second part might be.

While Deslon was not by nature a controversialist, he willingly entered the quarrel over Mesmerism because he thought it his duty to support his maligned partner, to defend the truth, and to labor for the good of humanity.

He opened his campaign in 1780 with his *Observations on Animal Magnetism,* an apologia that explains how he first became interested in Mesmerism and then convinced by it. He gives Mesmer all the credit for the method and its triumphs, rebuts hostile criticism, and meets the most common objection thus: "If M. Mesmer had no other secret except that of causing the imagination to work effectively in the interests of health, would not this be in itself a wonderful thing? For if the medicine of the imagination is the best, why should we not employ the medicine of the imagination?"

Deslon finessed the question of the universal fluid. Although he said he believed in a physical "influence" flowing from doctor to patient, and defended all of Mesmer's propositions, including those that referred to the universal fluid, he got away from the subject as quickly as possible and stressed practice rather than theory. He thought the real necessity just then was to persuade his readers that the cures alone should be sufficient to establish this truth, that Mesmerism was too successful to be left unused by the medical profession. The argument is couched in reasonable language, not polemics. The writing caused Mesmer to compliment Deslon: "He has applied all his art in his account to polish the verities I presented roughly in mine."

Deslon's book was something special in the literature of Mesmerism for several reasons, not least because he had one particular cure to rely on—his own. He said that ever since childhood he suffered from stomach pains and headaches, no treatment being able to alleviate them until he found Mesmer's. Deslon quotes Mesmer on the hard fact that no complete cure could be expected since the organs had degenerated physically too far, an example of candor and skill in diagnosis—Mesmer was no Cagliostro promising anything to get the patient's fee, no mediocre diagnostician fumbling with the evidence. This patient subjected himself to Mesmer's animal magnetism, went through his Mesmerian crisis, and came out really improved for the first time in his life.

"I would not refer to my personal case," Deslon concluded, "except that I want to defend my opinion on the basis of my experience."

In only one passage did he allude in a critical tone to the rejection of Mesmerism by the learned bodies: "As far as I can tell, it might be easier to make the four great rivers of France flow together in the same bed than to persuade the savants of Paris to hold an assembly to judge in good faith a matter that passes beyond the bonds of their principles."

One group of the "savants of Paris" took grave exception to Deslon's book, the Faculty of Medicine to which he belonged. For once he ran into no obstacle when he proposed a conference on Mesmerism. His enemies eagerly agreed because they wanted to put him on trial and to force a decision on whether he deserved to remain a member. The faculty convened on September 18, 1780, to hear arguments for and against.

Roussel de Vauzèsmes, speaking for the opposition, launched a derisive diatribe against Mesmer, Mesmerism, Deslon and Deslon's *Observations.* Vauzèsmes dredged up all the old tales about the Viennese failures, rebuffs, and scandals. He sprinkled his discourse with the names of Hell, Ingenhousz, Stoerck, Paradies, et cetera. He termed Mesmer a charlatan and Deslon the associate of a charlatan. He scoffed at the notion that animal magnetism ever cured anybody or was even a reality. He charged Deslon with promoting superstition in the guise of science.

Deslon delivered a moderate reply after protesting against the violence of his opponent. The main point in his reply, as in his book, was that the results obtained by Mesmerism ought to be examined with an open mind. Again he skirted around Mesmer's theory of a universal fluid, which he knew would be a stumbling block for most of those in the room. The cures were the thing.

Deslon's conciliatory message and tone did no good. The decision, formulated in four sections, went crushingly against him:

1. He was warned to be more circumspect in the future.

2. His voting rights in the faculty were suspended for one year.

3. He was threatened with the erasure of his name from the membership list unless he disavowed within one year the *Observations on Animal Magnetism.*

4. Mesmer's twenty-seven propositions were rejected.

The decision of the faculty was a serious threat to Deslon's career, but by now he was putting his faith in animal magnetism ahead of his career. He continued to practice what he took to be the most scientific and beneficial medicine available, and far from disavowing his book, he continued to write and speak in defense of its contents.

All the Mesmerians agreed that the faculty was adopting an unscientific attitude in refusing to investigate the evidence mentioned at the conference—the members were like the Aristotelians who refused to look through Galileo's telescope. The comparison seemed entirely inappropriate to the objects of this criticism, who complained that the data collected by Mesmer had been explained *ad nauseam.* The physicians of the corporation, putting aside those whose enmity warped their judgment, could see nothing to be gained from another catalogue of cures at Mesmer's clinic. So many individual doctors and groups and committees had investigated and come back with the information that the cures were factual but the explanation fantastic that less could be said for animal magnetism than for imagination, nature or some other cause, known or unknown. The faculty would not waste its time traveling down that road again.

Here the matter rested for the moment while Mesmer and Deslon rethought their position. They had adopted opposite strategies in the campaign to get animal magnetism accepted by the savants of Paris, and both strategies had failed. Mesmer, starting with his theory of the universal fluid, could not persuade the scientists to accept his cosmology—a rejection Deslon understood and tried to learn from. The theory was too abstruse and unsubstantiated in scientific terms. Deslon, starting with the medical facts in the clinic, could not persuade the physicians to accept his explanation of something physical joining doctor and patient— a rejection Mesmer understood and probably foresaw from his own experience with that strategy. The medical facts could too easily be attributed to something beside animal magnetism.

What course remained open to them? They could approach the court of Versailles in the hope that Louis XVI might appoint a royal commission to settle the issue. Deslon made the proposal to Joseph de Lassonne, the king's physician, who passed it on to the higher echelons at Versailles. An apparently hopeful start made the end harder to take when the negotiations fell through because the conditions could not be agreed on.

Mesmer's Vienna experience was repeating itself in Paris. Having run up against a stone wall in Vienna, he had left the city to its fate and looked elsewhere for recognition. Now up against a stone wall in Paris, he threatened to leave the city to its fate and look elsewhere for recognition. He would have put it in precisely that way. He always felt sorry for the place from which he was departing. He always deplored the fact that he must turn his back on ill and diseased human beings and that the innocent must suffer with the guilty.

The innocent in Paris suffered a minor panic at his announcement. He was besieged by the sick and the suffering, from whom there came cries of despair at the prospect of losing the one physician they trusted. Those titled ladies and devoted Mesmerians, the Princesse de Lamballe and the Duchesse de Chaulnes, were of one mind that Mesmer's disappearance would be a disaster. They made representations to the queen about the French government's tendering a formal contract that would lead him to change his mind.

Marie Antoinette would take no part in the affair directly, for her mother, Maria Theresa, Empress of Austria, had died in 1780, and she remained in mourning at Versailles. She did go so far as to turn the problem over to the Comte de Maurepas, the minister of state, with permission to act in her name. Maurepas had made a reputation in government service as a master of compromise. One British diplomat called him "calm, prudent, cautious." It seemed evident to the queen that he, if anyone, might bring order and tranquillity out of the furor over animal magnetism.

Obeying a summons with alacrity and anticipation after negotiating with go-betweens, Mesmer and Deslon arrived at Maurepas' office on March 28, 1781. There the two principals confronted each other, the diplomatic old minister (now over eighty) and the prickly visitor from Vienna. Maurepas had a license to offer Mesmer a substantial settlement in return for a commitment to stay on in Paris and continue to receive patients. The main clauses offered him an annual pension of 20,000 livres, plus 10,000 for the rent of a building he wanted for a school of animal magnetism, in return for which he would be required to accept into his establishment a number of pupils named by the government.

Mesmer turned the offer down in high dudgeon. He objected to the pupils who would be forced on him, regarding them as agents commissioned to take over the direction of the establishment as far as they could and to report periodically to the authorities on what he was doing. His only demand, apart from money, he told Maurepas, was official endorsement of animal magnetism and no pupils except those he chose himself. On that note the conference at Versailles came to an end.

Maurepas could only have been startled and confounded by the conversation. Here he was, a minister of state, speaking in the name of the Queen of France, offering a princely guarantee to a Viennese doctor with a dubious reputation who had been snubbed by the leading scientists and physicians of Paris—and here was the man not only rejecting the offer, but making counterdemands of his own and behaving like an aggrieved party. There was no dealing with such a person. So the minister reported to the queen.

Mesmer threw away a glorious opportunity with such cavalier disdain that one might suspect him of rationalizing his position, of producing bad reasons why he should reject an offer he did not want in the first place. His demand for official recognition of the scientific truth of animal magnetism partly explains his attitude, for his *idée fixe* was now entrenched in his mind. Still, might he not have waited for vindication by the savants to emerge in due time while he got on with his pension and his cures?

He might, if it had not been for another character trait. His repeated rebuffs had given him a persecution complex. He was suspicious about others, especially about what they would do to his discovery and to his rights as the discoverer. He began to fear that, having been too generous and forthright in making known his arts and techniques, he might lose control of his movement to unprincipled scoundrels exploiting them. It was excessive to become adamant about pupils who, on his analysis of the situation, would have to report wonderful successes from his workshop, but his feeling makes sense if he knew they would report more of his activities than he cared to have known.

Two contradictory motives moved him. He wanted to reveal his theory and practice to all in authority who could gain him scientific recognition. He wanted to conceal as much as he could from those who might steal his ideas. In judging his later conduct, it is often necessary to find out which of the two motives is uppermost in his mind on a specific occasion.

Mesmer refused to let his case rest with Maurepas. He set forth his reasons for behaving as he did when, on the day after the Maurepas meeting, he wrote the following letter to the queen herself.

MADAM,

I can feel nothing but the most sincere gratitude that Your Majesty deigns to take notice of me. Yet my predicament weighs heavily upon me. There are those who have told Your Majesty that my plan to quit France is inhuman and that I intend to abandon the ill who are still in need of my attention. I do not doubt that today some attribute to interested motives my refusal to accept the conditions Your Majesty has offered me.

I am acting, Madame, neither from inhumanity nor from avarice. I dare to hope that Your Majesty will allow me to place the proof before her eyes. But more than anything else, I should remember that she may blame me, and my first consideration must be to make clear my respectful submission to her slightest wish.

With that in mind, and only out of respect for Your Majesty, I tender the assurance of my extending my stay in France until next September 18 and of continuing until that date the treatment of those who continue to rely on my care.

I appeal to Your Majesty to believe that there is no ulterior motive behind this offer. Although I have the honor to make it to Your Majesty, I set aside every indulgence, every favor, and every hope except that of acting under the protection of Your Majesty in the deserved peace and security that have been accorded me in this country since I came here. Finally, Madame, in declaring to Your Majesty that I give up all hope of an agreement with the French government, I beg acceptance of my most humble, most respectful, and most disinterested deference.

I am seeking, Madame, a government that will see the necessity of not permitting a tardy introduction into the world of a truth that, through its effect on the human body, can work changes that knowledge and skill should maintain and direct from the beginning of an illness through a proper regimen to a proper cure. Since the conditions offered to me in the name of Your Majesty would not achieve this, my fixed principles forbid me to accept them.

Where a cause is primarily concerned with the good of humanity, money should not be anything more than a secondary consideration.

To your Majesty, four or five hundred thousand francs more or less, well spent, are nothing. Human happiness is everything. My discovery should be welcomed and myself rewarded with a munificence worthy of the monarch to whom I have appealed. What should acquit me unanswerably of every false imputation, in this respect, is that since my arrival in your country I have not victimized any of your subjects. For three years I have received monetary offers every day. I have had little time to read them, but I can say, without having made an exact count, that I have permitted large sums to slip through my fingers.

My conduct in Your Majesty's country has been always the same. Assuredly it is not because of avarice or desire for empty glory that I have exposed myself to the ridicule heaped on me by turns by your Academy of Sciences, your Royal Society of Medicine, and your Faculty of Medicine. I have done it because I thought I ought to do it.

After their rejection of me, I consider myself at a point where the government would surely take notice of me on its own account. Deceived in this expectation, I have decided to look somewhere else for that which I can no longer reasonably expect here. I have arranged to leave France next August. This is what some call inhumanity, as if my departure were not forced on me.

Striking a balance, twenty or twenty-five sick persons, whoever they may be, mean nothing compared to the human race. To apply this principle to one Your Majesty honors with her friendship, I have to say that to give Madame the Duchesse de Chaulnes alone the preference over the mass of people would be, at bottom, as wicked for me as to neglect my discovery because of my personal interests.

I have constantly found myself compelled to abandon the ill who were precious to me and to whom my care was still indispensable. This was true when I left the land of Your Majesty's birth. It is also my native land. Why did no one accuse me of inhumanity at that time? Why, Madame? Because that serious accusation would have been superfluous. Because my enemies had by more simple intrigues caused me to lose the confidence of your august mother and your august brother.

Madame, one like myself who is always mindful of the judgment of nations and of posterity, who is always prepared to account for his actions, will, as I have done, react to so cruel a check without arrogance but with courage. For he will know that if there are many circumstances in which kings ought to guide public opinion, there are many more in which public opinion irresistibly shapes royal opinion. Today, as I have been told in Your Majesty's name, your brother has only disdain for me. So be it! When public opinion decides, it will do me justice. If it does not do this in my lifetime, it will honor my tomb.

Without doubt, the date of September 18 that I have mentioned to Your Majesty will seem extraordinary. I would like the same date of last year to be remembered, when the physicians of your kingdom did not hesitate to dishonor in my name one of their colleagues to whom I owe everything. On that day was held the assembly of the Faculty of Medicine of Paris at which my propositions were rejected. Your Majesty knows them. I believed then, Madame, and I still live in the persuasion, that after a spectacle so base by the physicians of your city of Paris, every enlightened person should no longer have failed to examine my discovery and that the protection of every powerful person should have been given to it without demur. However that may be, on next September 18 it will be one year since I placed all my hopes in the vigilant and paternal care of the government.

At this time, I hope Your Majesty will judge my sacrifice to be sufficient and see that I have not fixed a limit out of fickleness, or vainglory, or pique, or inhumanity. I dare to flatter myself that her protection will follow me wherever destiny leads me away from her and that as a worthy protectress of the truth she will not disdain to use her influence with her brother and her husband to win their goodwill for me.

With the most profound respect I remain Your Majesty's most humble and obedient servant.

Mesmer

This astonishing missive is vintage Mesmer right down to his mention of money in terms specific enough for a Paris businessman. Unwittingly he reveals in his language, tone, and bearing why Maurepas considered him a crank. He sees himself as a persecuted martyr to the truth, a partisan of the light beset by fools and knaves. He is angry with those too stupid to see that they could be remembered forever as friends of the human race by granting him everything he desired. He nurses a grudge against those who thwarted him in Vienna and takes care to name the rascally corporations that rejected him in Paris.

As if these generalities were not enough, Mesmer becomes personal in a manner Marie Antoinette must have found a clear case of *lèse majesté*. He addresses the queen as if they were social equals, the deferential phrases in the letter being mere formalities of the epistolary idiom of the eighteenth century. He speaks to her in phraseology that, when not querulous, comes very close to insulting, most obviously in the references to Maria Theresa ("your august mother"), Joseph II ("your august brother"), and Louis XVI ("her husband"). It would have been bad enough to have written thus in a letter to a citizen of Paris. It would have been bad enough if Mesmer had confined his derogatory personal allusions to the queen's confidante, the Duchesse de Chaulnes. But to speak thus of the Empress of Austria, the Holy Roman Emperor, and the King of France! And to threaten the emperor with the judgment of posterity!

There is also an undercurrent of disingenuousness in the letter. Mesmer adopted in all his polemical writings any argument that occurred to him, and his utterances vary from the sound to the specious. He did not really mean that Deslon was "one of their colleagues to whom I owe everything." It just seemed the thing to say in this context. After their falling out, he wrote quite differently about Deslon. His request that the queen "use her influence with her brother and her husband to win their good will for me" cannot be treated as sincere after the hectoring that has gone before. This is the writer's pique showing. He is attempting to score a point, nothing more.

What Mesmer expected Marie Antoinette to do after reading this letter is difficult to imagine. Possibly he was surprised that she did nothing.

CHAPTER 13

Mesmer's Secret Society

As if to make good his threat, Mesmer left Paris, but he went no farther than Spa near Liège in the Belgian Ardennes. His choice of place is instructive. Spa was a watering spot so famous for its mineral springs and public baths that other health resorts across Europe took its name for a general designation of their trade. Mesmer needed rest after so much labor in Paris and so many emotional ups and downs. The waters of Spa would rejuvenate him, clear his brain, settle his nerves, and give him the vigor to conduct another campaign for animal magnetism wherever and whenever that might be.

Our psychosomatic physician was suffering from psychosomatic problems. He denied himself the logical move of requesting Deslon to magnetize him. Mesmer was too doctrinaire about himself as an animal magnet to contemplate subjecting himself to magnetism by another or to doubt that his faculties would right themselves in time. He had received his magnetic powers from nature, and nature would remagnetize him.

So he went to Spa, like any other person with a case of nerves, to bathe in the healing waters of the mineral springs. Spa was a tranquil town amid trees, mountains, and broad open fields. The sights and sounds of the country carried Mesmer back to his childhood on the shores of Lake Constance when he tramped with his father across the wooded domain of the archbishop, watched the creatures of the wild digging burrows and building nests, and peered in rapt admiration at the Alpine peaks off in the distance. His senses and his emotions expanded in the pure air and warm sunshine. He again felt his oneness with nature, with the earth and its creatures, with the infinite cosmos.

During his brief time on this first visit to Spa he completed his

Short History of Animal Magnetism, the best thing he ever wrote. The prose is limpid for him. It is infused with emotion, revealing him as a man of sentiment rather than merely a cold-headed scientist theorizing abstractly about physical facts. While he recapitulates his version of events in Vienna and Paris, renews in memory his feuds with Stoerck and Vicq-d'Azyr, prints his letter to Marie Antoinette, and demands to know how anyone can examine his cures and still reject animal magnetism, he nevertheless throws in here and there a touch of real eloquence.

Thinking of the rocky road he had traveled: "Oh truth! truth! Your empire is certain but your first steps are arduous!" Thinking of the Frenchmen with the capacity but not the will to rush to his support: "Oh cavaliers of France! What has become of your ancient pride?"

For the first time he reveals an unsureness in defending his theory: "I would like to be able to establish my argument with order, clarity, and precision, but the subject I am discussing escapes adequate treatment." This is more than a gloss on Proposition 3 of his *Memoir,* about the most basic laws of animal magnetism being unknown. It is also a reflection of his Romanticism, of the Rousseauist idea that nature appeals more to the instincts and the emotions than to the intellect. He shows a deepening tendency to become mystical. Of animal magnetism, he now says, "It is the universal means of healing and preserving human beings. It is an artificial sixth sense. . . .Only feeling can render the theory intelligible to us."

This volume is important in the Mesmer canon. In it he extends his ideas beyond logic and actual experience and begins to talk in exaggerated terms about the nonrational sources of knowledge. He has charted a new course for his thinking, and it will take him to some destinations that would have surprised the earlier Mesmer.

Looking back toward Paris from Spa, he returned to his conviction about himself as the possessor of truth too important to be ignored by anyone however exalted:

> To state briefly my feelings about the matter, I cannot enter into an agreement with a government that does not at the start recognize formally and validly the existence and utility of my discovery. To allege in reply that the royal dignity might be compromised, this is to state pos-

itively that one is not convinced, from which, although without complaining, I must infer that after all I have done conviction remains a plant foreign to French soil, and that the best thing for me to do is to cultivate land less unproductive.

Comment seems needless.

In spite of his petulance, arrogance, and minatory talk about looking elsewhere, Mesmer returned to Paris. It was the one city where, if success finally came to him, it would be a universal, European success. He had disciples there waiting for his return, so that he could resume his work overnight. Anywhere else he would have to begin at the beginning, and he could not face the time, drudgery, and humiliation of approaching more scientific organizations and medical faculties, begging for an inspection of the evidence for animal magnetism he held out to them.

Crucially, Paris was the place where Deslon was practicing in a clinic of his own. Mesmer, who had been angered that Deslon refused to follow him to Spa, was incensed that Deslon had set up as an independent. The faithful follower had become a turncoat. Grimm found the spectacle amusing:

> His disciple, Deslon, thought he should console Paris for the loss of his master by setting up an establishment for Mesmerian treatment. A beguiling personality, still possessing the advantages of youth and a pleasing demeanor, had brought Deslon the protection of some women of letters of the second rank. They undertook to create for their protégé a reputation in animal magnetism. . . . Mesmer . . . rushed back to Paris, and his first care, as one might expect, was to accuse of infidelity and ignorance a pupil who, instructed with difficulty in his doctrine and his principles, dared *to magnetize* without his approval and on his own account. He asked the public by way of the journals to ignore the same man whom six months before he had praised for his profound knowledge and practical skill in animal magnetism.

Deslon infringed Mesmer's proprietary rights to animal magnetism; he acted as if he had graduated from his teacher's tutorial. Mesmer would not overlook Deslon's defection any more than Freud overlooked Jung's, although it must be said that Jung was always more independent than Deslon. Jung created a new school of psychoanalysis while Deslon did not create a new school of Mesmerism. Except for hedging on the nature of the universal fluid, Deslon accepted Mesmer's doctrine as Mesmer had taught it to him. Deslon had learned from Mesmer that this healing method should be made available to the ill, he saw no reason to leave Paris, and like Mesmer, he would not refuse the Mesmerian balm to those who asked for it. To have closed up shop because Mesmer had, against his advice, left Paris would have been absurd in his eyes.

The two met and talked and patched up a peace. The fact that they agreed to join forces again is a tribute to Deslon, a moderate man who made allowances for Mesmer's pride and suspicion as understandable in a discoverer who felt he was being cheated out of the recognition and rewards of his achievement. They worked together again in the same establishment, yet the new alliance could not continue indefinitely because Deslon had matured as a mesmerizer. In spite of Mesmer's notion that no one but he really understood the doctrine and the technique, Deslon had mastered both. Knowing his own ability and proud of his success, Deslon would not play the pupil to Mesmer's teacher forever. Some of their followers realized the truth sooner than they did. Grimm picked up the gossip:

> This reunion . . . could not last long; it was impossible to reunite and persuade to live in peace the women who had worked together to build Deslon's reputation and Mesmer's; neither side could excuse the pretensions of the other. The *Mesmerians* could only be condescending in allowing the *Deslonians* the honor of sharing Mesmer's treatment with them. The Deslonians reserved for Deslon, whom they considered their property, and who remained the idol of their egotism, both their preference and a bias that made them reject all interests except those of Deslon. The masters rejoined one another in vain. Between the different sects there always existed a feeling of acrimony to which there soon succeeded all kinds of reproaches, and which finally ended in scenes as bitter as they were scandalous. They forced Mesmer and Deslon to separate again, and again the journals were filled with the recriminations of the master and the disciple.

Grimm's cynical view of the two great magnetiziers focuses on the outward show, which is reliable as far as it goes. Each leader *did* have ardent followers arrayed in defense of his reputation. Women *were* prominent on both sides among the intransigent partisans.

The division *was* a source of confusion to the faithful who could not understand how a single true doctrine was thus divided.The controversy *was* the cause of raillery by those outside the movement.

Yet these facts did not touch the reality that Mesmer and Deslon, if left entirely to themselves to work out their dilemma, must have reached a parting of the ways. Deslon was too important to be a subordinate, and Mesmer too dictatorial to have an equal. Therein lay the reason for their failure to come to an accommodation with each other.

They parted company, more or less amicably, in July, 1782. Mesmer returned to Spa, accompanied by a number of his patients, and set up a clinic there. Deslon in Paris came forward frankly as a master of animal magnetism, undertaking to heal and teach without deferring to anybody. He began to propagandize for the doctrine on his own, writing to the head of the Faculty of Medicine in an effort to gain another hearing. This letter contains a laudatory passage on Mesmer, but Deslon speaks for himself and asks for a vindication of their common ideas through his own work, which is mentioned as self-sufficient for a verdict. Gaining a hearing by the faculty on August 20, 1782, he appeared alone, defended the doctrine alone, met the hostility of the assembled physicians alone, received their condemnation alone—and ignored a letter from Spa demanding to know by what authority he arrogated to himself Mesmer's right to represent the theory of animal magnetism.

The break was not complete. The following year found them negotiating for further cooperation, but the negotiations failed when Deslon laid down the condition that Mesmer divulge to him the last of Mesmer's secrets. Mesmer refused because his only secret was that he had no secrets to which Deslon was not already a party. Increasingly Mesmer created an air of mystery about himself, hinting at unrevealed powers, intimating that there were all kinds of revelations to come for those who followed him faithfully, accepted his guidance without demur or quibble, and supported him with their voices, if not with money and influence.

Mesmer thought he found the man he needed in Nicolas Bergasse, a lawyer from Lyons and a vague theorist who dreamed cloudy dreams, in eighteenth-century fashion, of regenerating humanity by following Rousseau's "nature" into government, society, education, and even the fine arts.When in 1781 Mesmer alleviated

a pathological depression into which Bergasse plunged periodically, the latter became convinced that animal magnetism was a force
provided by nature through which mankind might enter a Rousseauist paradise where noble feelings, virtuous acts, and political
freedom would flourish.

Bergasse wore the unkempt clothing and bushy wig becoming to
a philosopher and the fixed, uncompromising, unsmiling expression becoming to a fanatic. He was the type who can think of little
except his cause. Having made Mesmer's cause his own, he threw
himself into it with the passionate commitment of a man ridden by
a single idea and pleased with his burden. As early as 1781 he wrote
his first defense of Mesmerism, an open letter in which he announced that he believed in cures by animal magnetism and
strongly condemned orthodox medicine.

The idea of a Mesmerian academy was the kind of thing that
would appeal to Bergasse, who shared the constitution-making, in-
stitution-building mentality of the time. Mesmer had thought of establishing a public institution that would develop his ideas and promote them after he was gone. That was a factor in his negotiations
with the French government. Keeping the Mesmerian movement
personal to himself while he lived, he anticipated a future in which
his spiritual descendants would labor collectively in his name. Marie Antoinette had failed him, and he had nowhere else to turn until
Bergasse alluded to the practicality of a private institution. The
idea charmed and excited Mesmer. This would be success more satisfying in its own way than backing from the Queen of France. Delay and disappointment would no longer be his twin afflictions.
There was no need to stand cap in hand waiting for public function-
aries to decide whether or not to bestow their indulgence on him.
The institution could be founded at once, and he would make the
rules.

Bergasse was the lawyer of the enterprise. The banker was Guil-
laume Kornmann, a financier from Alsace, another of Mesmer's
grateful patients. Kornmann's family affairs had made a nervous
wreck of him. His wife, whom he charged with adultery, managed,
after an involved conspiracy, to appear to be the injured party. She
reclaimed her dowry and gained control of the children. Since one
of the sons had been treated successfully by Mesmer, Kornmann
returned to the Mesmer clinic to have his own problem taken care

of. He, like Bergasse, followed Mesmer from Paris to Spa, where he took part, as the one who understood how to finance the project, in the plans for a Mesmerian institute.

They gave their organization the name Société de l'Harmonie. Bergasse and Kornmann, in concert with Mesmer, agreed that the basic strategy should be the following:

1. A charter subscription would be opened, inviting 100 members to join on payment of dues of 100 louis apiece, a sum that would belong to Mesmer, and subscriptions would be offered indefinitely after that.

2. Mesmer would undertake to teach the members how to control and apply animal magnetism.

3. Diplomas would be offered to qualified pupils allowing them to set up as practitioners of animal magnetism in their own establishments.

Bergasse set about promoting the Society of Harmony energetically and successfully. The list of subscribers included some of the greatest names in France—Lafayette, still basking in the glory he had won in the American Revolution; the Marquis de Chastellux, another French veteran of the American campaigns; the Comte de Puységur, who would bring artificial somnambulism into Mesmerism; and various other aristocrats, professional men, and members of the clergy. Deslon joined and stayed until his final break with Mesmer.

So superior a membership list reflected the existing tradition of would-be reformers and apostles of human betterment entering societies both secret and open. The best-known and most talked-about of the secret societies, the Freemasons, boasted the Princesse de Lamballe among its leaders. Lafayette and Chastellux both belonged to the (open) French antislavery movement. There was a host of groups, large and small, conspiratorial and promotional, scientific and occult, literary and technological, concerned for social programs, educational reform, and the dissemination of ideas on art and music.

Mesmer's Society of Harmony, secret, scientific, humanitarian, and promotional, found its place in this welter of causes. Everyone had heard of Mesmer. Many regarded animal magnetism as worth experimenting with, as much as electricity or gravitation. The cures proved it could be of immense benefit to humanity. Different motives combined to give Mesmer's institution a claim at least as good as most of the rest. There lay the reason for its popularity.

It *was* a secret society. Mesmer declared for secrecy at the start when he produced a contract for each member to sign upon joining:

> We the undersigned, A. Mesmer, doctor of medicine, on the one hand and N. on the other hand, have mutually agreed on the following, to wit:
>
> I, A. Mesmer, having always had the desire to spread the knowledge of animal magnetism among respectable and virtuous persons, undertake to instruct M. N., referred to above, in all the principles of that doctrine on these conditions:
>
> 1. He will not train any pupil, or transmit directly or indirectly to anyone whatever, either the whole doctrine of animal magnetism or any slightest idea relative to it, in any sense whatever, without my written consent.
>
> 2. He will not enter into with any prince, government, or community whatever, any negotiation, treaty, or accord of any kind relative to animal magnetism, this right being retained solely by myself.
>
> 3. He will not, without my express written consent, establish any clinic or gather the ill to treat them together by my method, he being allowed only to see and treat the ill individually and privately.
>
> 4. He pledges to me by his sacred word of honor, both verbal and written, to conform rigorously, and without any restriction, to the above conditions and not to set up, authorize, or favor directly or indirectly, wherever he may happen to live, any establishment without my formal agreement.
>
> And I, N., referred to above, considering that the doctrine of magnetism is the property of M. Mesmer, its author, and that he alone has a right to decide the conditions under which it shall be propagated, I accept all the conditions laid down in this document, and I extend in writing, as I already have done verbally, my most sacred word of honor to observe its import in good faith with the most scrupulous exactitude.
>
> This is agreed to by us both in the form of this contract, and we promise to ratify it in the presence of notaries on the first demand of one of the two parties, at the expense of the party who demands it.

Mesmer's contract contradicted the third clause of the Bergasse-Kornmann plan, a contradiction so irreconcilable that it shook the society apart within two years of the founding date, March 10,

1783. The seeds of discord went unnoticed in the flush of enthusiasm with which the enterprise began. Mesmer naturally assumed that his interpretation of the agreement was the only one, and by his interpretation all the members bound themselves to remain under his direction, revealing nothing of what they saw or heard at the secret sessions of the society, in its headquarters at the Hôtel de Coigny on the rue Coq Héron, for as long as it pleased him to hold them to their vow of silence.

Aristocratic and powerful men obediently took this oath, some under a misconception that Mesmer never intended to contravene the freedom of the Bergasse-Kornmann plan, others because they wanted to learn about animal magnetism at the feet of the master himself, becoming privy to the mysteries of what he liked to term "my discovery." Lafayette signed his contract with Mesmer on April 5, 1784.

Bergasse drew up the statutes covering the operations of the organization, the duties of the members, the rights of subordinate groups, and the parliamentary rules for general assemblies. He delivered the inaugural address at the opening session, welcoming the charter members and explaining the aims and objectives of their union.

Mesmer began a series of oral instructions, the information not to be divulged by his listeners. Since he maintained his new clinic in the same building, he could shift easily from theory to practice and back to theory. The clinic by itself enjoyed the success of his former establishments and enhanced his reputation as a healer.

Mesmer was not a good speaker. He spoke slowly and ruminatively in French encumbered with a strong Austrian accent. However, he had adjutants to supplement him in speech and writing, particularly Bergasse, of lively mind and facile expression. The staff ran the Society of Harmony through lectures, seminars, conversation groups, and written reports. Bergasse gave a series of lectures that became the substance of his book *Considerations on Animal Magnetism* (1784), in which the author filled in details of the cosmic system outlined broadly by Mesmer.

We know the structure of the society and its teaching program from recollections by some of its members, but principally from Caullet de Vaumorel, who procured notebooks of the courses and published the contents in his *Aphorisms of M. Mesmer, Dictated to a*

*Class of His Pupils in Which One Finds His Theory, His Principles and
the Methods of Magnetizing: The Whole Forming a Body of Doctrine Developed in 344 Paragraphs to Facilitate the Application of the Commentaries on Animal Magnetism* (1785).

The society was a combination institute, medical school, and clinic. Students pursued advanced theories of Mesmerism in the institute, largely through the lectures of Bergasse. They studied the
textbook phase in the seminars of the medical school, learning how
animal magnetism acted on the nervous system and the vital organs. They watched the practical application of animal magnetism
to patients in the clinic. All these departments together added up to
a comprehensive schooling in Mesmerism, abstract and concrete.

What took place when a man or woman walked into Mesmer's
office complaining of a malady? First, there was the medical examination in which Mesmer looked for the trouble and the cause as
any physician would. He asked for a description of the patient's
symptoms, considered his general health, probed the ailing area,
and made his diagnosis. If the illness was organic, he sent the sufferer to a conventional doctor for conventional treatment. If the
illness was functional, he prescribed a regimen of animal magnetism depending on age, sex, length of illness, type of illness, and so
on.

Mesmer advised his students that "the patient will show you the
place of the pain and often the cause, but ordinarily it is by touch
and your own knowlege that you will satisfy yourself as to the place
and the cause, the latter residing in most cases on the side opposite
to the affliction, especially in paralyses, rheumatisms, and other illnesses of that type." The magnetizer was expected to find the cause
when all else failed, by acting on the theory that animal magnetism
has poles just as mineral magnetism has. The poles were the explanation when an affliction and its cause were separated.

Remembering his long clinical training under De Haen, Mesmer
kept full case histories. He was as pragmatic in prescribing doses of
animal magnetism as any other physician in prescribing doses of
medicine. A person with a mild twitching or coughing might be
prescribed a single session at the baquet and sent home. Difficult
cases required several sessions, severe crises, and psychosomatic
symptoms from catalepsy to convulsions. Mesmer watched over his
patients solicitously during his séances, stroking their bodies or

wielding his wand to bring on the trance, directing his assistants to take the squirming, shouting, paralyzed patients to the crisis rooms. Then he followed the subsidence of the symptoms until he felt each individual had absorbed enough animal magnetism and was ready to be discharged.

The activities at the Society of Harmony brought Mesmer's Mesmerism to its fullest elaboration. They tell us precisely what his achievement was—namely, the control of the trance through scientific knowledge.

The trance from the beginning of time had been a monopoly of sibyls, oracles, faith healers, and occultists—strange people strangely endowed. Their art was personal to themselves, granted as a boon by a preternatural power, so that progress was impossible. The gifts of Greatraks and Gassner died with them.

Mesmer broke this monopoly. He brought the trance within the bounds of science. He created a scientific universe of discourse in which many minds could cooperate in a rational enterprise, the rationale of all progress in the sciences. He and his staff at the Hôtel de Coigny learned from one another, experimented, formed hypothesis, worked out techniques, and put together a coherent body of tested and verifiable information. They started the tradition of scientific investigation that continued from their time to ours and produced scientific hypnosis.

The explanation of the trance was scientific. So was the technique of inducing the trance—not prayer or mystical incantations, but such physical acts as fixing the attention of the subject on the moving fingers of the magnetizer. This type of act was repeatable by all practitioners of animal magnetism, and the ability to repeat an experiment under controlled conditions is another sign of genuine science.

The discarding of old theories in favor of new is also quintessentially scientific. This happened to Mesmerism. The theory of suggestion is just as scientific as the theory of animal magnetism, and Mesmer, by insisting on a scientific approach, made it possible for his followers to discard his pet theory of animal magnetism for suggestion when the weight of scientific evidence necessitated the change. All the experimenters who shifted Mesmerism away from Mesmer's theory—Faria, Bertrand, Braid, Bernheim—belong to Mesmer's tradition of scientific psychology.

In rising to this height, Mesmer had the assistance of an able, enthusiastic staff. These were men of ideas, willing to think for themselves about what Mesmerism was, where it was going, and how it ought to be managed. Like all teaching faculties, this one had individuals who were popular or otherwise with the student body. Bergasse's popularity grew until he became the "overmighty subject" of Mesmer's society. He took upon himself a larger share of the burden of running the organization as time went on, although "burden" is a misnomer since he enjoyed being the most prominent member after Mesmer—and not so far after, either, he told himself. Here there was a personality problem that might have been discerned before it disrupted the society.

The mother lodge in Paris gave rise to offshoots, daughter groups in the provinces and in other countries, in Strasbourg, Lyons, Bordeaux, Toulouse, Grenoble, Lausanne, Turin. Within a short time the numbers of the society as a whole were tabulated in the thousands. Nor were the provincial groups merely echoes of Paris. Strasbourg moved into the forefront of Mesmeric studies because it had Puységur when he was experimenting with artificial somnambulism. Each lodge created local interest and attracted converts.

The Mesmerian lodges were like cells ready to infect France with Mesmerism. Devoted loyalists and outraged enemies agreed on that, the first terming it a high promise, the second a deadly danger.

Lafayette was by his own account a true Mesmerian when he sailed for America in 1784. He made the fact known in Versailles, where, upon his paying his respects at the palace before leaving, Louis XVI said to him, "What will Washington think when he learns that you are Mesmer's apothecary's apprentice?"

While in Paris, Lafayette wrote to Washington about Mesmer. Mesmer, having been told about this letter, wrote to Washington himself. Washington's reply concluded this surprising correspondence.

Lafayette to Washington, May 14, 1784: A German doctor named Mesmer, having made the greatest discovery upon animal magnetism, has gathered pupils among whom your humble servant is called one of the most enthusiastic. . . . Before leaving, I will obtain permission to reveal to you Mesmer's secret, which, you may believe, is a great philosophical discovery.

Mesmer to Washington, June 16, 1784: The Marquis de la Fayette proposes to make known in the territory of the United States a discovery of much importance to mankind. Being the author of the discovery, to diffuse it as widely as possible I have formed a Society, whose only business it will be to derive from it all the expected advantages. It has been the desire of the Society, as well as mine, that the Marquis should communicate it to you. It appeared to us, that the man who merited most of his fellow-men should be interested in the fate of every revolution that has for its object the good of humanity. I am, with the admiration and respect that your virtues have ever inspired me with, Sir, Your Obedient Servant, Mesmer.

Washington to Mesmer, November 25, 1784: The Marquis de la Fayette did me the honor of presenting to me your favor of the 16th of June; and of entering into some explanation of the powers of Magnetism, the discovery of which, if it should prove as extensively beneficial as it is said, must be fortunate indeed for Mankind, and redound very highly to the honor of that Genius to whom it owes its birth. For the confidence reposed in me by the Society which you founded for the purpose of diffusing and deriving from it, all the advantages expected; and for your favourable sentiments about me, I pray you to receive my gratitude, and the assurances of the respect and esteem with which I have the honor, etc. George Washington.

Washington temporized on the matter of animal magnetism since he had no idea what was being confided to him. His repetition of Mesmer's language is the conventional tactic of a letter writer who wants his correspondent to be clear that he is, politely, not committing himself to anything.

Lafayette stood to his trust in promoting Mesmerism, at least in words, during this American tour, but he had to compete with political events, for the new nation had not yet straightened out its affairs under the Articles of Confederation. No one could say whether, having won its independence, it was not destined to founder because the states demanded semi-independence. The Constitution was four years in the future. Washington would not take office as President of the United States for five years. Officialdom was occupied with social unrest and the problems of administration.

Lafayette knew better than to press his American friends to accept his new creed, although he did lecture on animal magnetism at the American Philosophical Society in Philadelphia. The fact is that he lacked sufficient understanding of Mesmer's theories to expound and defend them. He had no solutions for difficulties with which he had never been made acquainted at the Society of Harmony. American savants could see holes in the argument as well as their European counterparts. They knew the basic question about the ether, a question now more than two centuries old: How can an imponderable fluid blowing through objects *move* them? They easily perceived that animal magnetism presented the same unsolvable problem. Wherever savants congregated, Lafayette would have run into queries about the possibility of animal magnets or the necessity for the crisis. The marquis was out of his depth at scientific sessions. He aroused interest but not conviction. When Mesmerism came to America, it came later and under different auspices.

The skepticism of Washington and other Americans may have shaken Lafayette's faith in the "great philosophical discovery" he had announced to Washington in his letter. At any rate, he paid little attention to it after his return to France; then he was caught up in the turbulence of the French Revolution, and belief in Mesmerism, not to mention proselytizing, became a dead issue with him.

Mesmer? He would not have been Mesmer if there had not flitted through his mind an image of George Washington presiding over Mesmerian séances at Mount Vernon, or even—why not?—summoning the discoverer to preach the pure milk of the word to sturdy republicans in the land of Rousseau's noble savage.

CHAPTER 14

An Official Investigation

When Mesmer set up as the leader of a secret society, he made himself more vulnerable than ever to the popular suspicion that he was either the hierophant of a cult or the strategist of a confidence game. There was so much coming and going under mysterious circumstances at the Society of Harmony, so much covert talk about undisclosed doctrine, so many sessions restricted to the initiated, so many louis d'or paid into the treasury by novices eager to part with their money if only they could become adepts of Mesmerism.

Mesmer heard echoes of the past in the rumors of the present. In Vienna the gossip had concerned his conduct with Maria Theresa Paradies in his Landstrasse clinic. In Paris it had fastened at first on his crisis rooms at the Hôtel Bullion. Now people wanted to know what went on behind the closed doors of the Hôtel de Coigny.

Questions flew around Paris. Was Mesmer a competitor of the Rosicrucians and the Freemasons, deceiving himself with the myth that he possessed a magical formula by which he could commune with and coerce nature? Was he a villain abusing the credulity of simpletons and outdoing in his effrontery Saint-Germain, Cagliostro, and Casanova? Popular rumor made much of each of these questions.

The professionals occupied the middle ground. They took the line that Mesmer was neither a Rosicrucian nor a Cagliostro, but an honest, muddleheaded man misguided enough to cling to a scientific hypothesis after it had been shown to be gratuitous. Holding fanciful ideas about science was no crime. Mesmer got into trouble because he applied his ideas in medicine, where to be wrong could have serious practical consequences and where he was challenging powerful vested interests.

His critics attacked him in a stream of publications. His partisans replied in kind. A veritable battle of the books raged in 1784.

One of the most persuasive criticisms came from Michel Augustin Thouret, whose *Investigations and Doubts Concerning Animal Magnetism* was intended to undermine Mesmer's reputation before he enticed any more physicians away from orthodox methods of healing. It remains a book to consult for the case against Mesmerism at the time of the great quarrel; the author systematically presents the arguments to be found piecemeal in many other sources, and he does so judiciously, restraining the animosity he shared with the corps of anti-Mesmerians. Since the Mesmerians answered him voluminously, the case *for* Mesmerism was also clearly stated before the quarrel died away.

Thouret devotes the first part of his *Investigations* to a history of Mesmer's fundamental idea and shows easily enough that the concept of a cosmic fluid is to be found in a succession of modern thinkers beginning with Paracelsus, continuing through Maxwell and Fludd. The Mesmerians countered that Mesmer had answered this charge beforehand in his doctoral dissertation when he explicitly stated that he was giving an old idea a new scientific basis. They suggested that Thouret, by his own reasoning, should reject Copernican astronomy since the theory of a moving earth had been judged, found fallacious, and set aside after Pythagoras propounded it in early Greek times.

Regarding Mesmer's cures, Thouret argues that there have been many healers able to do as much. He mentions Valentine Greatraks as the classic example of a healer who was believed to release "corpuscles" that entered the body of the patient and effected the cure. The similarity to animal magnetism was patent to Thouret, who therefore ruled out this type of explanation as an exploded fiction. The Mesmerians retorted that Mesmer had forestalled this criticism, too, in his analysis of Johann Gassner's cures—Greatraks did indeed transmit something physical, and that something, although he did not know it, was animal magnetism.

Thouret attributed Mesmer's successes to the imagination of his patients. The Mesmerians agreed that this was part of the truth inasmuch as Mesmer explicitly postulated the need of rapport, which involved imagination, before animal magnetism could freely penetrate the nervous system of the subject.

Neither side convinced the other in this battle of the books. The disputes went on and on; the same arguments, rejoinders, and sur-rejoinders appeared again and again. Mesmerism was not ruined by this passage of arms. It was the shock of events in 1784 that did the damage.

Claude Louis Berthollet, a member of the Academy of Sciences and the Faculty of Medicine and a significant figure in the developing science of chemistry, was a catch of the greatest moment when he joined the Society of Harmony. He was the great exemplar of the fact that all a real scientist needed was an open mind and an unprejudiced look at the facts to acknowledge the reality of animal magnetism. All the more shattering was Berthollet's defection from the movement, which he left in a high dudgeon, creating a scandal as he went. "I declare finally," he wrote, "that I consider the doctrine of animal magnetism, and the practice for which it serves as a foundation, as completely chimerical; and I permit anyone from this moment to use my declaration in anyway he sees fit."

Many saw fit to use it as a crushing retort to Mesmer, a refutation of the theory of animal magnetism, and a condemnation of the Society of Harmony.

While Mesmer and his Mesmerians were still reeling from Berthollet's secession, Court de Gébelin died. Gébelin was another prize catch, a scholar linguist and philosopher who wrote a well-received volume comparing the cultures of ancient and modern times. Suffering from a bad case of dropsy that made his legs swell agonizingly, he went to Mesmer in his extremity and in spite of an ingrained disbelief in animal magnetism. The success of Mesmer's treatment turned Gébelin into a vocal Mesmerian. He described the "wonderful effects of magnetism," condemned the notion that belief in it sprang from "simple ignorance, stupid credulity or vain superstition," and concluded: "Ignorance produces nothing useful. Superstition does not create, it abuses and corrupts."

Here again Mesmer could count an invaluable ally, a respected savant converted from skepticism to acceptance, from scoffing disbelief to passionate partisanship. Here again the outcome harmed the cause. Gébelin succumbed after a relapse. True, Mesmer had diagnosed the illness properly. Gébelin had understood that no complete cure could be anticipated and had praised Mesmerism for the relief it brought him in his wretched condition. The public did not choose to view the affair in that light. Gébelin "was cured by animal magnetism," as one satirist put it, "and he died."

A witty versifier had this comment on the fate of the savant who placed himself in Mesmer's hands:

> Here lies poor Gébelin
> Who spoke Greek, Hebrew, Latin;
> Admire his heroism;
> He was a martyr to magnetism.

Another squib ends with a variation on *Croire au magnétisme animal* ("Believe in animal magnetism"). The French line is adapted into a self-explanatory form: *Croire au magnetisme—animal!* Lampoons poured from the press, of which the following may be noted (it dates from 1786 but is typical of the whole pasquinade war on Mesmerism):

> A magician of importance
> Is Mesmer, who therefore
> Can make the melancholy dance
> Without knowing why or wherefore.

Two burlesques—*Modern Doctors* and *The Baquet of Health*—put Mesmerism on the stage for Parisians to laugh at. The former, one of the hits of the 1784 season, portrayed Mesmer ("Cassandre") and Deslon ("The Doctor") as a couple of rascals injecting credulous patients with animal magnetism and laughing at them behind their backs. (See appendix for the text of *The Baquet of Health*.)

Critics had a joyful time with this humorous spoof of a movement they were inclined to laugh at before they entered the theater to be entertained by a company of skillful comedians.

Jean de La Harpe:
    In the list of novelties at the Théâtre Italien . . . *Modern Doctors,* a vaudeville farce that is simply a very funny satire on animal magnetism. Some rigorists claim it is a personal satire and goes beyond the limits of propriety. Not at all! Animal magnetism is no longer Mesmer's secret; it is an epidemic infecting all France; and since for a century it has been permissible to satirize medicine on the stage, there is no reason why magnetic medicine should be respected more than any other branch.

Baron Grimm:

Franz Anton Mesmer at the height of his career.
From a drawing by Jules Poireau in the Bibliothèque Nationale

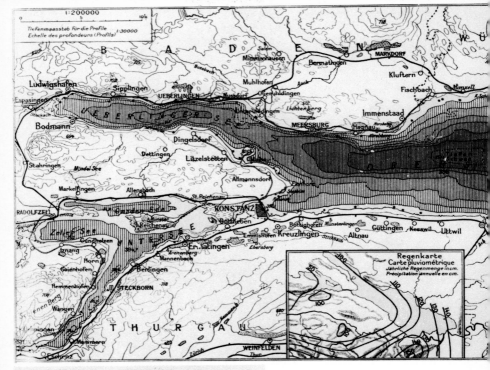

Gerhard van Swieten, who presided over Austrian medicine when Mesmer was a medical student at the University of Vienna.

From an engraving by Josef Axmann in the Nationalbibliothek

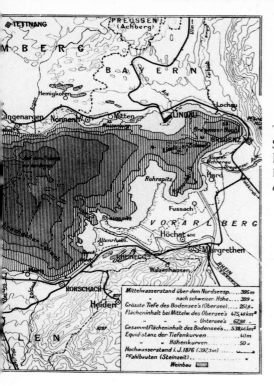

The Lake Constance region of Swabia and Switzerland where Mesmer spent most of his life. From the *Dictionnaire Geographique de la Suisse*

abella of Parma, the psy-
oneurotic member of the im-
erial House of Hapsburg
hose strange compulsions
ffled Van Swieten.
om a portrait in the Nationalbib-
thek

Left: Valentine Greatraks, the Irish Stroking Doctor of the seventeenth century, healing a patient by the laying on of hands. From a print in the British Museum

Right: The title page of the work in which Mesmer announced his discovery of animal magnetism to the world.
From a copy in the British Museum.

MÉMOIRE
SUR LA DÉCOUVERTE
DU
MAGNÉTISME
ANIMAL;

Par M. MESMER, *Docteur en Médecine de la Faculté de Vienne.*

A GENEVE;
Et se trouve
A PARIS,
Chez P. FR. DIDOT le jeune, Libraire-Imprimeur de MONSIEUR, quai des Augustins.

M. DCC. LXXIX.

Left: Nicolas Bergasse, Mesmer's friend and enemy, and the complete partisan of political Mesmerism.
From a portrait reproduced in the biography by Louis Bergasse

Above: Mesmer treating a fashionable lady at his baquet while she presses a bar protruding from magnetized water to the ailing part of her anatomy.

From a print in the Bibliothèque Nationale.

LE MESMERISME CONFONDU.

Above: Mesmer and his devotee collapsing in disarray before the thunderbolts of Truth and the scales of Justice.
From a cartoon in the Bibliothèque Nationale

Left: Cagliostro as he looked when he and Mesmer were considered twin charlatans by most Parisians.
From an engraving by Frances Bartolozzi

Left: Justinus Kerner, Mesmer's first biographer and a leader of occult Mesmerism during the nineteenth century.
From the frontispiece to *Kerners Briefwechsel*

Phineas Parkhurst Quimby, the American mesmerizer who influenced spiritualism, Theosophy, New Thought, and Christian Science.
From a photograph taken late in his ministry

Svengali, the villainous mesmerizer of *Trilby*, portrayed as a sinister spider weaving his web.
From the novel written and illustrated by George Du Maurier

Madame Blavatsky, the founder of the Theosophical Society and the last great Fluidist of animal magnetism in the tradition of Mesmer himself.
From a photograph taken when she was the world's foremost practitioner and theorist of Theosophy

. . . There is reason to believe that this little comedy will do more damage to the new sect than the reports of all the academies, and all the faculties, and all the verdicts of the council or the parlement that might solemnly proscribe both the doctrine and the practice.

The *Journal de Paris:*
First the arguments of those competent in physics and medicine, and then ridicule, that weapon so effective with us! When the remedy is pleasant, resisting it is difficult. That has become just now the secret of comedy.

The Mesmerians were incensed by *Modern Doctors,* and one of them, Duval d'Épremesnil, a paranoic, posturing character, nearly went out of his mind. At one performance he tossed to the audience copies of a manifesto comparing Mesmer to Socrates ridiculed by Aristophanes. He asked the Comte d'Artois to persuade the king to remove the burlesque from the boards, but the king merely laughed when he read the manifesto.

Louis XVI had already acted to satisfy himself about the merits of Mesmerism through royal commisions charged to look into the matter. The request for this action came originally from Deslon, who, no longer hampered by Mesmer's intransigence, won the king's assent. Baron de Breteuil, an official of the royal household, received an order to name distinguished members to two investigative bodies representing, respectively, the Academy of Sciences and the Royal Society of Medicine.

Benjamin Franklin, the American minister to France living at Passy, received the signal honor due his international eminence of being named to head the first commission. His age (seventy-eight) made his appointment nominal. His duties devolved on his colleagues, of whom the most eminent were Jean Sylvain Bailly, the leading French astronomer, and Antoine Laurent Lavoisier, who established modern chemistry. The Faculty of Medicine contributed, besides those now fallen into oblivion, Joseph Ignace Guillotin, who immortalized his name when he persuaded France to adopt the guillotine, the most humane instrument of execution in his opinion. The second commission had Laurent de Jussieu, a major figure in the history of botany.

The appointment of these commissions jolted Mesmer. Unable to comprehend how animal magnetism could be adequately examined except through him and his clinic, he wrote to Franklin protesting the decision to take Deslon's practice as a model.

Nothing could be done at that late stage.The king could not be asked to withdraw his assent, or the commissioners to switch magnetizers, even supposing Franklin agreed with Mesmer, which he did not. The official investigation went forward as planned, at Deslon's clinic.

The first commission convened on March 12, 1784, the second on April 5. The members attended Deslon's clinic faithfully during the next few months. They saw all the paraphernalia characteristic of Mesmerism—the baquets, the wands, the musical instruments, the principal magnetizer and his assistants in powdered wigs and lilac jackets.They saw all the phenomena characteristic of Mesmerism—the twitchings, crises, convulsions, trances, and sudden cures.

The fact of the cures was established and admitted. The reason for the cures remained in question. Deslon did his best to make his visitors agree that the explanation could only be a universal fluid or, at any rate, something physical that passed from him into the nervous systems of his patients. The commissioners challenged him to magnetize them, he accepted the challenge—and nothing happened. They considered the failure crucial, believing that if the cause were physical, they must feel it entering their bodies. Deslon produced the usual Mesmerian argument that it was a fluid too subtle to be detected and that its existence must be deduced from the effects. But they disagreed with him and looked, vainly, for tangible proof of its existence.

In a critical experiment, commissioners and magnetizers left the clinic and paid Franklin a visit. The official report of commission number one tells us: "Mr. Franklin, although his infirmities prevented him from going to Paris and assisting in the investigation going on there, was himself magnetized by M. Deslon, who went to Passy for that purpose. There was a big group present, and all were magnetized."

The results were negative. Some subjects failed to react when magnetized. Others reacted when not magnetized under the impression that they were. Thus, a commissioner impersonated Deslon to a woman who had her eyes bandaged. She had an immediate fit of trembling accompanied by spasms of pain.

The first commission, having satisfied itself that everything relevant had been gone into, issued its report on August 11, 1784. The conclusion of the report summed up the unanimous judgment of the members:

> The commissioners, having recognized that this animal magnetic fluid cannot be perceived by any sense, and that it has had no effect on them or on the ill shown to them; having assured themselves that the pressing and touching rarely cause changes helpful to the animal organism, and often cause agitation harmful to the imagination; having, finally, demonstrated by decisive experiments, that the imagination without magnetism produces convulsions, and that magnetism without imagination produces nothing; they have concluded unanimously, on the question of the existence and utility of animal magnetism, that nothing proves the existence of the animal magnetic fluid; consequently that this nonexistent fluid is without utility; that the violent effects that one observes in group treatment come from touching, from imagination provoked into action, and from mechanical imitation that makes us in spite of ourselves repeat that which strikes our senses. At the same time, we feel ourselves obliged to add, as an important observation, that the touchings, the repeated action of the imagination causing crises, can be harmful; that the spectacle of these crises is equally dangerous because of imitation, which nature seems to us to have made a law; and consequently that all group treatment where the methods of magnetism are employed must have, in the long run, harmful effects.

The scientific argument against animal magnetism was the old one that had been brought against the "subtle matter" of Newton and Huygens: If this substance affects material objects, then it must be detectable; if it is too ethereal to be detected, then it cannot affect material objects. That was the formal judgment of the academicians and the representatives of the faculty.

A majority of the physicians of the Royal Society of Medicine reached the same conclusion, terming animal magnetism an unnecessary hypothesis rather than a necessary deduction. To Deslon's contention that the Mesmerian crisis could be explained only by animal magnetism coursing through the patient's body, agitating and convulsing it, they replied that the primary cause was the stroking, which excited the patient's nerves and emotions. The secondary causes were such things as imagination, suggestion, and imitation. They agreed among themselves that the Mesmerian treatment was injurious because it tended to generate a habit of having convulsions.

One scientist in this group, Jussieu, filed a minority report. Jussieu thought there was something to be said for the theory of animal magnetism, at least in the sense that subjective factors could not by themselves explain all the phenomena he had seen, that something physical did appear to be operating in the crisis and the trance. He would not endorse Deslon's position, but he did call for a suspension of judgment until conclusive evidence could be accumulated: "The physicians who use the magnetic treatment without bias claim to have observed good effects. Let us invite those who practice it to renounce all reticence, to publish what they know, what they believe, and especially what they have observed."

At the end he was noncommittal: "CONCLUSION. The theory of magnetism cannot be accepted until it has been developed and vindicated by solid proofs."

Jussieu's dissent was too tepid to be effective. If he had been as aggressively for animal magnetism as the others were against it, he would have had a stronger impact. But he merely asked for the maintenance of an open mind so as not to foreclose the issue, and his colleagues could see no point in waiting any longer on the chance that scientific evidence for animal magnetism might turn up.

Each commission, after investigating the science and the morality of Mesmerism, condemned it on both counts. The academicians and the men of the faculty went further with regard to morality. They wrote a secret report containing matter so sensitive that it was intended for the eyes of the minister alone, not for publication. The subject was the erotic effects of Mesmerism, especially the effects on female patients treated by male magnetizers. Ailing women, Breteuil read, were in danger of a moral breakdown because of their weakened physical condition, and curious women because their curiosity knew no bounds. Any one of them might find herself in the following extremely perilous situation:

> The man who magnetizes ordinarily sits with the knees of the woman between his. The knees and the lower parts of their bodies are thus in contact. His hand strokes the abdomen and sometimes lower down in the region of the ovaries. The touch is then extended over numer-

ous areas and in the vicinity of the most sensitive parts of the body. Often while the man applies his left hand in this way, he passes his right hand around the woman's body. The tendency is for the pair to lean toward one another to make this double touching process easier. Their proximity becomes the closest possible, their faces nearly touch, their breaths mingle, they share all their physical reactions, and the mutual attraction of the sexes acts with full force. It would not be surprising if their feelings became inflamed.

Whatever use Breteuil may have made of this secret report, he did not use it as an excuse to close the Mesmerian clinics. He knew that Deslon and Mesmer had survived inquiries into the actual moral consequences of their treatment. Deslon, like Mesmer, had had to endure the innuendos and snickering of those who made him the victim of bawdy humor. Like Mesmer, he never had a moral case brought against him by an outraged husband, nor was any assistant of his ever accused of moral turpitude.

Two Americans should be introduced to have their say on Mesmerism, Benjamin Franklin because he put his name to one of the hostile reports and Thomas Jefferson, replacing Franklin as American minister to France, because he was an exceptionally perspicacious observer of men and events.

Franklin had been skeptical when the commision on which he nominally served convened in March:

> As to the animal magnetism so much talked of, I must doubt its existence till I can see or feel some effect of it. None of the cures said to be performed by it have fallen under my observation, and there being so many disorders which cure themselves, and such a disposition in mankind to deceive themselves and one another on these occasions, and living long has given me so frequent opportunity of seeing certain remedies cried up as curing everything, and yet soon after laid aside as useless, I cannot but fear that the expectation of great advantage from this new method of treating diseases will prove a delusion. That delusion, however may, and in some cases, be of use while it lasts.

Five months later Franklin had seen Deslon's experiments at Passy. They did nothing but confirm him in the skepticism he had felt at the start of the official investigation.

Jefferson received *his* information about Mesmerism at second hand. He felt, however, that it was valid enough for him to reject the ideas of the Viennese doctor, as he told one of his correspondents in a letter from Paris:

> The doctrine of animal magnetism after which you enquire is pretty well laid to rest. Reasonable men, if they ever paid any attention to such a hocus pocus theory, were thoroughly satisfied by the Report of the commissioners. But as the unreasonable is the largest part of mankind, and these were the most likely to be affected by this madness, ridicule has been let loose for their cure. Mesmer and Deslon have been introduced on the stage, and the contest is now who can best prove that they never were of their school.

Franklin, the oracle on electricity, could find nothing in Mesmerism comparable to the "fluid" he had traced up into the lightning in the sky. That failure disposed of animal magnetism for him, and he could not but believe that its practitioners would dwindle into a tiny sect clinging to outworn myth. Jefferson refused to allow Mesmerism that much vitality. Considering it moribund, if not already dead, he pronounced the funeral oration.

Franklin and Jefferson were, for once, poor judges and unreliable prophets. Mesmer's method of treating illnesses would not be abandoned, would rather attract a greater following in the years ahead. The funeral oration was premature.

Deslon tried to blunt the force of the blow by publishing his *Supplement to the Two Reports of the Commissioners*, the substance of which was another series of wonderful cures. To get around the argument from imagination and suggestion, he adduced a six-week-old baby cured of colic, a one-year-old cured of fever. An adult contributed a testimonial in which satire was used in defense of Mesmerism: "If I owe the health I enjoy to an illusion, I humbly ask the savants, who see so clearly, not to destroy the illusion. While they enlighten the universe, let them leave me to my error and permit me, in my simplicity, frailty and ignorance, to make use of an invisible agent that does not exist and yet heals me."

This volume of prodigies and its companions—for the Mesmerians rushed to their pens to scribble refutations of the commissioners—had no more effect on the doubters than those that had gone before. La Harpe wrote an outline history of Mesmer's ill fortune in France, attributing it to his charlatanism and cupidity, saying that an honest man would have gratefully accepted the generous offer made by the French government of a pension and a house for his clinic. Mesmer protested the use of Deslon's clinic rather than his own, yet he had rendered the choice inevitable by his autocratic demands—he wanted not an unbiased investigation, but one directed by himself. As for animal magnetism, La Harpe wrote: "I do not believe in occult medicine any more than in occult physics." His conclusion reflected a common opinion:

> Every science moves with the time, and what credulity it is, good God! to imagine that everything we learned about medicine from Hippocrates to Boerhaave is good for nothing, and that it was left to the later eighteenth century for a German doctor to come to Paris and reveal universal medicine to us, based on the action of a magnetic fluid of which scientists deny the existence!

The Faculty of Medicine formally outlawed the employment of animal magnetism in medical practice, obtaining willing obedience from most of its membership, resisted by a handful who believed in spite of all the condemnations that Mesmer could not be totally in error.

Mesmer found himself in a terrible predicament. If his doctrine was vindicated, his rival was vindicated; if his rival was rejected, his doctrine was rejected. He strove to divorce the two, appealing to the Parlement of Paris to order another investigation "so that my doctrine, so unworthily prostituted by M. Deslon, may be submitted to a more impartial examination than that of which the results have been puslished."

The appeal failed. Mesmer continued to protest the conduct of the commissioners, but his last word is in his letter to Franklin:

> I am like you, Monsieur, among those men whom one cannot insult with impunity, among those who, because they have achieved great things, retain their integrity under humiliation as strong men retain theirs under authority. Whatever the test, Monsieur, like you, I have the world for a judge, and while they may forget the good I have done and prevent the good I wish to do, I will be vindicated by posterity.

Nous soussignés, ANTOINE MESMER, Docteur en Médecine, d'une part, & *Et Monsieur le Marquis de la Fayette, maréchal de Camp, demeurant à Paris, rue de Bourbon* d'autre part, sommes convenus, double entre nous de ce qui suit, SAVOIR :

Moi, ANTOINE MESMER, ayant toujours desiré de répandre parmi des personnes honnêtes & vertueuses, la Doctrine du MAGNÉTISME ANIMAL, je consens, & je m'engage à instruire dans tous les principes qui constituent cette Doctrine, M. *Le Marquis de la Fayette* dénommé ci-dessus, aux conditions suivantes :

1°. Il ne pourra former aucun Elève, transmettre directement ou indirectement, à qui que ce puisse être, ni tout, ni la moindre partie des connoissances, relatives, sous quelque point de vue que ce soit, à la découverte du MAGNÉTISME ANIMAL, sans un consentement par écrit, signé de moi.

2°. Il ne fera, avec aucun Prince, Gouvernement, ou Communauté quelconque, ni négociation, ni traité, ni accord d'aucune espèce relatifs au MAGNÉTISME ANIMAL, me réservant, expressément & privativement cette faculté.

3°. Il ne pourra, sans mon consentement exprès & par écrit, établir aucun Traitement public, ou assembler des Malades pour les traiter en commun par ma Méthode, lui permettant seulement de voir & de traiter des Malades en particulier, & d'une manière isolée.

4°. Il s'engagera avec moi par le serment sacré DE L'HONNEUR verbal & écrit, à se conformer rigoureusement, sans restriction aucune, aux conditions ci-dessus, & à ne faire, autoriser, favoriser, directement ou indirectement, dans quelque partie du monde qu'il habite, aucun Etablissement, sans mon attache formelle.

Et moi, *Marquis de la Fayette* dénommé ci-dessus, considérant que la Doctrine du MAGNÉTISME ANIMAL est la propriété de M. MESMER son Auteur, & qu'il n'appartient qu'à lui de déterminer les conditions auxquelles il consent de la propager, j'accepte en totalité les conditions énoncées au présent Acte, & j'engage par écrit, comme je l'ai fait verbalement ; ma parole d'honneur la plus sacrée d'en observer teneur de bonne-foi, avec l'exactitude la plus scrupuleuse.

FAIT DOUBLE entre nous librement, sous nos seings, avec promesse de ratifier par-devant Notaire, à la première réquisition d'une des deux Parties, aux frais du requérant. A PARIS, le *Cinq avril mil sept cent quatre-vingt-quatre*

Lafay

CHAPTER 15

Schism in the Secret Society

While waiting for the royal commissions to publish their reports, Mesmer found sanctuary and consolation in his Society of Harmony, in the Paris mother lodge where he lived, and in the provincial lodges to which he gave more of his attention as they multiplied, flourished, and begged him to visit them. The Lyons lodge was one of the most active in the entire chain, directed by a renowned magnetizer, Jean-Baptiste Willermoz. Answering a call from Willermoz, Mesmer arrived in Lyons on August 9, two days before the first official report came out.

Prince Henry of Prussia was there, a swashbuckling soldier who had commanded armies in the wars of his brother, Frederick the Great. Henry had stopped off in Lyons, on a tour of France, and had asked to see an exhibition of Mesmerism at the local Mesmerism lodge. He described himself as an interested doubter, questioning the fact of animal magnetism but willing to act as a guinea pig and change his mind if a magnetizer could throw him into a trance. The men of the Lyons lodge felt that their royal guest deserved the Mesmerism treatment from no less an authority than the discoverer of the healing cosmic fluid and the founder of their society.

Mesmer enjoyed this kind of attention. He went to Lyons, met Willermoz for the first time, and was introduced to the rest of the lodge, all of whom revealed considerable excitement at having their leader on their premises. Prince Henry, arriving with his aide-de-camp, was noncommittal about Mesmerism, but Mesmer had met skeptics before and conquered their skepticism, and this time there would not be even the hint of a language problem, magnetizer and subject both being German. The circumstances looked favorable until Willermoz postponed the principal exhibition in order to show off some lesser cases.

He was interested in magnetizing animals, and he brought out a sick horse to be his subject, explaining to the prince, with Mesmer's approval, that if animal magnetism worked on human beings and inanimate objects, clearly it worked on everything in between, on all species of life. Willermoz made passes around the horse, which flinched, trembled, and gave hacking coughs when he reached the area of the throat. He therefore identified the throat as the ailing part of the animal's anatomy. An autopsy revealed a diseased larynx. Willermoz pronounced this a QED, only to have Prince Henry disagree because the horse might have shied nervously at the approach of the magnetizer's hands toward the painful area rather than reacted to an infusion of animal magnetism.

Again, the army commander in Lyons offered to attempt to magnetize a company of his soldiers for the Prussian general. Mass hypnotism is a reality to which armies are not unsusceptible, but little could be expected of the rank and file dragooned to watch their commanding officer stare at them, make odd gestures, and order them into a trance instead of through the manual of arms. Men thinking of the comforts of the barracks or the pleasures of the dives of the city were not readily turned into automata. They stayed wide awake, bored, and annoyed at having to fall out to take part in unmilitary nonsense and were dismissed by a disgruntled commander.

There remained Prince Henry, a subject for Mesmer himself to work on. We do not have a description of their sessions together. All we know is that Mesmer did his best to mesmerize the prince—and failed.

It should not have been taken for a humiliating failure since the nonreaction could be explained plausibly according to Mesmerian principles. No groundwork had been laid for the experiment. No rapport could be generated between the magnetizer working against time and the unimpressed subject, and therefore no flow of animal magnetism from the one to the other could reasonably be expected. Alternatively, Prince Henry might have been a natural, inevitable failure, one of those infused with the countervailing force of Mesmer's Propositions 18–19 that neutralized animal magnetism.

A younger Mesmer would have fastened on one of these excuses, insisting dogmatically that his role of an animal magnet remained uncompromised. The Mesmer of 1784 was fifty, badgered by his enemies, a prey to self-doubts. The Prince Henry failure gave him misgivings about a possible waning of his magnetic powers. Perhaps they were diminishing after the analogy of a mineral magnet losing its ability to influence metal objects. The universal fluid of the cosmos might, for some inexplicable reason, cease to flow into an animal magnet, depriving him of his capacity to pass it on to other people. Mesmer feared this was happening to him.

The Lyons visit proved unfortunate in every respect. Willermoz turned out to be a great disappointment, a devotee of Mesmerism but also a devotee of occultism. He dabbled in the esoteric lore and alchemical symbolism of the Rosicrucians; belonged to Speculative Freemasonry with its mystical views of the regeneration of humanity and the coming of a golden age; headed the Martinists of Lyons, a group that indulged in magical rituals; and founded the Chevaliers of the Black Eagle to promote an arcane philosophy built from these dubious sources.

Animal magnetism was but one of the ideas Willermoz tossed into the hopper. It emerged as "spiritual magnetism," an adulteration of Mesmerism that appalled Mesmer. After stating and reiterating so often that he was not an occultist but a scientist, here was his own lodge declaring, by implication, that his opponents were right who declared him to be not a scientist, but an occultist.

Willermoz was a frank, amiable individual, humble enough to take advice, not least from Mesmer, whom he admired. Unfortunately he also admired Martines de Pasqually, the founder of a mystical order called the Chosen Priests of the Universe that maintained lodges in cities where Mesmerian lodges were located. The two systems appeared complementary to those who belonged to both. If Mesmer based his claim on the fact that his system worked experimentally, so did Pasqually. Mesmerians went into trances as Mesmer predicted; Chosen Priests of the Universe enjoyed visions of the angels, as Pasqually predicted.

Willermoz did not accept *any* claim by *anyone* to preternatural knowledge. In that year of 1784 he refused to meet Cagliostro, who was creating a sensation in Lyons as a healer, because he believed the notorious crystal gazer was a charlatan posing as a seer. But the head of the Lyons Society of Harmony was a mystic by nature, and he looked at objective reality through a veil of mysticism. He could not see any fallacy in the logic that put Mesmer and Pasqually on an equal level of authority. Mesmer failed to convince him that there was one—namely, that mystical visions were the private property of the visionary and might be hallucinations, while Mesmeric trances were objectively verifiable under valid scientific safeguards.

Mesmer returned to Paris in a disturbed state of mind. Lyons occultism added to official condemnation by the royal commissioners left him moody and meditative beyond his wont, disillusioned about his followers faithfully following his doctrine, doubtful about what was happening to him personally.

The consummation of his afflictions was still to come. In 1785 his chief lieutenants in the Paris Society of Harmony rebelled against him.

Mesmer intended the society to be a benevolent despotism of which he would remain the despot. Animal magnetism was "my discovery." Therefore no one else fully understood it or had any right to contradict him on how it should be taught, used, and promoted. His concept was of willing, obedient subordinates accepting the doctrine as he was pleased to reveal it, transmitting it to the lower membership, and returning to him for enlightenment or direction when they ran into difficulties. He wanted no Deslons at the Hôtel de Coigny.

What he got was a faction of enemies who made Deslon look like a sycophantic henchman. Aristocrats like the Duc de Lauzun, the Comte de Ségur, and the Marquis de Jaucourt were themselves accustomed to giving orders, not taking them. One vice-president, Adrien Duport, was middle-class, but also an ambitious politician who would, only five years later, be a leader in the Estates-General and an advocate of the French Revolution. Chastellux, another vice-president, conducted scientific experiments and entertained personal views on the application of Newtonian cosmology to scientific problems.

D'Éprémesnil was a weathercock who, according to Condorcet, embarrassed every cause he served (the cause of Cagliostro was among those he served). Puységur, a courtly gentleman of the old school who conceded the founder's precedence in the society, nonetheless knew that just then he was contributing, through his studies of artificial somnambulism, more than Mesmer to the advancement of Mesmerism. Kornmann's primary loyalty was to Bergasse, and Bergasse's primary loyalty was to himself.

Mesmer expected—trustingly, unrealistically—that these men would bow to his will forever or at least that the recalcitrant would be summarily expelled on his demand. The first months of the society went smoothly enough to make him believe that such was the case. It did not bother him when he heard the word "Bergassism" rather than "Mesmerism." Bergasse was his right-hand man, his alter ego, his creature. Rebellion was unthinkable to Mesmer, and so he never thought of it.

As for Bergasse, he never had accepted the role of Mesmer's alter ego, let alone his creature, and by now he was questioning who was who's right-hand man. On the basis of actual constructive work at the society, he was himself the leader, Mesmer slipping little by little into the position of a figurehead. When Mesmer went on his travels or failed to appear for any other reason, the society got on without him—under Bergasse's direction. Bergasse gave the lectures, supervised the seminars, and ran the clinic where patients were received and treated with animal magnetism. The staff carried on at his behest. This being so, the thought crossed Bergasse's mind—it shows between the lines of his writings—that Mesmer just might be superfluous.

During Mesmer's absence in Lyons, Bergasse delivered some lectures at the Paris lodge to which nonmembers were invited. The staff and a group of students attended along with the general public. Mesmer, learning of this on his return to Paris, felt the old betrayal syndrome rising within him. Indignantly he told Bergasse:

> It is clear that the right you arrogate to yourself to divulge my doctrine, the chair you occupy so well during the public courses arranged by you, none of this do you do by your own authority. On the contrary, I find it expressly forbidden by a pledge of honor, the only one we both have sworn.

Bergasse was taken aback. He had had no intention of defying Mesmer because he had never considered that defiance might be involved. Public lectures had been envisaged in the third clause of the original contract establishing the Society of Harmony, the clause relating to the exploitation of animal magnetism for the good of all humanity. Everyone on the staff understood that. Having endorsed Bergasse's public lectures, they were as surprised as he by Mesmer's complaint.

Mesmer referred Bergasse to the secrecy contract and said accusingly about spreading Mesmerism everywhere in the world:

> I cannot remain silent, Monsieur. This pretension seems to me the height of injustice and blindness; and every honest man will think the same thing when he casts his eye over the engagements you have entered into, and when he reads there that I did not instruct you, any more than any other of my students, except on the express and preliminary condition that he would not make, with any prince or foreign government, either a treaty, or an accord, or negotiations relating to animal magnetism, this right being expressly and personally reserved to me. Can the right to dispense my gift belong to anyone except myself?

Bergasse responded wrathfully that the society had bought Mesmer's gift from him, and at a tidy sum. Other arguments entered into the quarrel. Bergasse accused Mesmer of overweening pride, of exploiting those who had labored on his behalf, and of using the Society of Harmony as his own plaything. Mesmer hurled the accusations back at Bergasse. When Mesmer threatened to go to London and found an English Society of Harmony that would be more loyal, Bergasse picked up the gauntlet, arguing that this in itself would render secrecy in Paris absurd—as if by decree of an absentee director the French members could be restricted to nothing more than teaching one another and learning from one another within the four walls of their headquarters. The personal duel of the head of the society and his lieutenant became biting and insulting.

The real dispute, nevertheless, was over money, over whether the society had or had not purchased "my gift" from Mesmer. Bergasse went back over the history of the concept of a Mesmerian institution.

It had been agreed by Mesmer, Bergasse, and Kornmann that subscriptions would be opened for 100 members, each of whom would pay 100 louis d'or (worth 24 livres each), so that there would be 240,000 livres in the treasury when this subscription closed. These 240,000 livres would be Mesmer's, in exchange for his tuition in his system, and until they were raised, the society would be run in the strictest confidence under his control.

The first 100 members came in quickly, a flood following them raised contributions well above the prescribed limit, and Bergasse backed by the staff, called for the society to cease to be secret. Members who had passed the course in animal magnetism and been awarded diplomas would be allowed to establish Mesmerism clinics of their own. Lectures at the Hôtel de Coigny would be thrown open to the public. Mesmer's pledge to disseminate his ideas about healing as widely as possible for the good of humanity would be honored.

For Bergasse, Kormann, Puységur, and the rest, there were to be two versions of the Society of Harmony, one secret and temporary, lasting until Mesmer's financial demands were met, and one public and permanent. Secrecy had been understood to apply only as long as the first subscription remained unfilled, for the obvious reason that if public lectures were given or if graduates made the doctrine known far and wide, the subscription would never be filled. No one would pay a large sum for information he could get for nothing. Mesmer's 240,000 livres would never be forthcoming. It was for his advantage that the secrecy contract was allowed during the first subscription drive. The sum agreed upon having been collected, and much more, Mesmer having been paid, the validity of the secrecy contract lapsed.

Bergasse traced the present troubles to Mesmer's besetting sin, cupidity:

> Last July, the Society of Harmony assembled and nominated a committee to draw up a new set of rules. Other affairs and absences pushed the work ahead to November. Then the committee held its meeting. The new rules were rapidly formulated. There was no mention of monetary contributions except for ordinary expenses. But M. Mesmer wanted us to demand, for instruction, at first 100 louis, then 50, and proportionate sums in the provinces, half for him and half for the society. The committee resisted his proposal. The subscription was

more than filled; to continue on the same terms would have caused benefactors to become businessmen, and would have made them extortioners of humanity.

Mesmer's riposte has an air of grievance about it, and also a touch of intellectual dishonesty since he gives something less than the whole picture regarding his negotiations with the ministers of the Crown:

> As to the pecuniary calculations with which you bored a respectable assembly, and of which you have dared to print a summary, I am too far above such petty details to give you an answer. I do not condescend to demonstrate the plain falsity of the whole thing. How is it that, having yourself published the fact that I refused a pension of 30,000 livres from the government, because I wished it to be granted as a reward for my achievement, not payment for a commodity, how is it that you can choose paltry means to accuse me of avarice?

The dispute was clearly going nowhere except to the disruption of the society. Lectures, seminars, and clinical demonstrations could not be carried on satisfactorily when the teachers were occupied with a quarrel over the very nature of the establishment. Students could not study with full concentration when they heard the director and his lieutenants bickering in the executive suite. Everything drifted while whispering went on in the corridors, frowns and smiles in the offices. A despairing voice was heard:

> In point of fact, who are we? A subscription has been undertaken in favor of M. Mesmer. Is it not filled? He objects that the government ought to give him a pension of 30,000 livres for the publication of his discovery. Well then! How much has he received? If he does not have his 30,000 livres, let us fill up that amount forthwith. But make an end of this discussion so that the public, with which M. Mesmer and the society have a commitment, may be served.

This generous proposal, and the support it drew from the members, showed that Mesmer was no victim of a heartless conspiracy. Puységur, the peacemaker of the society, put the matter to him in conciliatory language:

You are here in a circle of your friends and your defenders. Tell us what you still lack to complete your 30,000 livres. We will find the means to make up the sum. Only, let us chose the means. Meanwhile, let no more students be admitted for a fee. Also, the commitment we have made in your name and ours must be honored, the public must be informed about the merits and application of your discovery, and the men who wish to be benefactors of humanity must cease to play at your direction the scarcely honorable role of your officers and spoliators of the human race.

Puységur's only mistake was to suppose that Mesmer's obstinacy was entirely a matter of money. Secrecy for its own sake ranked high among his motives. Once so eager to place his knowledge before all comers, he had suffered too many disappointments; he had seen too many men making use of Mesmerism to his disadvantage, to remain frank and aboveboard. He did not want to lose control of the Society of Harmony. He sought to maintain control by dropping hints among the members about marvels not yet disclosed, a baited hook that took many a fish, binding much of the membership to him. Perhaps he salved his conscience with the thought that there were things not yet mentioned from his long career as a healer. We know from his later works that there were no marvels among them.

Bergasse, too, had mixed motives. If he wanted to aid humanity, as he did in his abstract Rousseauist fashion, he also wanted to make a name for himself on the platform. He fancied himself as a speaker, and an end to secrecy would place him in the limelight. He would deliver his lectures before large audiences, receiving cheers and applause to go with the tepid compliments offered to him in the intimacy of the lodge. He craved public recognition, something he had waited for, a reward for his labors of which Mesmer was trying to deprive him. Rather than knuckle under, he would break up the place.

Break it up he did. He and his group of rebels—Kornmann, Duport, Chastellux, D'Éprémesnil and a few others—seceded from the main body and began to hold sessions in Kornmann's Paris home. Feeling the pressure of the approaching Revolution, they deviated into political Mesmerism, proposing to reform society and the state, using Bergasse's *Considerations* as the point of departure for their radical theories. Jacques Pierre Brissot, the man who would become the leader of the Girondins during the Revolution, joined them. The political Mesmerians agreed theoretically that men and women should live according to nature, the creation of animal magnetism, and practically that the way to begin was to make a clean sweep of the unnatural institutions of France, including the absolute monarchy. They were ready in 1789.

The schism left Mesmer with a rump society. The loyalists were less significant members who could not make up for the loss of the leadership. Mesmer, disillusioned, soon abandoned them and Paris. The rump staggered along until the Revolution and then vanished.

No one will ever breathe life into the dry bones of this skeleton in the closet of Mesmerism. Much of the quarrel reached the public through the press, each side reporting what was said, or believed to have been said, inside the Hôtel de Coigny, and the arguments can be pieced together from their pamphlets. Bergasse caused to be published: *Sums Turned Over to Monsieur Mesmer to Acquire the Right to Publish His Discovery.* Mesmer replied with: *Letter by the Author of the Discovery of Animal Magnetism . . . Serving as an Answer to a Printed Work Having for Its Title: Sums Turned Over to M. Mesmer to Acquire the Right to Publish His Discovery.* Bergasse came back with: *Observations on a Writing by Doctor Mesmer.*

The titles are self-explanatory; the contents cover the essentials of the dialectic, such as it was.

The feud between Mesmer and his former friends, conducted in public, coming hard on the heels of his feud with Deslon, naturally made him more of a spectacle than ever. His penchant for secrecy caused him to be derided for a charlatan in gossip and cartoons. It was his bad luck that a genuine charlatan was in the public eye at that moment. If 1784 was the year of Mesmerism in Paris, 1785 was the year of Cagliostro and the scandal of the Diamond Necklace.

Cagliostro's notoriety matched Mesmer's during that year. Cagliostroism and Mesmerism were bracketed together—two charlatans, two absurd creeds for the credulous, two exposures. Cagliostro saw the inside of the Bastille, Mesmer went scot-free, and that was the difference between them. So said the broadsides hawked through the streets of Paris.

Mesmer capitulated. He could no longer rise after every fall. His depression did not dissipate as of old. His triumphs appeared fated to lead him into disappointments, his cures being followed by snubs. His disciples appeared fated to become turncoats. Deslon had been his ideal assistant, and Deslon had betrayed him; Bergasse, after giving him so much satisfaction by filling the place vacated by Deslon, had betrayed him. The Society of Harmony, on which he had pinned his hopes, was seen to be built on shifting sands, a flimsy structure that split wide open at the first gale.

He was back where he started, alone, friendless, devoid of prospects, wondering what the future held for him.

CHAPTER 16

Wanderings

The year 1785 marked a decisive turning point in Mesmer's life. Until then he was a determined advocate of his theory, always looking for a new quarter in which to promote it, always ready to do battle, in speech and in print, with those who thwarted him. The traumatic experience at the Society of Harmony changed his character. He subsided into a mere spectator of the movement he started, still taking patients on an occasional basis, but never founding a clinic comparable to the institutions he directed in Vienna and Paris. He would never launch another resolute campaign for the validation of animal magnetism. He had thirty years before him. In 1799 he would publish his last noteworthy book, and then he would have sixteen years as an extinct volcano.

Giving up on Paris in 1785 as he had given up on Vienna in 1777, he had to decide what to do next. He decided to travel.

His conscience might have reminded that the city on the Danube would be an appropriate choice for a destination—his wife was still there, waiting for him in the mansion on the Landstrasse. Being at a loose end, he might have made the return journey to see her again after eight years. He traveled to other parts of the Holy Roman Empire. To put Vienna on his timetable would have been no hardship to him.

Alas, Frau Mesmer was the reason he stayed away. He had left her behind when he went in pursuit of a will-o'-the-wisp, relegating her to a secondary role compared to the *idée mère* governing his thoughts. He had never sent for her even though she could have been of assistance in his Paris clinic as she had been in his Vienna clinic. No letter from one of them to the other has been found. Maria Anna vanished from his life and apparently from his memory, too, while he fought and lost the battle for animal magnetism on the banks of the Seine. Her own silence can be attributed to age and family pride. At sixty-one she felt no passionate desire for her husband, and as a Eulenschenk, she would not stoop to beg him to come back.

Still, her feelings were bruised by his indifference. Eight years are a long time for a deserted wife to wait for a wandering husband. Those eight years gave Frau Mesmer the time to nurse, cherish, and savor her resentment.

Mesmer realized what kind of reception he could expect. His Paris fiasco was common knowledge in Vienna, to the immense satisfaction of Stoerck, Ingenhousz, and the Viennese medical profession in general. He was afraid, with good reason, that Frau Mesmer would meet him at the door as she had seen him off in 1777, with an icy observation that he continued to play the fool at a time of life when he should know better. A scene like that was more than he could face in his despondency. He decided against Vienna.

Possibly, as some of his contemporaries said, he paid a visit to London, following up his threat to found a Society of Harmony there. His fame, or notoriety, had crossed the Channel, and the London of George III would surely have taken note of him. No journalist or letter writer did. No crowds of the ill came to him to be healed. No Mesmerian lodge was founded. *Ergo,* the London trip is a myth.

Gaps like this recur in his later biography because he was so often on the move. The longer stops are well documented, and the occasional letter by or to him pins him down momentarily. Guesswork fills in the rest.

Leaving his money and belongings in Paris since he intended to return eventually, he traveled through the French provinces in 1786, visiting lodges of the Society of Harmony that operated independently despite the civil war in the Paris lodge. The warm greetings extended to him by his followers cheered him, and he scored a particular triumph in Toulouse; but nothing could rejuvenate his spirits or restore him to his former vigor of mind and body.

This was the year Deslon died. Mesmer harbored a grudge against his old friend, subsequent enemy, and successful rival, but the passing of Deslon rendered his own life the poorer. He had treated Deslon for his fatal illness, and Deslon had been committed so entirely to Mesmerism that he consulted only practitioners of animal magnetism in his final agony, showing faith in Mesmer's discovery to the end.

Mesmer moved east through France into Germany and Switzerland, where 1787 found him at Lake Constance, in Zurich, and in Karlsruhe.

This was the year Kornmann published a pamphlet about his wife's adultery in which he named the dramatist Beaumarchais as a conspirator (not correspondent). It was the beginning of a war of words between Kornmann-Bergasse and Mme. Kornmann-Beaumarchais that lasted until 1789, when the Parlement of Paris handed down a decision against Kornmann. Bergasse paid the penalty of quarreling with a comedian. Beaumarchais made fun of him in the character "Begearss" of the play *The Guilty Mother,* a very substandard production by his standards, but enough to raise some chuckles around Paris at Bergasse's expense. The Kornmann suit was the final *cause célèbre* of the Old Regime. The reverberations reached Mesmer, but he had nothing to say on the subject.

The case ended just in time for Bergasse to play a role in a wider drama. He was elected a deputy of the third estate to the Estates General that gathered at Versailles on May 5, 1789. He came as a social critic demanding the eradication of aristocratic privileges in France, an attitude understandable in an ambitious bourgeois irritated by the restrictions on the third estate and consumed by a Rousseauist passion for personal, social, and political equality.

Mesmerism, which Bergasse never forsook, gave him a drive in the same direction. He invoked the doctrine of animal magnetism in support of revolutionary politics. As he had said in his *Considerations,* animal magnetism, the most basic of natural realities, implies the natural in everything from the state to the fine arts; it implies an extirpation of unnatural inequalities: "A new physical world must necessarily be accompanied by a new moral world." This thought fitted the broad indictment being brought against the government of Louis XVI by a host of would-be reformers, among whom the political Mesmerians were not the least.

Again, the Mesmerians were adversaries of the Establishment insofar as its official bodies—academies, institutes, and faculties of the traditional sort—oppressed them. They shared the bias against arrogant royal organizations, including absolute monarchy. The bloodstained rebel Jean Paul Marat, who created much havoc before Charlotte Corday arrived at his home with her knife—Marat fed a flaming hatred of the scientific corporations of France because they obstinately preferred Newton's physics to his. Although Bergasse disagreed with Marat's science, he shared Marat's feeling that the corporations ought to be transformed by filling them with freer spirits.

The years 1785–91 were the golden age of political Mesmerism, from the swing to the left after the breakup of the Paris society to Brissot's assumption of power under the Girondin administration. The theory of animal magnetism added an eddy to the whirlwind of the Revolution.

Mesmer stood apart from the political offshoot of his theory. It would have been absurd if he had repudiated Bergasse's argument that Mesmerism would propagate mental health, which would bring better institutions because they were run by saner people; conversely, that to replace the existing irrational institutions would improve the mental health of the people governed by them. But Mesmer held all this to be a side issue compared to the science of animal magnetism as applied to medicine.

Which is not to say that he was apolitical. A man of the Age of Reason, he applauded the rising of the French people in the name of a more egalitarian society. He had run his clinic for all classes, and he thought the government should be run for all classes. He simply refused to join the melee.

Bergasse was unwilling to remain that uncommitted because he could not stand the way France was governed. The system that gave power to a feckless king swayed by an extravagant queen and haughty courtiers had to be replaced. Bergasse mulled over innovative ideas on government, economics, and education that he longed to see put into practice. As a lawyer and a member of the rising middle class he would have been a reformer in 1789 no matter what. By an accident of his intellectual history, (the fact that Mesmer crossed his path) he came to Versaille as partisan of political Mesmerism.

Bergasse supported the early Revolution and its political reforms. He was among the deputies of the Estates General at Versailles who took the Tennis Court Oath to give France a constitution. The champions of political Mesmerism gravitated by instinct into moderate groups. They strove to remain integral constitutionalists in every crisis. They accepted the ideology of a constitutional monarchy, democratic guarantees, and a better life for the French people. When the war against the Austrians and the Prussians failed, and the Girondins fell, and Robespierre's Reign of Terror began, the political Mesmerians went into prison or exile or rode the tumbrels through the streets of Paris to the guillotine.

Brissot's head fell into the basket in 1793, D'Éprémesnil's in 1794. Duport got across the border in time to save himself. Bergasse, condemned by the Revolutionary Tribunal, was rescued from the guillotine on the Ninth of Thermidor when Robespierre was overthrown. He continued to write political brochures, outlasted Napoleon, discussed the Holy Alliance with Tsar Alexander I, watched the restored Bourbons come and go, and died in his bed in 1832, when Louis Philippe was King of the French.

Another political Mesmerian, Lafayette, for a time the most powerful man in France, deserted to the enemy out of disgust when the Revolution lurched toward the Terror. But the Prussians and Austrians did not trust him. They put him in prison and there he remained for five years.

Two men from the first commission that condemned Mesmerism lost their lives. Bailly was elected mayor of Paris, joined his authority to Lafayette's in suppressing a rioting mob of antimonarchists, fell from office, faced the Revolutionary Tribunal, and went to the guillotine. Lavoisier also felt the edge of the knife because he had been an associate of tax farmers before the Revolution and because "the Republic has no need of savants." Guillotin, by the most exquisite of ironies, would have been destroyed by his own machine except for the Thermidorian Reaction.

The tumultuous years of the Revolution saw Mesmer on his travels in the German lands and Switzerland. At the height of the Reign of Terror in 1793, he at last revisited Vienna, which he could do in comparative peace since his wife had died in 1790. Separated for thirteen years, they were virtual strangers when death decided that they should never meet again.

Mesmer found the city changed since he had left sixteen years before. Empress Maria Theresa, Emperor Joseph II, and Emperor Leopold II, who followed them, were gone. Kaunitz lived in retirement and out of favor. Francis II, the son of Leopold, ruled the Holy Roman Empire from Schönbrunn Palace and did his best to contain the French Revolution with his armed forces. The news from the French frontier was generally good when Mesmer arrived toward the end of the year. No one had yet heard of a soldier named Bonaparte.

Mesmer's old adversaries in the university and the Faculty of Medicine had vanished with one great exception. De Haen had died in 1779, Hell in 1792. Ingenhousz had returned to London. Stoerck remained. There would have been no sense in approaching him, for Mesmer knew that Stoerck knew what had happened to him in Paris. Mesmer remained discreetly aloof from his principal opponent in the Paradies episode.

The musical scene had a different look and a revolutionary sound. Mozart and Gluck were dead. The new star was Ludwig van Beethoven, who had come to Vienna in 1792 and now dominated the salons and musicales as a performer at the keyboard. Beethoven played with the fire and the fury he would put into his titanic compositions, forcing Western music out of the decorous drawing rooms of the eighteenth century into the passionate world of the Romantic movement.

Mesmer had seen in Mozart's music evidence for the reality of animal magnetism flowing into human beings and moving them emotionally. How much more might he not have read into the music of Beethoven! Mesmer and Beethoven did not meet in Vienna, and it is impossible to say whether Mesmer heard enough of the titan's works in later life to draw an analogy between this music and animal magnetism, each being "natural" in its own way.

Mesmer hardly had a chance to meet anyone in Vienna. He came back to the Landstrasse hoping to hold a reunion with his relatives and old friends. Most of them, including his stepson, were no longer in the city, and before he could meet the survivors, he met Princess Gonzaga.

The princess was renting part of the Mesmer mansion, and so he paid his respects to her as her landlord. The conversation turned to the topic of the moment, the French Revolution. She abominated the regicides. Mesmer tried to differentiate between the excesses of the Jacobins and the justified struggle for freedom under the Girondins. The discussion became warm, the princess became strident and ordered him out of her suite. Then she reported that he was a dangerous radical who sympathized with the wild men of the

Seine who had murdered their king and established a bloodstained republic. These accusations gained added force in that while Mesmer was in Vienna, the Reign of Terror claimed Marie Antoinette, the former Austrian Archduchess Maria Antonia, who was executed on October 16, 1793.

The authorities had Mesmer picked up by the police, thrown into jail, and investigated. He spent two months behind bars while a dossier on him was put together. Nothing incriminating being found, he was released, but the authorities ordered him out of Vienna because any partisan of the French Revolution, even in its early form, was *persona non grata* in the capital of the Hapsburgs when Austria was at war with France.

Mesmer went back to Lake Constance. Two of his sisters, Ida and Genoveva, were living in Meersburg, and he spent some time in the company of them and their families, the Schorpfs and the Strohmayers. Family ties were beginning to tug at him. His parents were long since gone, and as he passed his sixtieth birthday, he felt his old love of company, conversation, and the surroundings of his youth. His nieces and nephews took the place of his stepson. Human relations once more competed with animal magnetism for his attention.

Another reason for keeping in touch with his relatives was a financial pinch. He had intended to return and draw on the money accruing to him from the Society of Harmony, but the time stretched on and on, and the French Revolution intervened, and everything he owned was sequestrated. In 1798 he was forced to borrow 600 florins from his nephew, Konrad Strohmayer, *Burgomeister* of Meersburg.

It was not in Mesmer's character to write off the debt owed to him by the French government. He returned to Paris in 1798 to claim his rights in the courts. The French people had put the Terror four years behind them. The man of the hour was Napoleon Bonaparte, who, after crushing the Austrian armies in Italy, was off on his Egyptian adventure.

Mesmer's identity card gives a description of him at this period of his life, using the metric system introduced to France by the Revolution: "Age 64, height 1 metre 76 centimeters, hair and eyebrows brown, eyes the same, chin double, face full, forehead high, nose and mouth medium."

He lived in Paris and Versailles during the years 1798–1802, remaining aloof from politics and Mesmerism. Political Mesmerism no longer existed, and in any case Mesmer could not be reconciled to the men who had disrupted his Society of Harmony. He would not pay a call on the veteran of the feud, Bergasse. Medical Mesmerism, reviving after the Revolution, was in the hands of men who were developing it in ways he disapproved. Animal magnetism was talked of less in terms of a cosmic fluid than in terms of personal magnetism or some other deviation from the doctrinal purity he had defined.

Mesmer lived close to the center of events as Revolutionary France became Napoleonic France. Crossing the Mediterranean from Egypt, Napoleon joined the Consulate at the head of the French government (1799), took the Great St. Bernard Pass through the Alps to Italy and defeated the Austrians again at Marengo (1800), arranged a concordat with Pope Pius VII (1801), and signed the Treaty of Amiens (1802) bringing peace between France and Great Britain.

Mesmer could feel secure in Napoleonic France. He sued for his losses under the Revolution and was awarded roughly one-third the worth of his property and a life annuity that enabled him to live in a modicum of comfort.

While waiting for a court decision on his case, he wrote to the Swiss minister of Arts and Sciences in Lucerne regarding animal magnetism. Styling himself a "Swiss citizen" and "Member of the Faculty of Medicine of Vienna and of the Academy of Science of Bavaria," he suggested that Switzerland might be willing to accord him the support denied to him elsewhere by the "disbelief or jealousy" of stupid or interested men. Except for that one typical sentence, the tone of the letter is so mild, for him, that he cannot have entertained much faith in its efficacy and therefore cannot have been disappointed when he received a negative response.

The Swiss minister may well have been put off by a package he received along with the letter. The package contained Mesmer's new book.

CHAPTER 17

The Occult Sciences

The title of the book was *Memoir of F. A. Mesmer, Doctor of Medicine, Concerning His Discoveries* (1799). Nothing in the author's past prepared his reading public for this work. It fell into his pattern of rewriting his old ideas and then adding new things to the existing theory, but here the word "new" meant novelties of the kind he had rejected when put forward by Mesmerians in the past. This is a treatise on the occult sciences. Of course, he does not call it that and would have resented the intellectual insult of hearing it so described. His purpose was to push his doctrine into one more field, and that field was the one where you find such things as clairvoyance, mental telepathy, and precognition.

The author abandoned his old polemical and propagandist tone in favor of a plain expository rhetoric, his aim being no longer to confute opponents or convince skeptics, but to set forth his system in a simple logical manner for readers willing to understand and to learn. He could not resist mentioning his disappointments in Vienna and Paris or animadverting on the conduct of the shallow men who rebuffed him. To quarrel with opponents was not, nevertheless, his concern. He intended this work to be a general statement of his system and a guide for future research. If his ideas were to be extended into fresh areas of human experience, well, he would describe the manner in which he had done just that, and others could learn from him.

He had passed beyond the limits of his earlier thought and, for all his disclaimers, was now working outside science in the Newtonian sense. Wandering from one place to another, he no longer had a laboratory and clinic as in the old days. He no longer submitted his mind to the scientific discipline of such institutions but let it roam freely whither it would go. Nor did he have to play devil's advocate

189

with himself, imagining objections he would be expected to answer in meetings with scientists and physicians. There would be no more official conferences of the Vienna-Paris variety.

Thus liberated from corrective reality, he proceeded by a natural progression into the occult without realizing what he was doing. Mesmerism had uncovered phenomena foreign to conventional science. It had shown that inexplicable and even stupefying things were simply true—controlled trances, artificial somnambulism, hypnotic memory, posthypnotic hallucinations. Who could set bounds to further developments just as strange? Who could rationally deny that Mesmerism might uncover more hidden realities and explain more convoluted enigmas?

Mesmer was held in this book by only one check, logical deductions from the facts he accepted, the deductions to be made according to his theory of animal magnetism. His thought is rigorously this-worldly. He sets the supernatural and the preternatural to one side, allowing no place for faith healing, spiritualism, demonology or the practice of magic through mystic rituals, alchemical symbolism, or incantations chanted in the light of the full moon. Willermoz and the Chosen Priests of the Universe would never hold any attractions for him.

Since Mesmer based himself on "the facts," the critical question is what he considered factual. He began with the ability of men and women, under the influence of animal magnetism, to activate strange powers within themselves, to gain insights into cosmic truths hidden from most of humanity by a veil of ignorance. He had observed subjects, and the annals of Mesmerism recorded many more, who manifested super-normal powers. He could no longer be sure where the real sciences left off and the occult sciences began. He was certain that all genuine phenomena could be accommodated within his system, but he could not define "genuine" in such a way as to protect himself from fantastic speculations.

He had written in his doctoral dissertation, and repeated in a series of writings, that hoary fallacies could be shown to have essential truth within them when interpreted scientifically—astrology, alchemy, oneiromancy, divination. Now he will explain them through animal magnetism. He sets down in a series of questions "the facts" to which he will apply himself:

1. How can a sleeping man diagnose his own illnesses and even those of other people?

2. How, without having any instruction, can he identify the best means of effecting a cure?

3. How can he see objects at any distance, and how can he predict future events?

4. How can a man receive impressions from a will other than his own?

5. Why is this man not always endowed with these faculties?

6. How can these faculties be perfected?

7. Why is this state more frequent, and why does it appear in its most developed form, when the methods of animal magnetism are employed?

8. What have been the effects of ignorance of this phenomenon, and what are they today?

9. What are the evils resulting from the abuse of it?

The first two of these questions refer to a belief held by Mesmer, Puységur and many of their colleagues in the Mesmerian movement, the belief that subjects placed in a trance often became sensitive to what was wrong with the ill and therefore could guide the physician. Number 3 admits the reality of clairvoyance and precognition. Number 4 does the same for mental telepathy. The rest concern animal magnetism as the agent responsible, its controlled use to heighten supernormal powers, and precautions against its misuse.

Such are Mesmer's premises. He proceeds to his conclusions by following his theory that hypnotic sleep is a condition in which the outer senses become subservient to the inner sense, and the inner sense becomes in tune with the objective world.

The question here is how the senses, inner and outer, organize reality. The individual lives in a bewildering world, and it is the specific function of each sense that makes it possible for him to sort his experiences into a coherent order. The eye is responsive to rays of light, the ear to waves of sound. The inner sense unifies the perceptions of all the outer senses, meshing them together into the experience of one individual. This thought goes back to Aristotle, whom Mesmer had read in his student days.

But there is a far more extraordinary function of the inner sense.

He tells us that the inner sense responds to animal magnetism as the eye responds to light. This means that it receives messages directly from the cosmos.

Here we have Mesmer's explanation of somnambulism. As the outer senses shut down, the somnambulist begins to receive messages and commands from his inner sense, which acts as a surrogate and permits him to "see" when his eyes are closed, to "remember" when memory has lapsed, to answer questions intelligibly when the other avenues to his intelligence are closed.

Mesmer does not go into the sensory lapses of the somnambulist—hypnotic blindness, et cetera—but the explanation from his thesis is evident. These are psychosomatic symptoms attending the crisis. Animal magnetism rushing through the nervous system affects the outer senses, and just as it may make them more acute, it may paralyze them, depending on the individual, the condition of his nerves, and the commands of the mesmerizer. The inner sense is affected in the same way, sometimes failing, sometimes becoming acute to an astonishing degree.

The inner sense, he says, is at the bottom of faculties that seem mysterious. Acting in one way, it is instinct; acting in another, it is esthetic taste. Mesmerian rapport, that intimate feeling of complete trust between persons, comes from the communication of inner sense and inner sense. The same analysis explains a whole range of ideas obtained in a nonrational way, from mere hunches to profound mystical experiences.

Momentous consequences follow. Since the inner sense is in touch with the cosmos and with all the interrelated parts of the cosmos, reacting to them in their timelessness, therefore, there seems to be ideally no limit to human knowledge (whatever practical impediments there might be).

Extrasensory perception is only to be expected, to put the matter in modern language. The eye cannot see a suit of cards face down on the table because light is reflected from the backs only. The inner sense can "see" the faces because animal magnetism flows everywhere, through and around objects. The outer senses must have their objects within a limited range. The range of the inner sense is limitless, so that there is no reason why an individual might not be clairvoyant enough to perceive things on the opposite side of the earth.

Mental telepathy works through animal magnetism as its medium. One mind thinks thoughts into it, and it carries those thoughts to another mind. There is nothing more puzzling here than the act of the mesmerizer sending animal magnetism streaming into the nerves of his subject.

So much of Mesmer's case is extreme enough, stated with the starkness of occult physics, not experimental science. The occult is more extravagant in his treatment of precognition.

In an evil hour, Mesmer undertook to explain the seers, sibyls, oracles, and fortune-tellers. He came to the conclusion that the genuine articles could predict the future because they broke the time barrier. Time in his view is merely a form of our human ex- perience imposed by the outer senses on the material reaching them. The cosmos itself is timeless—past, present, and future being "different vectors in the entire universe." The inner sense, making direct contact with the cosmos, can see these vectors as they are and follow any of them. To the visionary it is all one. To his listeners he seems to be speaking of what is, has been, or will be, since their finite outer senses must react in a time frame.

The conquest of time gives certain people a privileged view of the "eternal now," a partial and fragmentary view, no doubt, but still valid. When in their dreams they touch the cosmic source of knowledge, they become capable of predicting future events. Sometimes, when they do not understand the revelation vouch- safed to them, their dreams may be interpreted by those who do understand, and that is the truth in oneiromancy.

The fortune-tellers fall within the same definition. The inner sense is able, with the assistance of animal magnetism, to see every- thing in the present. What we call the future is available to it. Per- ception of the future is therefore no mystery.

Since somnambulism is by definition a condition governed by the inner sense, somnambulists have all the occult capacities that have puzzled mankind down the ages. They can see through objects, in- terpret dreams, prophesy. They can diagnose diseases because the bodies of the ill lie open to their inspection.

The above refers to those in the right mental and physical condi- tion. The degree of reception of animal magnetism determines a particular case. No more than the outer senses is the inner sense the same in all people, or in the same state in the same person at different times.

Circling back to his first thought, Mesmer applies his reasoning to superstitious folklore, in which he finds a kernel of truth. From time immemorial humanity has given credence to oracles, prophets, thaumaturges, witches, magicians, demonologists. The old beliefs were a mixture of true and false, rational and irrational, fact and fraud. Whatever was true, rational and factual came from individuals consulting their inner senses responding to animal magnetism.

These visions appear to those in a pathological condition. Sibyls often inhaled fumes and magicians took drugs so that they might lose control of their normal faculties before entering the prophetic state. The fumes and drugs made them more receptive to animal magnetism. Somnambulism, too, is always pathological, a crisis of one suffering from some mental or emotional abnormality. The somnambulist needs animal magnetism, which while curing him may also vouchsafe him visions and revelations. The healthy person cannot react to animal magnetism and therefore cannot enjoy the visions and revelations.

The remaining visionary states—catalepsy, epilepsy, madness—are imperfect forms of somnambulism. Thus, pathology and Mesmerian visions invariably go together.

The above argument refers to human beings, but animals, being subject to animal magnetism, also possess extraordinary gifts. Instinctive behavior, so beautifully and mysteriously linked to biological needs, as in the case of bees building a honeycomb, follows from knowledge arrived at in a manner equivalent to the enlightenment of the human seer. Can animals foresee the future? Mesmer held that they could.

He had been interested in the lower orders ever since his boyhood days on Lake Constance. In later life he kept pets and collected animal stories, out of fondness for both and because they instructed him in high philosophy, cosmological theory, natural history, scientific law, and human behavior. When he amused his friends with fables and anecdotes toward the end of his life, and they accused him of going absurdly far beyond the evidence, inferring broad conclusions that the premises could not possibly sustain, he replied that the instinct of the lowest living thing has a universal significance through animal magnetism. His prime example was the story of the gray poodle of Paris.

During the winter of 1784, while Mesmer lived in the French

capital and employed animal magnetism to heal the ill, his Viennese servant, Antoine, encountered this poodle on the street one day. It followed him, persistently dogging his heels in spite of his efforts to shoo it off and send it home. Arriving at the Mesmer clinic, Antoine reported that the dog was hanging around the door, whereupon Mesmer went outside and tried to make friends with it. The animal backed away from him, refusing to be touched, refusing to leave. It was not frightened, angry or hostile, just determined, as if on a set course from which it would not be forced or enticed.

For six weeks the poodle remained on guard at the clinic, foraging for food in refuse heaps, camping at the door in the cold and the snow, scrambling to its feet when the door opened, and padding after Antoine when he emerged. This odd canine behavior impressed Mesmer, who watched to see what the outcome would be.

At the end, Antoine went on an errand to the rue d'Orléans, the poodle tenaciously accompanying him as always. The man went into a bistro to ask for directions. The dog sat down outside and patiently waited for him.

Suddenly a voice called to the animal, which leaped to its feet, raced to a window where a man was leaning out, and went into a transport of delight at the meeting. The man told Antoine he had raised the dog in Moscow, had lost it on arriving in Paris nearly a year before, and never expected to see it again.

Mesmer, analyzing the significance of the gray poodle, asked himself a series of questions. Did the dog choose his servant because it somehow knew he would lead it to its master? Did it refuse to enter the clinic for fear of being trapped inside on the great day? Did it expect its master to look in its direction from the window at the precise moment?

Mesmer felt sure that the animal knew what it was doing. Since intelligence clearly could not explain the facts, even if a dog were capable of complex logical reasoning, he argued that instinct was the faculty operating here. According to his theory, reason depends on the senses, but instinct has a direct connection with nature and therefore has certain powers denied to reason. Instinct's use of animal magnetism makes the difference.

Animals and human beings alike testify by their strange powers to the truth of Mesmerism, the only system capable of explaining the hitherto-inexplicable facts Mesmer has been dealing with.

Such is Mesmer's system in its full development. He still is not concerned to expand his ideas in the manner of Bergasse into sociology and esthetics, but sticks precisely to animal magnetism and its influence on the individual. He still wants to show what the scientific implications are, granted the existence of the cosmic fluid and its capacity to affect living things.

The ultimate consequences as far as he can determine them are worked out in this *Memoir*, and he has little to add when he has described the impact of the cosmic fluid on the inner sense. His system is complete. The reader can subject it to a fundamental criticism.

Mesmer's mental attitude causes the first reservation. The animal magnetism theory offers no check to wild imaginings. Mesmer does not say that human beings can perceive events on distant stars, but his occult astronomy allows the possibility. There is no reason, in his terms, to doubt the crassest forms of occult physics like the antics of the ouija board. Logically, Mesmer had no right to draw the line before any department of the preternatural or to complain about Mesmerians like Willermoz who wandered down lurid byways where he himself refused to go.

While Mesmer has said rightly enough that skepticism can be stupid, he himself is not skeptical enough. His credulity is unlike him, one might say unworthy of him. Until 1799 he tried to be empirical. Now he is following logic beyond the bounds of common sense. His acceptance of parapsychology could be a sign of wisdom if only he had not attributed its success to occult properties of animal magnetism. He is totally vulnerable to an argument long alleged against him—namely, that the phenomena he is dealing with can be explained, supposing them to be true, by some other agency than his universal fluid.

Moreover, Mesmer involves himself in a contradiction his philosophical studies should have protected him against. He says that animal magnetism is essentially movement, pure motion, and that it is outside time, such that past and future can be subsumed under a universal present. But there is no such thing as movement without time since movement involves "before" and "after" in getting from "here" to "there." Mesmer must have known this. He forgets it in his customary fashion of not letting inconvenient difficulties hamper him when he is immersed in the system he thinks must be true.

Again, his treatment of time equates the human mind with the divine mind. God may see everything in a unison beyond space and time. Human beings, in their finiteness, cannot share that experience. Mesmer has given no reason to suppose they can.

His position on somnambulism, that it is essentially pathological, can be controverted from the evidence. Natural somnambulism happens to people in a normal, healthy state, and Puységur proved he could induce the artificial variety in the case of people who were not ill. It is no answer to say that some degree of abnormality will invariably be found if the investigation is pushed far enough—as much could be said of any effort of the mind or will if "abnormality" is defined with an eye to the right answer. All animals would be abnormal all the time since they always are under the guidance of instinct. Less than ever before will Mesmer allow for chance, accident, coincidence, or misjudgment of the evidence, any of which might explain the nearest fortune teller or the gray poodle of Paris.

This *Memoir* damaged Mesmer's reputation. He had, in the view of skeptics and scientists, finally exposed himself by going over overtly into occultism, declaring himself a devotee of the mystic arts—oneiromancy, second sight, fortune-telling. Everything he had written before became confused and confounded by the welter of strange beliefs to which he confessed. His opponents had been saying all along that he was mystic or a charlatan. Now they said— take your pick, and admit we were right. Those with a bias toward occultism reinforced the argument by welcoming Mesmer over his protests and placing him in the long line of teachers of esoteric wisdom.

That was how Mesmer appeared during the nineteenth century. Researchers with no axes to grind copied the picture they saw in the mass of material about him dating from his last years and the decade or so after his death. If they read his 1799 publication for themselves, they took it to be the final proof that the picture was an authentic intellectual likeness. It is not uncommon to find Mesmer so described today. He is often pigeonholed with Nostradamus, Madame Blavatsky, and the devotees of Isis and Osiris.

Mesmer himself was largely responsible for the distortion.

Granted that he had lost his sense of proportion and scientific proof, he might, after so many misunderstandings of his doctrine, have had the prudence to realize what would be made of his excursion into fields hitherto restricted to seers and imposters. He wanted to build his structure of ideas simply with regard to truth, ignoring what anyone might think. Yet by compromising himself, he created one more obstacle to the attainment of his primary objective, which was to ensure that posterity would accept Mesmerism and side with him against the obscurantists who rejected and ridiculed him in his own time.

It would have been better for him if he had written qualifications and limitations into his philosophy of timelessness and cosmic perception. It would have been best of all if he had never given any serious thought to the *modus operandi* of the fortune-tellers.

CHAPTER 18

Mesmer's Last Years

When Mesmer left Paris in 1802, he bade farewell to the centers of European power and culture. The last thirteen years of his life would be spent in remote areas of Switzerland and Swabia around Lake Constance, where he would remain for the most part "forgetting and by the world forgot."

He spent most of those years at Frauenfeld in Switzerland on the south shore of the lake. Switzerland was in a tumultuous state when he arrived. The French invasion of 1798 had led to the formation of the Helvetic Republic, on the model of the French Republic, designed in Paris by the Revolutionaries, a violent transformation that caused civil war between Swiss representatives of the old and new orders. Mesmer reached the relatively peaceful sanctuary of Frauenfeld when the conflict was at its height in the stronger, more populated regions.

The Helvetic Republic lasted for five years, until Napoleon, realizing it was not working, replaced it with the Swiss Confederation based on the decentralized cantons traditional to the people of Switzerland. Mesmer's area was directly affected because six cantons were added to those already existing, and one was Thurgau, the province in which Frauenfeld lay. Switzerland, after the fall of Napoleon and the return of the Swiss land taken by the French, settled down to the system of independence and neutrality that has maintained its integrity ever since.

Mesmer allowed the furor to pass him by. He may have preferred the Helvetic Republic, as he preferred the French Republic, for its greater equality and rationality; but he was still no politician, and he accepted the Swiss Confederation without any difficulty. It left him to his own devices, which was all he asked of any government at this time of his life. He had no further claims to make on any state officials, and he hoped they would make no claims on him. The city fathers of Frauenfeld never disturbed him, the main reason why he stayed there for ten years.

He was no longer promoting Mesmerism in any public way. He did not even keep up with developments in the movement, being only too aware that various schools existed—Puységur's, for instance—and that no unity could rationally be expected under the banner of animal magnetism that he had carried aloft for so long. He had not changed his mind one iota about the cosmic fluid working through animal magnets to cause Mesmeric crises and trances. And he did not want to meet anyone who differed with him on that, however much the individual might profess to be a mesmerizer. Much less would Mesmer listen to dissidents bent on convincing him that the agent of Mesmerism was, not a mythical cosmic fluid, but the very real force of suggestion in the mind of the subject. He was content to ignore and remain ignorant of what was being done in his name.

In Frauenfeld he successfully avoided the mainstream of European thought, steadfastly refusing invitations to visit friends and admirers who lived away from the region of Lake Constance. Paris and Versailles knew him no more despite the pleas of the doctors Johann Loos and Georg Würtz, the latter of whom graciously offered to prepare his Versailles home to meet his special needs.

Mesmer settled into permanent retirement. The pattern of his life was set by his seventieth birthday in 1804, and he never deviated from the pattern during his last years. A relative, Anna Maria Seeger, kept house for him while he practiced a little medicine among the local people to help them and to prove to himself that he still possessed magnetic powers. Visitors found him cheerful and talkative, enjoying wine and conversation, readily persuaded to read from his latest manuscript or perform a solo on the glass harmonica. Ever and anon the old combative Mesmer would show through the placidity of his old age, and he would launch into an acrimonious retelling of his misfortunes among the rogues of Vienna and Paris.

The years passed by. Then, out of the blue, came the communication from the Berlin Academy of Science. Since Mesmer would not come to the academy, the academy went to him—in the person of Professor Carl Wolfart, who made the journey to

Frauenfeld to see the master in 1812, wrote some of the best eye-witness notes we have on Mesmer, and took the final Mesmer manuscript away with him to be published under the title *Mesmerismus* (1814).

This volume, although a substantial one of 350 pages, is of little consequence in the Mesmer canon. The only interesting thing about it is that Mesmer seems to have been reading, or at least remembering, his bête noire, Bergasse. Whole sections of *Mesmerismus* sound like paraphrases of Bergasse's *Considerations*.

The Bergasse manner of system building is at work in these pages. Many Mesmerians were writing of animal magnetism within a framework of theology at one end and politics at the other, and that is how *Mesmerismus* treats the subject. The sections are broken down in standard form: (1) Physics; (2) Man; (3) Morality. God is the First Cause in this interpretation. The cosmology marches in Mesmer's fashion from matter and motion through gravitation, magnetism, electricity, light, fire, and so forth, all the phenomena owing to the ebb and flow of animal magnetism through the universe. The cure of illness by animal magnetism is described, and the function of somnambulism analyzed.

The final chapter on society, law, education, and human affairs in general is essentially what we find in Bergasse and other Mesmerian theorists about the need to be "natural" in everything. It is hard to see why Mesmer took so long to write this tome or why he considered it worth the labor.

One of Wolfart's letters, printed by Justinus Kerner in his biography of Mesmer, gives the last description of a patient responding to the master's application of animal magnetism. She was a teenage girl suffering from disorders of the spleen and liver, a victim of insomnia, lassitude, bouts of partial suffocation, and an inability to speak because of degeneration in the muscles of her throat. Her personal physician brought her to Mesmer on October 8, 1812, confessing himself defeated by her illness.

Mesmer made a diagnosis that the cause was functional, "stroked" the girl into a trance, sat her at the baquet for perhaps an hour, and sent her home, still mesmerized, with a prediction that she would go into a violent crisis preparatory to convalescence toward restored health. The next day she suffered from a series of agonizing cramps and debilitating nausea. Her frightened parents, fearing she would die, protested to Mesmer, who replied that the illness was proceeding as he expected and that the patient would be well enough on the following day to walk to his office. She was, and she did.

In 1813 Mesmer crossed the lake onto Swabian soil and settled in Constance for about a year. The historic political system into which he had been born was gone. Even the majestic Holy Roman Empire had been unable to withstand Napoleon Bonaparte, who dispatched it and all its ornate trappings into history in 1806 following his shattering victory at Austerlitz. The monarch ruling in Vienna in 1813 had gone through unique transmutation from Francis II to Francis I—that is, from Holy Roman Emperor to Emperor of Austria.

On April 11, 1814, Mesmer signed his testament, which shows what was on his mind just before his eightieth birthday:

> In my last will I name as my universal heirs the six remaining children of my two sisters, to wit, Mathias Schorpf, forester, Crescentia Frostin, widow, Cajetan Strohmayer, Burgomeister of Meersburg, Xavier Strohmayer, doctor, Theresa Maurus, widow, Augusta Fetscherin, saddler, of Meersburg. These six shall divide my entire estate in six equal parts. Anna Maria Seeger of Riedetsweiler shall for her several years of true service rendered to me be paid one hundred gulden after my death. As for my burial, I request that my body be dissected and that the area of the bladder be specially inspected to find out the cause of pains I have suffered for many years. A louis d'or is to be given to the dissector. As in life I held no office or title, therefore I wish to be buried like any ordinary man. This is my last will, which I have written with my own hand, signed and sealed.

That summer he moved to Riedetsweiler on the north shore of the lake. Kerner, searching for relics of this stay, heard from old-timers how Mesmer lived in a house with a courtyard and received the ill in his quarters, dispensing animal magnetism to the young as he himself grew more feeble.

His final move was to Meersburg, for reasons connected with the belief in the occult that haunted his old age, specifically, his belief in fortune-tellers. During his Paris period a gypsy had prophesied that he would die in his eighty-first year. The time allotted him would lapse before his next birthday, and convinced that the gypsy had seen his future in her communing with the cosmic fluid, he shifted to Meersburg to be near his relatives when the end came.

He took quarters near his nieces and nephews and their children. The ailment mentioned in his will curtailed his activities, for he could no longer walk easily, but he kept a carriage for daily rides into the countryside, where he could feel at one with nature. His gift of drawing animals to him remained, the gift he had first noticed, as he told Kerner, in his childhood. This, too, persuaded him that his hold on animal magnetism remained strong. On one occasion he visited the island of Mainau in Lake Constance where a bird fancier had successfully settled a flock of canaries. One canary perched on his boat when he sailed back to Meersburg, followed him home, and became the pet mentioned by his visitors in the final months.

Prince Dalberg, a man he had treated and converted to faith in animal magnetism, was a friend of his. Since Mesmer loved music, he felt the prince did him a return favor by inviting him to be a regular guest at weekly musicales. Doctors Johann Waldman and Johann Hirzel, friends with whom he could discuss his physical condition and the meaning of the human condition, were close to him.

Mesmer returned to the Catholic Church, from which he had lapsed for most of his life. Two priests, Schreiber and Fessler, visited him to hear him talk about nature and religion. Schreiber, cured of an illness by Mesmer, became his fervent partisan, holding that no conflict existed between animal magnetism and Catholic dogma. Kerner tells us that Mesmer seldom went to church, but the fact that he went at all was a significant change from the past.

On February 26, 1815, Mesmer felt a general sense of discomfort that caused him to remain in the house. He was not particularly worried about a touch of gout or a pain settling in his lower back because these generally afflicted him during the winter at Lake Constance. This time, however, the condition refused to respond to Hirzel's treatment. When Mesmer entertained some of his relatives on March 1, he had to keep to his bed and his speech was impaired. He sank into a coma shortly afterward, rallied, and lingered in paralysis, although conscious of those around him.

On March 5, with the end imminent, he asked if Fessler would come over and play the glass harmonica for him. The priest hurried to the bedside of the dying man, but Mesmer died quietly before he got there. Kerner says that the pet canary "neither ate nor sang again, and was soon found dead in its cage."

Hirzel performed the autopsy according to Mesmer's instructions. He found a deformation of the urinary tract that must have been extremely painful. Mesmer had borne it so stoically that even his personal physician had had no idea of the full extent of his ailment.

Meersburg insisted on a more splendid funeral than he had intended. He was no "ordinary man" to the relatives, friends, and patients who congregated at the cemetery, where Fessler delivered the eulogy, a moving tribute to a great man and a benefactor of humanity.

The members of the Berlin academy later placed a monument over his grave. It is a triangular block of marble raised on a circular pediment with three steps. The top of the block bears the image of a compass, the emblem of animal magnetism. One side has an eye within a triangle, the symbol of the Trinity, emitting rays above the name "F. A. Mesmer." A second side represents the solar system in which the orbit of the earth is inscribed with the words "born on 23 May" above the year "1734." The third side shows a star emitting rays above a torch (wisdom), a palm branch (peace), and the words at the bottom, "died on 5 March, 1815." He had died in his eighty-first year as the fortune-teller had predicted.

CHAPTER 19

From Mesmerism to Hypnotism

At the time of Mesmer's death in 1815, Mesmerism had split into three distinct varieties: scientific, occult, and political.

Political Mesmerism died in the French Revolution.

Occult Mesmerism continued, and continues, more or less adulterated, to this day. It started in Mesmer's lifetime when the Chevalier de Barbarin founded his Animist Society of Harmony, signifying by the name that he stood for an "Animist" rather than a "Fluidist" interpretation of Mesmerism. Denying that anything physical was involved, Barbarin discovered the meaning of the trance in simple faith healing, a point of view that allied him with Gassner as much as with Mesmer. He held prayer sessions, encouraged the ill to rely on divine intervention to heal them, and created a school of his own under the umbrella of Mesmerism.

Mesmer's friend and biographer, Kerner, took Mesmerism all the way into spiritualism. He was the mesmerizer of Frederike Hauffe, the Seeress of Prevorst, who, when he put her into a trance, talked animatedly with the dead. Kerner drew the inference that the trance of Mesmerism and the trance of spiritualism were identical, so that somnambulists might be expected to communicate with the phantoms of the next world. The Seeress of Prevorst conversed with them so persuasively that Kerner's book about her visions made her a celebrated figure of European occultism, the woman who inspired a succession of mediums trafficking in solace for the bereaved.

Mesmerian spiritualism flourished most abundantly in the United States, always a land hospital to strange creeds and odd cults. In 1838 Charles Poyen arrived from France and demonstrated animal magnetism around the country. Poyen made converts, one of

whom remains part of American religious history because he
influenced a major creed.

Phineas Parkhurst Quimby took to Mesmerism after hearing
Poyen, worked cures, mulled over their meaning, and became convinced that his patients were curing themselves through their mental attitudes. Abandoning animal magnetism, he pronounced illness to be a delusion inflicted by the sufferer on himself, not an objective fact to be dealt with through animal magnetism or any other
objective treatment. This idea was picked up by one of his patients,
Mrs. Mary W. Patterson, later, after her last marriage, Mrs. Mary
Baker Eddy.

The mother of Christian Science was cured of chronic backache
by Quimby, about whom she wrote fulsome tributes before and after his death. However, a spill on an icy sidewalk that wrenched her
spine more painfully than ever and a complete cure she worked on
herself by meditating on the Bible convinced her that she had
made a mistake. Repudiating Quimby and all his works, she developed a creed that she considered her creation alone, humanly
speaking, the creed above all others that makes illness a delusion
and the medical profession anathema.

Quimby had been a mesmerizer, and she feuded with practitioners of animal magnetism whom she considered materialists mis-
leading people with nonsense about an all-encompassing cosmic
fluid. They were enemies of the light, deniers of the truth of faith
healing. Hence the otherwise inexplicable ferocity with which she
attacks them. In *Science and Health,* published in 1875, the chapter
"Animal Magnetism Unmasked" states her position: "In no instance is the effect of animal magnetism, recently called hypnotism,
other than the effect of illusion. Any seeming benefit from it is pro-
portional to one's faith in esoteric magic."

Constantly seeing conspiracies against her by the Mesmerians,
she ran a series of essays in the *Christian Science Journal* under the
heading "Malicious Animal Magnetism." As her literary executor
wrote: "Animal Magnetism was her Devil." Her followers are still
writing against it. A pamphlet published in 1969 bears the title
What Is Animal Magnetism? The reader receives the answer that it is
"the sum total of evil."

Another formidable lady, Helena Petrovna Blavatsky, also at
work in the year 1875, when she founded the Theosophical Socie-

ty, gathered devotees to study and disseminate the wisdom of the East, which she claimed to have learned from the lamas of Tibet. Madame Blavatsky agreed with Mrs. Eddy that animal magnetism was "esoteric magic," only the Theosophist parted company with the Christian Scientist on its merits. Magic was her specialty.

Another difference—Madame Blavatsky went back and read Mesmer's works. They gave her a foundation for mysticism. She appropriated animal magnetism, making it the "carrier" of visions, prophecies, and clairvoyant perceptions. She was as good a "Fluidist" as Mesmer himself, insisting on the physical reality of the cosmic fluid, the cause of the aura of the individual and of his existence on the astral plane. Moreover, animal magnetism explained her theory of reincarnation—that the soul gathers a portion of the cosmic fluid and returns to earth in a new body.

Madame Blavatsky's *Isis Unveiled* has a number of flattering references to Mesmer, with this summation: "Mesmerism is the most important branch of magic; and its phenomena are the effects of the universal agent which underlies all magic and has produced in all ages so-called miracles."

Christian Science and Theosophy have survived as powerful creeds, overshadowing lesser movements such as the New Thought of Horatio W. Dresser, whose purpose it was to raise healing "to the spiritual level," and the doctrine of omnipotent autosuggestion preached by Émile Coué, whose formula for healthful, happy living was the repeated intonation of the daring assertion "Day by day, in every way, I am getting better and better." Dresser and Coué were both belated followers of Mesmer's followers. Since their time, New Thought has shown signs of aging, and Coué's system has deteriorated. Their successors in the "mind over matter" tradition can scarcely be called Mesmerian, although echoes of Mesmer can sometimes be heard in phrases like "magnetic spiritualism." The inspiration of the gurus of Transcendental Meditation comes from elsewhere.

Scientific Mesmerism is in the true tradition of Mesmer, the line of straight descent from his discoveries in abnormal psychology and therapeutic psychiatry. His genuine legacy, which he would not have admitted for one moment, was the problem of preserving Mesmerism while getting rid of animal magnetism.

The process began within his lifetime when, ignoring his protests that his discoveries belonged to physics, some Mesmerians took the first steps toward the psychological explanation that ultimately prevailed. After that, it was a matter of moving on to a more'precise understanding of what occurred during the Mesmerian trance.

The Mesmerian crisis and the Mesmerian séance were parts of the original apparatus dismantled, during the height of Mesmer's career, by Puységur, who achieved Mesmer's results without them. The baquet and the wand gravitated into the hands of wizards and charlatans and remained there. Deslon stressed the place of imagination more than Mesmer did. Puységur went further, putting imagination in the forefront and calling on the subject to bring his mind, volition, and emotions into play according to the admonition "Believe and Will."

Theories of Mesmerism proliferated so rapidly that, as early as 1813, before Mesmer's death, J. P. F. Deleuze was able to publish a *Critical History of Animal Magnetism*. Deleuze writes from the standpoint of a Fluidist, but a Fluidist with a difference since he denies Mesmer's universal fluid. Forget the cosmic tides swirling around in great gusts from the stars to the earth. The fluid in question is personal. Deleuze found that "most somnambulists see a luminous and brilliant fluid enveloping the magnetizer and flowing with greatest force from his head and his hands." The sight mesmerizes them.

The writer appears to be talking about something comparable to the aura of the occultists. In any case, it is a physical reality, and Deleuze invokes it to explain one phenomenon he described fully before anyone else—posthypnotic suggestion. The fluid, entering the nervous system during the Mesmerian trance, takes "impressions" and "stores" them such that the subject can record commands while in this artificial sleep and act upon them, without realizing what he is doing, after awakening.

Alexandre Bertrand in his *Treatise on Somnambulism* (1823) made what would prove to be a cardinal point: "If, for any reason whatever, somnambulists have the will to remember anything, they never fail to remember it." This raises the vexed question of the extent to which the mesmerizer can control the volitional life of the subject. Bertrand would have smiled at the total control of Trilby by Svengali in George du Maurier's novel. Today Bertrand seems justified, although no precise line can be drawn beyond which the mesmerizer's power cannot go. The tales of mesmerized people committing horrible crimes at the prompting of criminals are tales, and nothing more—the staple of the Gothic mystery to which they should be restricted.

Bertrand is notable in the annals of Mesmerism because he started as a Fluidist, came to doubt the existence of the fluid, and continued as an Animist. His personal intellectual history epitomizes the history of Mesmerism.

The first man who seems like our contemporary in this progression is the Abbé Faria, a Portuguese priest working in Paris, whose chief work, *On the Cause of Lucid Sleep* (1819), could almost have been written today. Faria clears away all the lumber left by Mesmer—animal magnetism, the baquet, the séance. "I have," he says, "replaced the phrase 'animal magnetism' with the word 'concentration.'" This means that a person can be mesmerized when his attention is concentrated on the single idea of going to sleep at the mesmerizer's command. The state that supervenes is "lucid sleep" in Faria's language, "somnambulism" in Puységur's.

Faria's method of inducing the state required no stage props. He would have his subject sit down in a comfortable position. Then he would tell him to lean back, relax, close his eyes, clear his mind of extraneous ideas, and concentrate on sleep. This involved confidence on the part of the subject, Mesmer's rapport. With a willing subject, the abbé would issue the final command "Sleep, sleep." The individual would drop off into a lucid sleep.

Faria developed techniques for dealing with difficult subjects, those who could not relax and follow orders. Sometimes he would spread his fingers and move them close to the face of the subject, forcing him to shift the focus of his eyes to follow the movement, thus capturing his attention and maneuvering him into concentrating on the commands given to him.

The cases described in this book include hypnotic paralysis and blindness, induced hallucinations and posthypnotic suggestion. Faria declares that most people cannot be induced into lucid sleep, a condition he attributes to their obstinate refusal to cooperate rather than to Mesmer's countervailing force impeding the flow of animal magnetism. He was wrong about the fact, right about the interpretation. Most people can be put into a trance. Those who cannot are unwilling.

That Faria's analyses and techniques are now fundamental hardly needs to be said. They failed to revolutionize Mesmerism when the book came out because it fell stillborn from the press. Faria had to wait until the end of the nineteenth century for his discoveries to be discovered and estimated at their true worth.

Millions of people have heard of the abbé without knowing it. He is the Abbé Faria of *The Count of Monte Cristo,* the prisoner of the Château d'If who spent years tunneling inch by inch through the wall of his cell only to arrive, not in the open air, but in another cell, that of Edmond Dantes. Dumas fastened on Faria's reputation for bizarre beliefs and behavior and turned him into one of the enduring characters of the picaresque novel.

Since Faria did not give Mesmerism a permanent bent toward psychology over physics, the debates between Fluidists and Animists continued. The subject became ever more complicated. Fluids of different types were introduced to explain the endless list of authentic cures. Nonphysical causes, from Providence to imitation, were bandied about.

Paris was the scene of most of the advances in Mesmerism until 1837, when Baron Dupotet brought a Fluidist interpretation to London and created a nine days' wonder with his displays of induced somnambulism. Dupotet's technique impressed John Elliotson of the London University Hospital, who adopted it with so much conviction and success that the authorities forced him into the dilemma of giving up either Mesmerism or his professorship. He gave up his professorship. Elliotson was less significant for theory than for practice. He promoted animal magnetism in his magazine *The Zoist: A Journal of Cerebral Physiology and Mesmerism* (1843–56). He used Mesmerism to anesthetize patients before operating, one safe painless method before the discovery of chloroform. He was the last of the great Fluidists of scientific Mesmerism.

The man who changed everything was James Braid of Manchester, who replaced "Mesmerism" with "hypnotism" in the lexicon of psychology. Coined from the Greek word for "sleep," Braid's neologism filled a language gap so well that it became the standard word for the scientific methods of inducing artificial somnambulism or lucid sleep. All the cognates come from the same root— "hypnosis," "hypnotist," "hypnotize," "hypnotic." The word "mesmerize" and its cognates are still in use referring to something broader and not so technical: trancelike semiparalysis caused by astonishment or fear.

Turning to theory, Braid rejected Fluidism in his *Neurypnology: or, the Rationale of Nervous Sleep, considered in Relation with Animal Magnetism* (1843):

> It will be observed, for reasons adduced, I have now entirely separated Hypnotism from Animal Magnetism. I considered it to be merely a simple, speedy, and certain mode of throwing the nervous system into a new condition, which may be rendered eminently available in the cure of certain disorders. I trust, therefore, it may be investigated quite independently of any bias, either for or against the subject, as connected with mesmerism.

Braid established the fact that the fundamental cause of hypnotism is subjective rather than objective, psychological rather than physical, the whole point being to make the subject will to do what the hypnotist wants him to do. That cause is suggestion. The hypnotist offers a suggestion that the subject adopts and obeys as a motive for action. Hypnotist and subject may be one and the same person, for autosuggestion and self-hypnosis are realities. As for technique, Braid assimilates Faria's major point about concentration—the subject must clear his mind of everything else and bring it to a focus on the single concept of sleep. Faria's success with his hand movements is explained by fatigue of the eye muscles causing the lids to close. Summing up:

> In time, from a careful analysis of the whole of my experiments, which have been very numerous, I have been led to the following conclusion—that it is a law in the animal economy, that by a continued fixation of the mental and visual eye, on any object which is not itself of an exciting nature, with absolute repose of body, and general quietude, they become wearied; and, provided the patients rather favour than resist the feeling of stupor of which they will soon experience the tendency to creep upon them, during such experiments a state of somnolency is induced, accompanied with that condition of the brain and nervous system generally, which renders the patient liable to be affected, according to the mode of manipulating, so as to exhibit the hypnotic phenomena. As the experiment succeeds with the blind, I consider it not so much the optic as the sentient, motor and sympathetic nerves, and the mind, through which the impression is made.

On Braid's analysis, the mind becomes fatigued by the effort to concentrate on one idea; there is a corresponding physiological fatigue in the effort to concentrate on one object; and the combination makes the subject vulnerable to suggestion and the activity of his imagination as directed. Braid compares normal sleep to Faria's lucid sleep, pointing out that just as concentration on one subject causes ordinary dreams, so does it cause the phenomena of artificial somnambulism.

Correct thus far, Braid failed to extract pure hypnotism from its cocoon of adventitious and wrong ideas because he accepted the phrenology of his period. The nineteenth century was dogged by the pseudoscience of Franz Joseph Gall and Johann Kaspar Spurzheim, according to which an individual's character and abilities can be inferred from the "bumps" on his skull. Braid, believing there was something in this, thought he could arouse ideas or emotions of a specific kind by stroking the areas of the head associated with them, making the subject feel anger, for example, by stimulating the area indicating the locus of this passion in the brain. Braid practiced phreno-hypnotism, a blind alley soon recognized to be such by his more knowledgeable readers.

Briad's ideas crossed the Channel into France, where they were picked up, winnowed, and more closely defined by a number of adept hypnotists of whom Ambroise Auguste Liébault was the leader. Liébault started from the fact that the artificial sleep induced by hypnosis is of the same nature as ordinary sleep, from which it follows that hypnotized subjects do not enjoy the preternatural powers ascribed to them by Mesmer, Puységur, and the line of mystical Mesmerians—no clairvoyance, mental telepathy, or ability to see through opaque objects and, of course, no escaping from time into the "universal now" of the cosmos.

Liébault's practice supported his theory. All his experiments with the occult came out negative. He gave his subjects orders to see visions and predict the future, which none of them obeyed. They failed at mental telepathy. This being demonstrated, Liébault refined his notions of what hypnotism actually was. Achieving a higher percentage of successes than anyone before him, he carefully tabulated the phenomena of hypnotic and posthypnotic suggestion and concluded: "The characteristics of active somnambulism are what the hypnotist makes them by mobilizing the nervous energy accumulated as a usable power in the mind through suggested ideas."

Liébault made suggestion unequivocally the key to hypnotism. The subject's mind is unable to operate by itself but remains dominated by the last suggestion from the hypnotist. This explains such things as catalepsy and paralysis. If he is told that he cannot move his arm, then he cannot move it because the thought of moving it does not enter his mind. The hypnotist must give him the thought, doing for him what his mind would do if he were awake.

Modern hypnotism was born with this analysis. Liébault's talented pupil Hippolyte Bernheim brought the analysis to its full development. They were the leaders of the Nancy school of hypnosis, the rival of which was the Salpêtrière school led by Jean Martin Charcot.

The name of the latter school came from Charcot's association with the Salpêtrière Hospital in Paris. The main point at issue between the two schools was the normality or abnormality of the hypnotic state.

Charcot was a specialist in hysteria who widened the scope of this neurosis to include many forms of abnormal behavior, of which he considered hypnosis to be one. It was "an artifically caused morbid condition" proceeding by three stages according to his *Lessons on Illnesses of the Nervous System* (1880–83). First there was lethargy, the stage of sleep; then there was catalepsy, the stage of bodily rigidity; and finally there was somnambulism, the stage of complete surrender to suggestibility. (The first two steps were sometimes transposed.) Charcot, comparing the conditions of hypnosis with those of hysteria, thought there could be no doubt of the truth. The two were allied.

Consequently, only people showing hysterical symptoms, or at least affected by incipient hysteria, could be hypnotized. This meant a minority of human beings, the whole mass of nonhysterical human beings being ruled out. Guided by his theory, Charcot found what he looked for. His subjects who submitted to hypnosis were victims of hysteria. Since he treated hysteria as a basically physiological problem, he did the same with hypnotism, a department of abnormal psychology in his system.

Bernheim, basing himself on Liébault's work and his own experience, denied Charcot's premises and therefore his conclusions. Psy-

chology rather than physiology was the key to hypnosis for Bernheim, a distinction of theory that allows us to draw up a rough analogy—Bernheim is to Charcot as Puységur is to Mesmer.

Bernheim's book *Suggestive Therapeutics: A Treatise on the Nature
and Uses of Hypnotism* (1888) holds its place as the most recent of the
masterworks on the subject. Not only did the author refute Charcot and place the psychological interpretation of hypnotism beyond
question, proving at the same time that it belonged to normal psychology, but he surrounded his thesis with a wealth of practical
data drawn from thousands of cases of hypnosis. One paragraph
from his preface assembles the essential ideas:

> No: hypnotic sleep is not a pathological sleep. The hypnotic condi-
> tion is not a neurosis, analogous to hysteria. No doubt, manifestations
> of hysteria may be created in hypnotized subjects; a real hypnotic neu-
> rosis may be developed which will be repeated each time sleep is in-
> duced. But these manifestations are not due to the hypnosis—they are
> due to the operator's suggestion, or sometimes to the autosuggestion
> of a particularly impressible subject whose imagination, impregnated
> with the ruling idea of magnetism, creates these functional disorders
> which can always be restrained by a quieting suggestion. The pretend-
> ed physical phenomena of the hypnosis are only psychical phenome-
> na. Catalepsy, transfer, contracture, etc., are the effects of suggestion.
> To prove that the very great majority of subjects are susceptible to
> suggestion is to eliminate the idea of a neurosis. At least it is not an ad-
> mission that the neurosis is universal, that the word hysteria is a syno-
> nym for any nervous impressionability whatever. For, as we all have
> nervous tissues, and as it is a property of such tissues to be impression-
> able, we should all be hysterical.

Bernheim shows how this understanding of hypnosis makes
sense of all the authentic medical cures recorded by the Mesmerists
from Mesmer onward. He treats extensively of posthypnotic
suggestion, remarking on this oddity: A subject after being wak-
ened cannot be hypnotized again if told while in hypnosis that such
will be the case. He makes the point that while most people are susceptible to hypnosis, only a minority can be induced into deep hypnosis or artificial somnambulism. He notes the dangers attending
frequent hypnotization such as the habit of falling into hallucina-

tions (one of the arguments used back in 1784 by the commissioners investigating Deslon) and offers a warning that hypnotists should be kept under surveillance to be sure all proper precautions are being observed (Deslon's answer to the commissioners).

Bernheim's book marks the consummation of the psychological interpretation descending from Faria through Braid and Liébault. The controversy between Nancy and Paris continued with some bitterness and pettiness, but the superiority of the Nancy school emerged more clearly all the time. Bernheim's proof appeared cogent to most of the hypnotists who tested his ideas in the consulting room and the hospital. Charcot's three stages dropped out of the debate, and a diminishing number of specialists identified hypnosis with hysteria, even at the Salpêtrière, where to defend Charcot was virtually an article of faith.

Hypnosis understood as suggestion compelled medical psychologists to investigate the human psyche in an entirely new manner. Posthypnotic phenomena—amnesia, paralysis, blindness—indicated that personality was immensely more complex than had ever been guessed before. An individual might appear to be one person while hypnotized and another while awake, each person being unaware of the other and acting on different ideas and motives. The structure of the mind and the dynamics of behavior needed rethinking.

Pierre Janet analyzed dissociation in his *Mental State of Hystericals* (1892), meaning by this a condition in which an aggregate of ideas clusters around one dominating idea, this aggregate being dissociated from the rest of the contents of the individual's mind and capable of motivating him as an independent cause. Dissociation proved to be often subconscious (Janet's word) when it would give rise to conscious maladjustments baffling to the victim. Janet used hypnosis to uncover such psychodynamic tensions, to understand them, and to cure them.

In America, Morton Prince developed the notion of multiple personality. The case that forced him to accept its reality was a woman with no less than four personalities vying for possession of her body. The account in his *Dissociation of Personality* (1906) of how he hypnotized and treated this patient advanced the study of abnormal psychology and the writing of weird psychological thrillers about multiple personality (although Robert Louis Stevenson, with an artist's insight, had beaten him into the field with *Dr. Jekyll and Mr. Hyde*).

Sigmund Freud, a pupil of both Charcot and Bernheim and the translator of *Suggestive Therapeutics* into German, began with hypnosis, which he pursued with his colleague Joseph Breuer. When he switched to free association as a better instrument for probing the unconscious and when he gave psychoanalysis the impetus to dominate the study of personality for a generation, he caused a slackening of interest in hypnosis. There is a regression back to hypnosis, now that psychoanalysis has been shown to be fallible. One of the recent novelties in therapeutic psychiatry is a combination of Mesmer and Freud in the science of hypnoanalysis.

What actually occurs in hypnosis remains a vexed question to which many answers have been given. Why does the subject submit? Is the explanation physiological—a breakdown of communication along the nerves, say, or a suspension of activity in the cerebral lobes of the brain? Is it psychological—a form of masochism, self-assertion, sexual gratification or self-fulfillment? All these might be true to some degree, varying as individuals vary. No single key has been found that will unlock the door and reveal the truth.

The above brief history of an idea, in which so many partial views and connecting links have perforce been left out, shows how Mesmerism was gradually clarified by a succession of great psychologists and psychiatrists who brought it to the condition in which we see it today. Of Mesmer's original system, the following can and must be said:

1. Animal magnetism is a myth. There is no such cosmic fluid as Mesmer imagined.

2. Animal magnets are therefore a myth.

3. Nothing physical passes from hypnotist to subject.

4. The Mesmerian crisis is a myth. No physical action-reaction takes place in the nervous system, at least in Mesmer's sense.

5. The Mesmerian trance is a reality.

6. The trance can be handled scientifically. Mesmer was wrong in his scientific theory, but he made it possible for scientists to take the trance away from the occultists.

Mesmer's tragedy was that he had the right facts and the wrong theory. If he had not had the theory of animal magnetism, he might have realized that his cures were psychological, and he might have carried the Western mind forward into psychosomatic medicine at a single bound. On the other hand, if it had not been for his theory, he might never have effected his remarkable cures, investigated their meaning so pertinaciously, or persuaded others to join him in a search for the explanation. Scientific hypnosis would not have developed when it did except for him.

His impress is clear on psychiatry, psychosomatic medicine, personality studies, and group therapy. He was the Columbus of modern psychology, which is enough of an achievement for any explorer.

Chapter 20

A Note on Poe and Mesmerism

If to the three varieties of Mesmerism, scientific, occult, and political, we were to add a fourth, it would be literary Mesmerism.

The work of Mesmer and his followers contributed to the decline of the Augustan Age and the birth of the Romantic movement. When the classical rules and lofty certitudes of Voltaire and Dr. Johnson gave way to the *Sturm und Drang,* the Storm and Stress, of Byron, Leopardi, Victor Hugo, and the young Goethe, the Mesmeric trance and its mysteries contributed to this basic shift in the mental and moral climate of the West. Mesmerism coalesced with the other elements of Romanticism—excessive individualism, passionate protest, uncanny fantasy, Gothic horror, and sentimental belief in nature.

Writers became interested in the trance as such during the middle of the nineteenth century when a second generation of mesmerizers was practicing in Europe and America. When John Elliotson, the focus of a scandal in the medical profession, refused to back away from Mesmerism, writers were among those who asked what he was doing that he made his colleagues so angry. Elliotson defended Mesmer publicly against the profession: "He employed means without knowing more than the fact of their power; so do you." He described a mysterious influence working through human beings, and that description was enough to stir the literary imagination.

Balzac in France and Tieck in Germany exploited the trance, but English letters were most prolific in literary Mesmerism. Bulwer-Lytton, novelist and occultist, knew enough to differentiate between Mesmer and Puységur in *A Strange Story.* Harriet Martineau, cured of a troubling illness, published her appreciative *Letters on*

Mesmerism. Thackeray, an accumulator of strange ideas and Gothic fancies, dedicated *Pendennis* to Elliotson. Du Maurier wrote *Trilby.*

During the year before their marriage in 1846, Elizabeth Barrett and Robert Browning put a dozen or more references to Mesmerism into their letters, out of interest in the phenomenon and hope that it might be a cure for her physical debility. He was of the opinion that it could succeed where her doctors had failed. She recoiled from the idea because of "something ghastly and repelling to me in the thought of Dr. Elliotson's great boney fingers seeming to 'touch the stops' of a whole soul's harmonies—as in phreno-magnetism."

On the other hand, she kept coming back to Mesmerism as to something with a repellent fascination. In her poem *Aurora Leigh,* she mentions Karl von Reichenbach, the German mesmerizer, who said he had identified an "odylic force" or "Mesmeric influence" emanating from people and things and visible to somnambulists, and she has a line in the same poem about "Mr. Strangways, the Leeds Mesmerist." In 1846 she noted a "horrible Mesmeric experience" she had just read about. It was by an American, Edgar Allan Poe.

The work referred to was "The Facts in the Case of M. Valdemar," Poe's third tale exploiting Mesmerism. Poe had a good grasp of the subject. He was twenty-nine when Charles Poyen came to America to demonstrate animal magnetism. He knew Andrew Jackson Davis, the Poughkeepsie Seer, who was inspired by Stanley Grimes, a pupil of Poyen. He reviewed William Newnham's *Human Magnetism* for the *Broadway Journal* when he was its editor. He read Chauncey Hare Townshend's *Facts in Mesmerism,* which went through several editions in London and New York.

Poe learned most of his Mesmerism from Townshend's book. It crossed the Atlantic with the prestige of an author "late of Trinity Hall, Cambridge." The introductory epistle was addressed to John Elliotson. The theory defended was animal magnetism in Mesmer's sense, supported by dozens of cases Townshend had witnessed illustrating action-at-a-distance, artificial somnambulism, heightened sensory awareness, and occult powers. Poe admired Townshend's description and analysis. Commenting on Newnham, he wrote: "Most especially do I disagree with the author of this book in his (implied) disparagement of the work of Chauncey Hare Townshend—a work to be valued properly only in a day to come."

Poe fastened on Townshend's contention that there exists around us an elastic fluid that can be stirred by the human will in such a way as to influence the nervous system of another human being and dominate his ideas, volitions, and emotions. Townshend claimed that this act turned the second party into a "sleep-waker," Elliotson's word for Puységur's "somnambulist," signifying a condition between sleep and waking that veers toward one or the other depending on the intensity of the trance. Townshend stresses the occult implications of this premise, especially thought transference over long distances and the ability of the sleep-waker to perform feats of extrasensory perception.

Poe believed what he read in Townshend, an unimportant point compared to his perception of its artistic usefulness. Mesmerism, will dominating will, thought transference, sleep-waking, occult knowledge—these moved his imagination and made him feel that they could be the ingredients of popular literature. His three short stories resulted.

In "A Tale of the Ragged Mountains," Poe refers explicitly to Mesmer and to Mesmerian rapport between hypnotist and subject, in this case between Dr. Templeton and Augustus Bedloe. The relationship is an adaptation of cases Poe found in Townshend:

> At the first attempt to induce the magnetic somnolency, the mesmerist entirely failed. In the fifth or sixth, he succeeded very partially, and after long-continued effort. Only at the twelfth was the triumph complete. After this the will of the patient succumbed rapidly to that of the physician, so that, when I first became acquainted with the two, sleep was brought about almost instantaneously by the mere volition of the operator, even when the invalid was unaware of his presence.

Having established the Templeton-Bedloe rapport, the narrator describes how Bedloe went for a walk in the woods, experienced a series of extraordinary hallucinations of violent events in an Oriental city, and returned to recount his experience. The explanation is that Bedloe's hallucinations were caused by thought transference by way of animal magnetism, Templeton being engaged at the same time in writing up an episode that had taken place in Benares long ago. Metempsychosis as well as Mesmerism is involved in the entire explanation, but the theory of animal magnetism is fundamental.

Poe is more strictly Mesmerian in "Mesmeric Revelation," where he begins with the challenging statement:

> Whatever doubt may still envelop the rationale of Mesmerism, its startling *facts* are now almost universally admitted. Of these latter, those who doubt, are your mere doubters by profession—an unprofitable and disreputable tribe. There can be no more absolute waste of time that the attempt to *prove*, at the present day, that man, by mere exercise of will, can so impress his fellow, as to cast him into an abnormal condition, in which the phenomena resemble very closely those of *death*, or at least resemble them more nearly than they do any other normal condition within our cognizance; that, while in this state, the person so impressed employs only with effort, and then feebly, the external organs of sense, yet perceives, with keenly refined perception, and through channels supposed to be unknown, matters beyond the scope of the physical organs; that, moreover, his intellectual faculties are wonderfully exalted and invigorated; that his sympathies with the person so impressing him are profound; and, finally, that his susceptibility to the impression increases with its frequency, while, in the same proportion, the peculiar phenomena elicited are more extended and more *pronounced*.

The story that follows is about a subject, Vankirk, using the preternatural powers of the sleep-waking state to penetrate the mysteries of matter, motion, and their laws. His mind is able to understand things unsolvable when he is awake and using his senses as the channels of information and experience. Thus, he expatiates, on the basis of mental perceptions alone, about the gradation of matter from the coarsest to the most rarefied, an ultimate, indivisible matter that he perceives to be God. This cosmology is gradually revealed in a rational conversation about ultimate things. Part of the dialogue resembles the source in Townshend when the mesmerizer questions the somnambulist:

Townshend:
Can the soul ever die?
Certainly not. It is the soul which is the only true existence, and which gives existence to all we apprehend.
Whence came the soul?
From God, who by his thoughts created the universe.
Is there a future punishment for evil-doers?

Undoubtedly, a great one.
In what will it consist?
In seeing themselves as they are, and God as he is.

Poe:
Does the idea of death afflict you?
No—no!
Are you pleased with the prospect?
If I were awake I should like to die, but now it is no matter. The mesmeric condition is so near to death as to content me.
I wish you would explain yourself, Mr. Vankirk.
I am willing to do so, but it requires more effort than I feel able to make. You do not question me properly.
What then shall I ask?
You must begin at the beginning.
The beginning! But where is the beginning?
You know that the beginning is GOD.

At the end of Poe's story, the mesmerizer wakens the subject only to see him die, gently, peacefully, in a manner befitting the conclusion of the story.

Quite different is "The Facts in the Case of M. Valdemar," a macabre tale in which Poe relates the sleep-waking state to death itself. He may have been influenced by Townshend's account of Signor Valdrighi, something hinted at in the similarity of the names. The Valdrighi case concerned the immensely heightened sensory awareness of a dying man:

> The same physician related to me the following occurrence: Visiting a gentleman who had an abscess, he found that the patient had not many hours to live; this, however, he did not tell him, but answered his inquiries about himself as encouragingly as he could. Taking his leave, he shut the door of the sick chamber, and, passing through two other rooms, the doors of which he also carefully shut, entered an apartment where some friends of the patient were assembled. To those he said, speaking all the time in that low and cautious tone which every one, in a house where illness is, unconsciously adopts, "The Signor Valdrighi" (that was the name of the invalid) "is much worse. He cannot possibly survive till morning." Scarcely had he uttered these words when the patient's bell was heard to ring violently, and, soon after, a servant summoned the doctor back into his presence. "Why did you deceive me?" exclaimed the dying man; "I heard every word you

said just now in the farther apartment." Of this extraordinary assertion he immediately gave proof by repeating the exact expressions he
had made use of.

It has also been said that Poe based his story partly on the final
scene in Justinus Kerner's *Seeress of Prevorst,* a book translated into
English in the same year (1845) that Poe wrote "Valdemar." The
Kerner passage runs thus:

> She often called loudly for me, though I was absent at the time; and
> once, when she appeared dead, some one having uttered my name,
> she started into life again, and seemed unable to die—the magnetic re-
> lation between us being not yet broken. She was, indeed, susceptible to
> magnetic influences to the last; for when she was already cold, and her
> jaws stiff, her mother having made three passes over her face, she lift-
> ed her eyelids and moved her lips. At ten o'clock, her sister saw a tall
> bright form enter the chamber, and at the same instant, the dying
> woman uttered a loud cry of joy; her spirit seemed then to be set free.
> After a short interval, her soul also departed, leaving behind it a total-
> ly irrecognizable husk—not a single trace of her former features re-
> maining.

If Poe did borrow from Townshend and Kerner, he transmuted
their leaden paragraphs into golden prose when he wrote his short
story, the effect of which differs not only in degree but in kind from
the Valdrighi-Seeress vignettes. Poe's imagination takes command
of his material, and he creates an artistic unity far beyond the ability of his sources. His narrator proposes an ultimate experience
with the trance;

> My attention, for the last three years, had been repeatedly drawn to
> the subject of Mesmerism and about nine months ago, it occurred to
> me, quite suddenly, that in the series of experiments made hitherto,
> there had been a very remarkable and most unaccountable omis-
> sion:—no person had as yet been mesmerized *in articulo mortis.* It re-
> mained to be seen, first, whether, in such condition, there existed in
> the patient any susceptibility to the magnetic influence; secondly,
> whether, if any existed, it was impaired or increased by the condition;
> thirdly, to what extent, or for how long a period, the encroachments
> of Death might be arrested by the process.

Valdemar is the subject, a dying man whom the narrator mesmerizes just before the end, arresting his condition and giving him a lease, not on life precisely, but on an intermediate condition between life and death. What follows is a description of the subject hovering uncannily over the grave, showing ever more clearly the attributes of a corpse, yet able to think about his condition and to comment on it. He unnerves the observers at his bedside by exclaiming: "Yes;—no;—I *have been* sleeping—and now—now—*I am dead!*" Finally he cries out: "For God's sake!—quick!—quick!—put me to sleep—or, quick!—waken me!—quick!—*I say to you that I am dead!*"

The narrator decides to make the attempt to snatch him back from the grave by wakening him:

> As I rapidly made the mesmeric passes, amid ejaculations of "dead! dead!" absolutely bursting from the tongue and not from the lips of the sufferer, his whole frame at once—within the space of a single minute, or less, shrunk—crumbled—absolutely *rotted* away beneath my hands. Upon the bed, before that whole company, there lay a nearly liquid mass of loathsome—of detestable putrescence.

Neither Townshend nor Kerner gave Poe that ending! His imagination created it out of nothing, and so powerfully that he received letters from readers who found the verisimilitude convincing. They thought he was describing a real event. Elizabeth Barrett, writing to Robert Browning of this "horrible Mesmeric experience," could not make up her mind whether it was fact or fiction. A Bostonian reported:

> Your account of M. Valdemar's case has been universally copied in this city, and has created a very great sensation. It requires from me no apology in stating, that I have not the least doubt of the *possibility* of such a phenomenon, for I did actually restore to active animation a person who died from excessive drinking of ardent spirits.

Poe was amused and gratified that his tale had this effect on his audience.

He was the greatest writer to exploit Mesmerism in a direct way, using the form of the hypnotist-subject relationship employed by practicing mesmerizers. His three short stories on the theme are skillfully varied in typical Poe fashion. Just as the narrators of "The Black Cat" and "The Tell-Tale Heart" are homicidal maniacs who could never be confused with one another, just so are his three mesmerized subjects—Bedloe, Vankirk, Valdemar—quite different personalities. Bedloe is a mental telepathist sensitive to gorgeous visions, Vankirk a preternaturally enlightened philosopher, Valdemar a mere voice in the darkness.

What would Mesmer have thought if he had read Poe's tales? He could have accepted the thought transfer of the first, the occult wisdom of the second. One guesses that, like Elizabeth Barrett Browning, he would have shuddered at the third.

Appendix

A French Burlesque of Mesmerism

During the *annus mirabilis* of 1784 when Mesmer reached the summit of his success as a practitioner of animal magnetism, when his Society of Harmony flourished under his direction, when Mesmerism was condemned by two royal commissions, when all Paris was talking about him in fervent, patronizing, or hostile terms, when he was the subject of eulogies and tirades, of prayers and lampoons—in that same year the troupe at the Théâtre Italien performed *Modern Doctors* and *The Baquet of Health*. These two burlesques were a commentary on current events in the idiom of the Paris stage, similar in inspiration to *Bastien et Bastienne,* the popular parody of Rousseau's all-too-serious pastoral romance, *Le Devin du village.*

Mesmer was but one of those in the public eye who suffered from the facile pens of Pierre Yves Barré and Jean Baptiste Radet, coauthors who wrote rapidly enough to put an incident on the boards before it lost its immediacy. As soon as one of their comedies slowed down because their patrons were tired of the subject, they were ready with another, and they compiled a long list of successes, most of which are impossible to revive, being too dependent for their vitality on long-dead issues buried in the back files of eighteenth-century publications. The fame of Barré and Radet has been as ephemeral as their plays, but in 1784 they were fashionable literary men whose latest work always arrived amid excitement and anticipation.

They made a great success with whatever happened to be the talk of the town, and in 1784 that was Mesmerism, about which they quickly worked up *Modern Doctors* and *The Baquet of Health,* the former a substantial comedy, the latter an epilogue, short, boisterous, intended to keep the audience in an uproar of laughter and applause. The main drama having been presented, the troupe had a romp with *The Baquet of Health,* which is filled with farcical scenes interspersed with absurd doggerel, all presented in the framework of a Mesmerian séance. One must imagine the patients around the baquet chanting in the manner of a chorus from Aristophanes.

The main character, representing Mesmer, is "Cassandre," named for the Greek prophetess whose fate it was to tell the truth and never to be believed. Deslon is "The Doctor," playing the main supporting role. The assistant "Pierrot" is a stock character from French farce, a buffoon in a baggy costume with his face painted white. To call one character simply "A Gascon" is to say that he is a fiery individual from Gascony, the province of D'Artagnan in *The Three Musketeers.*

Barré and Radet could take for granted some understanding of such stage directions as "a baquet" and "crisis room." Thus the audience knew part of what was to come before the curtain rose on opening night, November 27, 1784.

To recapture the feelings of that audience is impossible. Mesmerism was a scandal recently condemned, the subject of an ongoing quarrel, so that Parisians could catch topical references that escape us. The slang and doggerel cannot be translated. Still, something comes across in a rendering into English, and the following adaptation will give the reader some idea of what Mesmer had to endure.

The Baquet of Health

Dramatis Personae

CASSANDRE, a Mesmerian physician   A GASCON, a patient
THE DOCTOR, his confederate   A LAWYER, a patient
PIERROT, his assistant   A MALE PATIENT
AGLAE, a curious woman   A FEMALE PATIENT
HORTENSE, a young married woman   CHORUS OF PATIENTS

The curtain rises on a large room. At the rear is a door with the legend over it: CRISIS ROOM. At the front of the stage, a cuckoo clock stands at one side and a glass harmonica at the other. In the center of the stage there is a baquet surrounded by patients. Pierrot is in attendance.

Scene One

A MAN'S VOICE:

> Let us hold hands so that we will be joined together. Be thankful to destiny for the ties that bind us. While unbelief reigns in the two hemispheres, let us here at the baquet of health, laugh at ordinary doctors.

A WOMAN'S VOICE:

> No more black clothes and dusty wigs for us! Here the doctors are gallant and the female patients charming. A voice soft and musical, a soothing stroke with a practiced hand—these dispel insensitivity and bring us wisdom.

A MAN'S VOICE:

> In vain discredited common sense and uncouth reason try to defeat the wise with vain arguments. One day the Faculty of Medicine, silenced and its torch extinguished, will seek for light around the baquet of health.

ANOTHER VOICE:

> Where is the great man who should be here to give us

his aid? His delay makes us fret and anxiety grips us.
Soon, soon, very soon, hastening hither, he will come
to treat us. He will not let us perish.

CHORUS OF PATIENTS:

Soon, soon, very soon, hastening hither he will come
to treat us. He will not let us perish.

Scene Two

The same with Cassandre and the Doctor.

FIRST VOICE:

Behold him!

SECOND VOICE:

Behold him!

THIRD VOICE:

Behold him!

FOURTH VOICE:

Behold him!

CHORUS OF PATIENTS:

Behold him, the true model of science and zeal!

THE DOCTOR:

And his confederate—me.

PIERROT:

And his assistant—me.

A VOICE:

This event should be faithfully recorded. Humanity
will read it a thousand years hence. And in reading it,
each one will say—"Behold the true model of science
and zeal, the true doctor, behold him!"

CHORUS OF PATIENTS:

Behold him, the true model of science and zeal, the
true doctor, behold him!

CASSANDRE *(sotto voce)*:

And behold the dupes!

*The patients leave the baquet and force money on Cassandre, Pierrot
and the Doctor, who feign unwillingness but accept it.)*

CASSANDRE *(to a patient)*:

Ah, Monsieur, I am glad to see you again, It has been

a long time. Gentlemen, please have a little patience.
Do not cry so loudly.

PATIENTS *(in unison):*

Ah, already your concern makes your patients feel
better.

CASSANDRE:

Now then, let each one return to his place around the
baquet. Go, each one in his turn.

Scene Three

The same with Aglae and Hortense.

AGLAE:

As you can see, my dear Cassandre, I have kept my
word.

CASSANDRE:

You do me a great honor, sweet lady.

AGLAE:

I believe you will be happy to display your science.
This is why I have brought Hortense, for whom I will
answer as for myself. My gratitude compelled me to
do what I promised.

THE DOCTOR:

When one is pleased, it is common to wish to share
the pleasure with one's friend.

THE PATIENTS *(in unison):*

But, Doctor, it is my turn—

THE DOCTOR:

One moment, gentlemen, one moment!

HORTENSE:

Good heavens! What an infernal noise!

AGLAE:

That's nothing. You should see the crisis. You have
no idea of the things they do then.

CASSANDRE *(to the patients):*

Control your impatience. It is inevitable, let me be
frank, that when I see Beauty, I attend to it first.

HORTENSE:

Well, isn't he gallant!

AGLAE:
>As I told you, he's charming!

HORTENSE *(to Cassandre)*:
>Monsieur, are all these people mad?

AGLAE:
>Of course!

CASSANDRE:
>Well, they're not too bright.

THE DOCTOR:
>Luckily for us.

HORTENSE:
>What's wrong with them?

CASSANDRE:
>Each one to his own complaint.

THE DOCTOR:
>This one suffers from shortness of breath.

CASSANDRE:
>That one from an irritation. The twitching of his nose bothers him.

THE DOCTOR:
>Some have obstructions and fluxions—

PIERROT:
>Which, refracted, fill their heads with hallucinations.

AGLAE *(to one patient)*:
>Madame, how long have you taken this treatment?

PATIENT:
>Two years, madame.

AGLAE:
>And do you find yourself getting better?

PATIENT:
>Much better, madame. It used to be that I never had more than one crisis a week. Now I have two a day.

HORTENSE *(to Cassandre)*:
>Now then, Doctor, tell me candidly and in confidence. Does your magnetism do any good!

CASSANDRE:
>Well, I can assure you that it does *me* a lot of good.

THE DOCTOR:
>Me too.

PIERROT *(jingling his coins)*:
>Me too.

HORTENSE:

Who is that dark man with the serious air?

CASSANDRE:

He is an old lawyer who has suffered from violent headaches ever since he married a young wife—

HORTENSE:

A young wife!

AGLAE:

An old lawyer!

HORTENSE:

Headaches! *(looking at him)* Oh! it's my husband!

AGLAE:

It certainly is! Oh, what a lovely sight! He should have his portrait painted! *(pointing to the rod extending from the baquet)* What is he pressing against his head?

CASSANDRE:

That's the Magnetic Branch.

HORTENSE *(sotto voce)*:

Quiet. Let's get out of here.

CASSANDRE:

But, Madame—

HORTENSE:

We'll come again another time when I feel more at ease. Doctor, tell me, don't you make house calls?

CASSANDRE:

I do when there's a need, at least if I'm asked in the right way.

HORTENSE:

That's for me. Come on, my friend.

AGLAE:

Yes, that's well said. Let's go.

HORTENSE *(to Cassandre)*:

I hope you will be discreet.

CASSANDRE:

Whom are you addressing?

AGLAE:

Doesn't your husband look fine from here!

HORTENSE:

You're being silly. Come along.

(They exit giggling.)

Scene Four

The same.

THE DOCTOR:
>I was afraid he'd recognize them.

PIERROT:
>I hoped he would!

CASSANDRE:
>This fellow is too occupied with what he's doing to notice anything. *(to the patients)* Ladies and gentlemen, let us proceed. Pierrot, go to the harmonica.

(Pierrot plays an air while Cassandre and the Doctor wave their wands to magnetize the patients.)

CHORUS OF PATIENTS:
>What quick and sudden heat! Falarira, larira, dondon, dondane! Ah, my mind is whirling! dondon, dondaine, falarira, dondon!

LAWYER:
>It's odd. I don't feel anything.

(Pierrot repeats the music on the glass harmonica.)

THE GASCON *(quitting the baquet with a nosebleed):*
>To the devil with your cursed remedy!

THE DOCTOR:
>What's wrong? Why this violent emotion?

THE GASCON:
>There's no need to help me by making my nose bleed.

CASSANDRE:
>So much the better. You've reached your crisis.

THE GASCON:
>My crisis! This is too much! *Good-bye!*

Scene Five

The same.

THE LAWYER:
>Haven't I had enough of this holding myself with my beak in the water like a crane?

CASSANDRE:

> Monsieur, you are there just like the others. *(to the Doctor)* Here, my friend, I have kept this cure for you—the lawyer.

THE DOCTOR *(to the lawyer):*

> We will see, Monsieur, the two of us.

THE LAWYER:

> Listen, gentlemen. Shall I speak frankly? I don't believe in your Magnetism.

PIERROT:

> What! You don't believe in Magnetism?

THE DOCTOR *(to Cassandre):*

> My friend, he doesn't believe in it.

CASSANDRE:

> Let's discuss the problem. The imagination is affected by Animal Magnetism, but advanced methods have to be used.

THE DOCTOR *(to Cassandre):*

> Don't be disturbed. *(to the lawyer)* To begin with, Monsieur, haven't you felt—

THE LAWYER:

> That's just it, I *have* felt. This awkward posture makes my headache worse.

THE DOCTOR:

> So much the better. When the pain becomes worse, it's a sign you're getting better. *(He magnetizes him by touching his forehead with the wand.)* What do you feel now?

THE LAWYER:

> I feel that I'm suffering dreadfully.

THE DOCTOR:

> Splendid. Everything is proceeding nicely.

THE LAYWER:

> What do you mean by "proceeding nicely"?

PIERROT:

> Oh, that means you're going to have a crisis.

THE LAWYER:

> Well, I would like to see that. And after the crisis, will I be cured?

PIERROT:

Obviously, since you have been told so.

CASSANDRE *(to the Doctor):*

The Magnetized Mirror.

THE DOCTOR:

I agree.

Pierrot brings the mirror to the lawyer.

PIERROT:

Monsieur, don't give up hope. In a minute you'll see—

THE LAWYER *(looking in the mirror):*

What do I see? Doctor, enough! This bothers me! *(rubbing his forehead)* Stop! Enough! Take it away!

THE DOCTOR:

I trust your crisis is beginning.

THE LAYWER:

I'm appalled by what I thought I saw in the mirror.

PIERROT:

That's nothing. We'll make you see more, I guarantee you.

CASSANDRE *(to the Doctor):*

We must give him a shock, and I see how to do it with my Magnetized Clock.

THE DOCTOR:

Allow me to diagnose the effect.

CASSANDRE:

Your zeal does you honor.

THE DOCTOR *(to the laywer):*

Come over here if you please. Look at this clock and see what time it is.

THE LAWYER:

Well, it will soon be three o'clock.

THE DOCTOR:

The hour is about to strike. Listen carefully.

(The cuckoo sounds.)

THE LAWYER:

Aie! *(Cuckoo!)* Aie! *(Cuckoo!)* Aie, aie, aie, my head! My head, aie, aie, aie!

CASSANDRE:

Quick, a chair!

(The music becomes louder while the lawyer is in a crisis. The refrain is repeated.)

THE LAWYER:

> Aie, aie, aie, my head! My head, aie, aie, aie!

(He collapses into a chair.)

THE DOCTOR:

> Ouf! it's difficult to lift a lawyer!

CASSANDRE:

> Don't worry.

THE DOCTOR:

> I thought I'd never see this attack. But by its success I am rewarded for my pains.

THE LAWYER:

> And I am suffocating!

THE DOCTOR:

> Well, Monsieur, who makes so much noise—

THE LAWYER *(recovering)*:

> Ah, ye gods! What a crisis! No! it is certainly not an ideal treatment!

THE DOCTOR:

> With all due respect . . . believe now in Animal Magnetism, believe now in Magnetism.

THE LAWYER:

> Ah, my friends, I am finished!

CASSANDRE:

> Calm yourself. Accept our treatment. If you don't improve, at least you will be in the company of many others.

THE LAWYER:

> I'm going out of my mind. Where will you put me?

CASSANDRE:

> In the Crisis Room.

TWO VOICES:

> We're both mad. Where will you put us?

CASSANDRE:

> In the Crisis Room.

THREE VOICES:

> We three are mad. Where will you put us?

CASSANDRE:

> In the Crisis Room. Off you go, all of you.

(The rest go into the Crisis Room leaving Cassandre and the Doctor alone. They come forward and sing a duet while jingling the money they have received from the patients.)

THE DOCTOR:

> To our baquet full of health, see, see how they come. Profit is certain for us. This is a wellspring of riches. Digue, digue, digue, and din, din, din! Digue, digue, digue, money without end!

CASSANDRE:

> Into many weak minds, in which our country abounds, enthusiasm readily enters. The harvest is plentiful.

THE DOCTOR AND CASSANDRE:

> Away with the followers of Galen! We close our ears to their cries. Plutus, the god of wealth, will be our bulwark and our guide.

THE DOCTOR:

> If this method, which is so pleasing, should betray us, we'll look for something new.

CASSANDRE:

> The times may change. Let us profit from our luck and be ready to get out with a full purse. You approve of me, then?

THE DOCTOR:

> I do, with all my soul.

CASSANDRE:

> You approve of me?

THE DOCTOR:

> Magnetism is marvelous.

CASSANDRE:

> You consider it good?

THE DOCTOR:

> Money enchants me.

DUET:

> By hope of gain are we united, comrades to the end.

CASSANDRE *(to the audience)*:

> Judge indulgently, we pray you, the follies of vaudeville, that spoiled child. To hear your verdict, the Author is waiting for you—in the Crisis Room.

THE END.

Bibliography

Since this biography is intended for the general reader, there are no footnotes and titles are given in translation except where the original is self-explanatory. The bibliography is by its nature more scholarly, but more than that, it can be used as an independent guide to the literature rather than merely as a reflection of the text or a justification of what is said there. It has its own internal logic, complementing that of the text by approaching the same subjects from different angles. The bibliographical headings differ from the chapter titles precisely so that the two lists may serve as foils for one another in an understanding of Mesmer and Mesmerism.

Works

There is no collected edition of Mesmer's writings. The best selection is *Le Magnétisme animal,* oeuvres publiées par Robert Amadou, avec des commentaires et des notes de Frank A. Pattie et Jean Vinchon (Paris, 1971). The most important of Mesmer's individual works, *Mémoire sur la découverte du magnétisme animal,* has been translated under the title *Mesmerism* by Captain V. R. Myers, intro. Gilbert Frankau (London, 1948). The 1799 *Mémoire* is available as *Memoir of F. A. Mesmer, Doctor of Medicine, Concerning His Discoveries,* tr. Jerome Eden (Mount Vernon, New York, 1957). Frank A. Pattie's article, "Mesmer's Medical Dissertation and Its Debt to Mead's *De Imperio Solis ac Lunae,*" *Journal of the History of Medicine and Allied Sciences,* Vol. XI (1956), pp. 275–87, is essential for the proto-history of the theory of animal magnetism.

Life

The best encyclopedia entry is by Robert Darnton, "Mesmer, Franz Anton," *Dictionary of Scientific Biography,* ed. Charles Coulston Gillispie, Vol. IX (New York, 1974), pp. 325–28. The standard biography in English is D. M. Walmsley, *Anton Mesmer* (London, 1967). Karl Bittel, *Der Berühmte Hr. Doct. Mesmer, 1734–1815* (Überlingen, 1939), is a monograph with a valuable "documents and sources" section. The same author in collaboration with Rudolf Tischner produced a substantial "life and thought" treatise: *Mesmer und sein Problem: Magnetismus—Suggestion—Hypnose* (Stuttgart, 1941). Jean Vinchon, *Mesmer et son secret* (Toulouse, 1971) is useful, although marred by too much explanation of Mesmer's character in terms of narrow Freudian psychoanalysis. Bernhard Milt deals with his subject's life in Switzerland in *Franz Anton Mesmer und seine Beziehungen zur Schweiz: Magie und Heilkunde zu Lavaters Zeit* (Zurich, 1953). Justinus Kerner awaits a translator who will reveal to English-speaking readers the fund of personal information in his *Franz Anton Mesmer aus Schwaben, Entdecker des Thierischen Magnetismus* (Frankfurt-am-Main, 1856). Mesmer's city is described from experience by Michael O'Kelly, *Reminiscences* (London, 1826) and historically by Marcel Brion, *Daily Life in the Vienna of Mozart and Schubert,* tr. Jean Stewart (London, 1961). J. C. Rosenberg notes a unique combination of interests in "Friendship Between Viennese Physicians and Musicians," *Bulletin of the History of Medicine,* Vol. XXXII (1958), pp. 366–69. The Mesmer-Mozart friendship can be followed in *The Letters of Mozart and His Family,* tr. Emily Anderson (London, 1938). The origin of the Mozart opera Mesmer commissioned, *Bastien und Bastienne,* is the subject of Eric Blom, whose title refers to Jean-Jacques Rousseau, Mme. Favart, and Mozart: "The Philosopher, the Actress, and the Boy," *Stepchildren of Music* (London, 1926).

Medicine

George Barton Cutten chronicles the subject to which Mesmer made so great a contribution in *Three Thousand Years of Mental Healing* (New York, 1911), as does Gregory Zilboorg in his *History of Medical Psychology* (New York, 1941). The transition from early modern medical practice to the age of Hermann Boerhaave and Gerhard Van Swieten is described by Arturo Castiglioni, *Adventures of the Mind,* tr. V. Gianturco (New York, 1946). The healing properties ascribed to kings and queens are explained by Marc Bloch, *The Royal Touch: Sacred Monarchy and Scrofula in England and*

France, tr. J. E. Anderson (Montreal, 1973). There is no good book on Valentine Greatraks or Johann Gassner. Louis Trenchard More, *The Life and Work of the Honourable Robert Boyle* (OUP, 1944), discusses Greatraks briefly and prints Boyle's interpretive letter on the Stroking Doctor from Ireland. Eyewitness observations of Gassner are recorded by Christoph von Eschenmayer, "Über Gassners Heilmethode," *Archiv für Thierischen Magnetismus,* Vol. VIII (1820), pp. 86–135. An overall view of Mesmer's profession in Mesmer's time is provided by Lester S. King, *The Medical World of the Eighteenth Century* (Chicago, 1958). Max Neuburger deals with the university where Mesmer got his training in "British Medicine and the Old Vienna Medical School," *Bulletin of the History of Medicine,* Vol. XII (1942), pp. 486–528. A. J. Gerster portrays the man who made the school in "The Life and Times of Gerhardt van Swieten," *Bulletin of the Johns Hopkins Hospital,* XX (1909), 161-68. Frank T. Brechka, *Gerard van Swieten and His World, 1700–72* (The Hague, 1970), has written the fundamental study.

Controversies

The furor surrounding Mesmer was reported by many writers. The most entertaining is Friedrich Melchior, Freiherr von (Baron de) Grimm, *Correspondance littéraire, philosophique et critique* (Paris, 1829–30), followed by Jean François de La Harpe, *Correspondance littéraire* (Paris, 1801–07). Feminine skepticism is in Madame Du Barry, *Mémoires de la Comtesse dû Barri* (Paris, 1829) and Elisabeth Louise Vigée-Lebrun, *Memoirs,* tr. Gerard Shelley (London, n.d.). There are numerous references in *Mémoires secrets pour servir à l'histoire de la republique des lettres en France* (Paris, 1784–85). The most thorough negative criticism by a physician is Michel Augustin Thouret, *Recherches et doutes sur le magnétisme animal* (Paris, 1784). The anonymous *Antimagnétisme* (Paris, 1784). is less able and more satirical. Jean-Sylvain Bailly edited the official verdicts by Franklin's committee: *Rapport des commissaires chargés par le roi de l'examen du magnétisme animal* (Paris, 1784) and *Rapport secret sur le mesmérisme* (Paris, 1784). Editions and translations of these are noted by Denis I. Duveen and Herbert S. Klickstein in *A Bibliography of the Works of Antoine Laurent Lavoisier* (London, 1954). Antoine Laurent de Jussieu dissented from the negative judgment of his colleagues: *Rapport de l'un des commissaires chargés par le Roi de l'examen du mag-*

nétisme animal (Paris, 1784) Charles Deslon wrote his own dissenting opinion: *Supplément aux deux rapports de MM. les commissaires de l'académie et de la faculté de la médecine et de la societé royale de médecine* (Paris, 1784). The periodicals of the time should be consulted passim for the years 1778–86, *Journal de Paris, Journal litteraire et historique, Journal encyclopédique,* and so on. A key to Mesmer references in the last named is Albert Couvreur, *La Pharmacie et la thérapeutique au XVIIIe siècle vues à travers le Journal encyclopédique de Pierre Rousseau, à Bouillon* (Paris, 1953).

Scientific Mesmerism

The most complete bibliography of the use of hypnosis in medical practice is Margaret Brenman and Merton M. Gill, *Hypnotherapy: A Survey of the Literature* (Topeka, 1947). The standard source books are Ronald E. Shor and Martin T. Orme, *The Nature of Hypnosis: Selected Basic Readings* (New York, 1965) and Maurice M. Titerow, *Foundations of Hypnosis from Mesmer to Freud* (Springfield, Ill., 1970). The big history is Henri F. Ellenberger, *The Discovery of the Unconscious: The History and Evolution of Dynamic Psychology* (New York, 1970). Dominique Barrucand's *Histoire de l'hypnose en France* (Paris, 1967) is a monograph with a poor opinion of Mesmer and a good bibliography of hypnosis. Margaret Goldsmith traces the fate of the man and his idea in *Franz Anton Mesmer: A History of Mesmerism* (New York, 1934). Stefan Zweig links the two great psychotherapists in *Mental Healers: Franz Anton Mesmer, Mary Baker Eddy, Sigmund Freud,* tr. Eden and Cedar Paul (New York, 1932). J. P. F. Deleuze, *Histoire critique du magnétisme animal* (Paris, 1813), is the best survey dating from Mesmer's lifetime. Charles Deslon was Mesmer's assistant when he gathered the material for his *Observations sur le magnétisme animal* (Paris, 1781). Nicolas Bergasse extended Mesmer's principles into a broad philosophy in *Considérations sur le magnétisme animal, ou sur la théorie du monde et des êtres organises* (La Haye, 1784). The Marquis de Puységur produced one of the momentous documents of Mesmerism, the first systematic account of hypnotic hallucinations: *Mémoire pour servir à l'histoire et à l'établissement du magnétisme animal* (Paris, 1784). The development of Mesmerism into hypnotism in the nineteenth century emerges as a step-by-step process in the masterworks on the subject: Abbé Faria, *De la Cause du sommeil lucide* (Paris, 1819); Alexan-

dre Bertrand, *Traité du somnambulisme* (Paris, 1823); John Elliotson, *The Zoist: A Journal of Cerebral Physiology and Mesmerism* (London, 1843–56); James Braid, *Neurypnology, or the Rationale of Nervous Sleep, Considered in Relation with Animal Magnetism* (London,
1843); Ambroise Auguste Liébault, *Du Sommeil et des états analogues*
(Paris, 1866); Jean Martin Charcot, *Leçons sur les maladies du système
nerveux* (Paris, 1873); Hippolyte Bernheim, *Suggestive Therapeutics:
A Treatise on the Nature and Uses of Hypnotism,* tr. Christian A Her-
ter (New York, 1888); Pierre Janet, *The Mental State of Hystericals,* tr.
Caroline Rollin Corson, intro. Jean Martin Charcot (New York,
1901); Morton Prince, *The Dissociation of Personality* (New York,
1906). Only a few titles can be mentioned here from the small library of books on hypnotism in the twentieth century. Jean Dau-
ven, *The Power of Hypnosis,* tr. Joyce E. Clemow (New YOrk, 1969), is
an easy introduction with a helpful chronology and thumbnail bio-
graphies of hypnotists from Mesmer to the present. More
advanced is *Therapy Through Hypnosis,* ed. Raphael H. Rhodes
(New York, 1952). Charles L. Hull, *Hypnosis and Suggestibility: An
Experimental Approach* (New York, 1933) and Claude Scott Moss,
Hypnosis in Perspective (New York, 1965) are textbooks for students.
Gordon Ambrose and George Newbold address specialists in different fields of medicine with their *Handbook of Medical Hypnosis,* 3d
ed. (London, 1968). Lewis R. Wolberg covers the field in his two-
volume treatise, *Medical Hypnosis* (New York, 1948). The Society
for Clinical and Experimental Hypnosis publishes *The International
Journal of Clinical and Experimental Hypnosis* (Baltimore, 1953–).

Political Mesmerism

The best book on Mesmer's Society of Harmony, the schism
within it, and the deviation of the dissidents into radical politics is
Robert Darnton, *Mesmerism and the End of the Enlightenment in
France* (Harvard, 1968). Eugène Louis concentrates more closely
on Mesmer's Mesmerism in *Les Origines de la doctrine du magnétisme
animal: Mesmer et la Société de l'Harmonie* (Paris, 1898). Caullet de
Vaumorel preserved the system of ideas taught within the confines
of the society: *Aphorismes de M. Mesmer* (Paris, 1785). Duval d'É-
prémesnil launched his counterattack against the satirists of Mesmerism with *Refléxions préliminaires à l'occasion de la pièce intitulée les
"Docteurs modernes" jouée sur le theatre italien, le 16 Novembre 1784*

(Paris, 1784). Mesmer's leading advocate and then leading opponent in the society is the subject of Louis Bergasse, *Un Defenseur des principes traditionels sous la révolution, Nicolas Bergasse* (Paris, 1910). Etienne Charavay discusses Lafayette's Mesmerism in *Le Général La Fayette* (Paris, 1898), where the contract between Lafayette and Mesmer is reproduced in facsimile.

Occult Mesmerism

Louis Figuier categorizes Mesmer among the bizarre personalities of his period in *Histoire du merveilleux dans les tempts modernes* (Paris, 1860), a theme pursued also by Augustin Cabanès, "Autour du baquet de Mesmer," *Moeurs intimes du passé*, quatriemè série (Paris, n.d.), pp. 343–92. Frank Podmore, *Mesmerism and Christian Science: A Short History of Mental Healing* (Philadelphia, 1909), sees Mesmer as mainly a charlatan who opened the door to spiritualism, Theosophy, New Thought, and Christian Science. Justinus Kerner became a convinced believer in occult Mesmerism from the visions of Frederike Hauffe, of whom he wrote in *The Seeress of Prevorst*, tr. Mrs. Crowe (London, 1845). Two influential women who founded enduring institutions wrote about occult Mesmerism, which had attracted them in their earlier days. Mary Baker Eddy repented of her youthful indiscretion, into which she had been led by Phineas Parkhurst Quimby, and denounced animal magnetism in *Science and Health* (Boston, 1875). Helena Petrovna Blavatsky maintained a firm faith in animal magnetism and applauded Mesmer for being a "magician" in her fundamental theosophical treatise, *Isis Unveiled* (London, 1877). For Quimby's pilgrimage from Mesmerism to spiritualism, see *The Quimby Manuscripts, Showing the Discovery of Spiritual Healing and the Origin of Christian Science*, ed. Horatio W. Dresser (New York, 1921).

Literary Mesmerism

The history of literary Mesmerism is still to be written. The effect of the theory of animal magnetism on the Romantic movement has been demonstrated by Auguste Viatte in *Les Sources occultes du romantisme: illuminisme—théosophie, 1770–1820* (Paris, 1928). Robert Lee Wolff describes the use of the trance and the occult in one phase of English literature: *Strange Stories and Other Explorations in Victorian Fiction* (Boston, 1971). Harriet Martineau can be seen in the act of going over to John Elliotson's system in *Letters on Mesmerism* (London, 1845). Chauncey Hare Townshend, *Facts in Mesmerism* (New York, 1842), is the principal link between Mesmer and Edgar Allan Poe. Andrew Jackson Davis, *The Harmonial Philosophy* (Chicago, n.d.), is worth looking at if only because Poe listened to the Poughkeepsie Seer on the kind of Mesmerism expounded here. S. E. Lind wrote "Poe and Mesmerism," *Publications of the Modern Language Association*, Vol. LXII (1947), pp. 1077–94. The Brownings' interest in Mesmerism can be found in *The Letters of Robert Browning and Elizabeth Barrett, 1845–46* (Harvard, 1969). The best part of literary Mesmerism is, of course, in the great writers who used it creatively—Honoré de Balzac and Victor Hugo, Ludwig Tieck and E.T.A. Hoffman, even the philosophical pessimist Arthur Schopenhauer. Scholars read Edward Bulwer-Lytton's "A Strange Story." Everybody reads at least one of Poe's three stories with Mesmerism for a theme—"A Tale of the Ragged Mountains," "Mesmeric Revelation," "The Facts in the Case of M. Valdemar." Everybody ought to read *Trilby* for George du Maurier's period piece presentation of Mesmerism.

Index

254

Index